SIMPLE
CISSP

Exam Questions

Phil Martin, CISSP

SIMPLE CISSP EXAM QUESTIONS

Copyright © 2017. All rights reserved. Except as permitted under the Copyright Act of 1976, no part of this publication may be reproduced or distributed in any from or by any means, or stored in a database or retrieval system, without the prior written permission of the publisher.

OVERVIEW OF CONTENTS

ABOUT THE AUTHOR ... 1
ABOUT THE EXAM ... 2
WHAT'S IN THIS BOOK ... 4
HOW TO USE THIS BOOK ... 5
SECURITY AND RISK MANAGEMENT DOMAIN ... 6
ASSET SECURITY DOMAIN ... 65
SECURITY ENGINEERING DOMAIN ... 81
COMMUNICATION AND NETWORK SECURITY DOMAIN ... 198
IDENTITY AND ACCESS MANAGEMENT DOMAIN ... 324
SECURITY ASSESSMENT AND TESTING DOMAIN ... 383
SECURITY OPERATIONS DOMAIN ... 405
SOFTWARE DEVELOPMENT SECURITY DOMAIN ... 467
WHAT'S NEXT? ... 521

CONTENTS

ABOUT THE AUTHOR 1

ABOUT THE EXAM 2

WHAT'S IN THIS BOOK 4

HOW TO USE THIS BOOK 5

SECURITY AND RISK MANAGEMENT DOMAIN 6
- DEFINITIONS 6
- TERMS 34
- QUIZ 63

ASSET SECURITY DOMAIN 65
- DEFINITIONS 65
- TERMS 72
- QUIZ 79

SECURITY ENGINEERING DOMAIN 81
- DEFINITIONS 81
- TERMS 134
- QUIZ 188

COMMUNICATION AND NETWORK SECURITY DOMAIN 198
- DEFINITIONS 198
- TERMS 253
- QUIZ 308

IDENTITY AND ACCESS MANAGEMENT DOMAIN 324
- DEFINITIONS 324
- TERMS 352
- QUIZ 380

SECURITY ASSESSMENT AND TESTING DOMAIN 383
- DEFINITIONS 383

Terms	393
Quiz	403
SECURITY OPERATIONS DOMAIN	**405**
Definitions	405
Terms	433
Quiz	461
SOFTWARE DEVELOPMENT SECURITY DOMAIN	**467**
Definitions	467
Terms	493
Quiz	519
WHAT'S NEXT?	**521**

vi

About the Author

Phil Martin, **CISSP**, has more than 20 years of experience in the technology industry, including software development, infrastructure management and security practitioner. He currently works in the financial industry designing secure platforms for SaaS within enterprise security frameworks. Some of his certifications include CEH, CHFI, ISO 27001, CCENT, ITIL and of course, CISSP.

About the Exam

The exam consists of 250 multiple-choice, drag and drop, and Hotspot questions that must be answered in 6 hours.

- Multiple Choice – select a single option from many
- Drag and drop – select one or more answers and drag them to a drop area; occasionally the order matters
- Hotspot – click a visual item that does or does not answer the question

There is no penalty for guessing, so be sure not to skip a question. However, you must manage your time well – if you run across a question that you are not sure of, go ahead and guess but then flag it for review. When you have completed all other questions, go back to each flagged question and spend more time on it.

Of the 250 questions, only 225 will be graded – 25 are used for research purposes. Therefore, you may run across questions that are completely unfamiliar or appear to be too vague to answer properly – go ahead and answer them to the best of your ability, but don't worry too much about these critters – they may very well be one of the 25 research questions. Each test taker is given a random sampling of questions pulled from a much larger pool of questions, so you will not be taking the exact same test as the person sitting next to you. You will need to correctly answer 70% of the questions (175 questions).

An important fact to note is that there will be no questions that are specific to a platform (Windows, Linux, etc.). While this book does contain information that is specific to a platform, that content will not be highlighted (see How to Use This Book) – in other words you will not need to remember specifics, just the concept.

While most questions are direct, there will be some scenario-based questions that present a situation and then ask one or more questions about that scenario.

About the Exam

Once you have passed the exam, you will still need to provide proof that you possess the experience required to obtain the certification. This will include having a CISSP-certified individual sponsor you.

What's in This Book

This book contains over 4,400 questions in 3 formats:

- Definition – given the definition, provide the term described
- Term – given a term, provide the definition
- Quiz – a question is asked that has a specific answer – quiz questions are the hardest

The book will test you on topics as they appear in the Simple CISSP book, ordered by domain. Within each domain, the subject matter will follow the outline of the book.

Note: The format of the questions in this book will not represent how questions will appear on the test. The actual exam will provide questions in multiple formats, whereas this book is designed to test your knowledge, not to emulate the test experience itself.

How to Use This Book

You will be asked a question, and the answer will follow on the next line. Simply use a piece of paper folded in half, or an index card, to cover the answer while reading the question. Within the first section, if you want to learn more about the answer, it should be relatively easy to locate the section in the corresponding Simple CISSP book (sold separately) as they both follow the same general outline.

An audio version of this print book is available on audible.com!

Security and Risk Management Domain

Definitions

Question:
What is a term that describes confidentiality, integrity and availability?

Answer:
'CIA'

Question:
What provides a high level of assurance that information is kept from unauthorized parties?

Answer:
'confidentiality'

Question:
What results in a measure of harm or damage if information were to be disclosed?

Answer:
'sensitivity'

Question:
What is shown by a person when choosing to control disclosure of information to limit damage?

Answer:
'discretion'

Question:
What dictates how critical to a mission information is considered to be?

Answer:
'criticality'

Question:
What is the act of hiding or preventing disclosure?

Answer:
'concealment'

Question:
What is the act of keeping something a secret?

Answer:
'secrecy'

Security and Risk Management Domain

Question:
What is the act of keeping information confidential that is personally identifiable or that can cause damage if disclosed?

Answer:
'privacy'

Question:
What is achieved by storing something in an out-of-the-way manner?

Answer:
'seclusion'

Question:
What is achieved when we keep something separate from others?

Answer:
'isolation'

Question:
What is achieved when information remains unaltered (and can be proven to be so) except by authorized parties, prevents both intentional and accidental modifications, and ensures consistency remains valid?

Answer:
'integrity'

Question:
What is achieved when usable access to a resource is always provided in a timely and uninterrupted manner?

Answer:
'availability'

Question:
What is an abbreviation for authentication, authorization and auditing?

Answer:
'AAA'

Question:
What occurs when a subject claims a specific identity?

Answer:
'identification'

Question:
What occurs when a subject proves they are who they claim to be?

Answer:
'authentication'

Question:
What is the act of deciding what object a subject can access and how it can be used?

Answer:
'authorization'

Security and Risk Management Domain

Question:
What is the act of recording the activities of a subject in a log?

Answer:
'auditing'

Question:
What occurs when logs are reviewed to check for compliance?

Answer:
'accountability'

Question:
What is a weakness in a system that allows a threat to compromise security?

Answer:
'vulnerability'

Question:
What is the danger that a vulnerability might be exploited?

Answer:
'threat'

Question:
What occurs when a vulnerability is taken advantage of by an attacker?

Answer:
'exploit'

Question:
What is a person or process that exploits a vulnerability?

Answer:
'threat agent'

Question:
What is the likelihood that a threat agent will exploit a vulnerability combined with the damage that could result?

Answer:
'risk'

Question:
What is a single real-world instance of a vulnerability being exploited by a threat agent?

Answer:
'exposure'

Question:
What mitigates a risk?

Answer:
'control'

Security and Risk Management Domain

9

Question:
What is a type of management control that includes training, security policies and documentation, and managing risk?

Answer:
'administrative control'

Question:
What is a type of control comprised of software or hardware elements such as hashing or encryption, firewalls and enforcing authentication?

Answer:
'technical control'

Question:
What is another name for a technical control?

Answer:
'logical control'

Question:
What is a type of control comprised of external lighting, locked doors, fences, card keys and security guards?

Answer:
'physical control'

Question:
What occurs when we use multiple categories of controls in a layered approach?

Answer:
'defense-in-depth'

Question:
What is a control that can avoid an incident?

Answer:
'preventative control'

Question:
What is a control that can discourage an attacker?

Answer:
'deterrent control'

Question:
What is a control that can identify an intruder?

Answer:
'detective control'

Question:
What is a control that can fix a component or system?

Answer:
'corrective control'

Security and Risk Management Domain

10

Question:
What is a control that can bring environments back to normal operation?

Answer:
'recovery control'

Question:
What is a control that can provide an alternative control if the first choice is unavailable?

Answer:
'compensating control'

Question:
What is an approach on how to recognize and deal with weaknesses?

Answer:
'security framework'

Question:
What is the only framework geared specifically to security?

Answer:
'ISO 27000 series'

Question:
What is a set of policies, processes and systems to manage risk?

Answer:
'ISMS'

Question:
What is a standard that sets forward an ISMS?

Answer:
'ISO 27001'

Question:
What is a standard that provides a code of practice for implementing an ISMS?

Answer:
'ISO 27002'

Question:
What addresses the more general structure and behavior of an entire organization?

Answer:
'enterprise architecture'

Question:
What is a 2-dimensional matrix with 5 different audiences on the Y-axis, and 6 different views on the X-axis?

Answer:
'Zachman Framework'

Security and Risk Management Domain

11

Question:
What defines 4 types - Business, Data, Application and Technology - and is created by the Architecture Development Method (ADM)?

Answer:
'Open-Group Architecture Framework, or TOGAF'

Question:
What was created by the US military and ensures a common communication protocol as well as standard payloads?

Answer:
'Department of Defense Architecture Framework, or DoDAF'

Question:
What is the British version of DoDAF?

Answer:
'Ministry of Defence Architecture Framework, or MoDAF'

Question:
What is a framework like Zachman but focused on security; also, a methodology and process, not just a framework?

Answer:
'Sherwood Applied Business Security Architecture, or SABSA'

Question:
What is achieved when the needs of the business are met as well as all legal or regulatory requirements?

Answer:
'strategic alignment'

Question:
What is achieved when we acknowledge the importance of security while not losing sight of the reason for an organization's existence?

Answer:
'business enablement'

Question:
What is achieved when security actually increases an existing process' efficiency?

Answer:
'process enhancement'

Question:
What ensures that ISMS controls have achieved the desired results?

Answer:
'security effectiveness'

Question:
What is a framework that ties private industry IT, business and stakeholder goals together and provides for IT governance?

Answer:
'Control Objectives for Information and Related Technologies, or COBIT'

Security and Risk Management Domain

Question:
What is a framework that ties federal agency goals to FISMA?

Answer:
'NIST SP 800-53'

Question:
What is a framework that provides corporate governance (COBIT is a subset for security)?

Answer:
'Committee of Sponsoring Organizations, or COSO'

Question:
What is a process management tool that focuses on SLAs between IT and internal customers?

Answer:
'ITIL'

Question:
What is a process management tool that measures process quality using statistical calculations by identifying defects?

Answer:
'Six Sigma'

Question:
What is a process management tool that determines the maturity of an organization's processes by assigning 1 of 6 levels?

Answer:
'Capability Maturity Model Integration, or CMMI'

Question:
What is a process in which the last step feeds into the first step iteratively?

Answer:
'Process Life Cycle'

Question:
What contains the following activities: identify changes needed, create architecture, select solutions, and get approval?

Answer:
'plan step'

Question:
What contains the following activities: assign duties, create baselines, create blueprint, implement, enable monitoring, and define SLAs?

Answer:
'implement step'

Question:
What contains the following activities: monitor, carry out tasks, and ensure SLAs?

Answer:
'operate step'

Security and Risk Management Domain

Question:
What contains the following activities: review and identify changes for the next iteration?

Answer:
'evaluate step'

Question:
What is any activity that deals with a computer-based crime?

Answer:
'computer crime law'

Question:
What are the 3 following categories: computer assisted, computer-targeted and computer is incidental?

Answer:
'categories of computer crime law'

Question:
What is a computer-crime category in which the computer is a tool?

Answer:
'computer-assisted'

Question:
What is a computer-crime category in which the computer is the victim (and indirectly the computer's owner)?

Answer:
'computer-targeted'

Question:
What is a computer-crime category in which the computer was involved but was not the victim or did not play a significant role in the crime?

Answer:
'computer is incidental'

Question:
What are unsophisticated individuals who use pre-built tools?

Answer:
'script kiddies'

Question:
What are patient criminals who will spend weeks or months probing for weaknesses?

Answer:
'Advanced Persistent Threat, or APT'

Question:
What is the first step in gaining access by using phishing or zero-day attacks?

Answer:
'foothold step'

Security and Risk Management Domain

Question:
What is the second step in gaining access by installing back doors on vulnerable machines?

Answer:
'install step'

Question:
What is the third step in gaining access by using lateral movement to other accounts or systems?

Answer:
'lateral step'

Question:
What is the fourth step in gaining access by gathering data from servers and preparing for exfiltration?

Answer:
'gather step'

Question:
What is the fifth step in gaining access by exfiltrating the data via various means to a compromised machine hosted elsewhere?

Answer:
'exfiltrate step'

Question:
What is an international organization providing guidelines dealing with data transferred between countries?

Answer:
'OECD'

Question:
What is an OECD core principle stating that collection of personal data must be limited and lawful, and with the knowledge of the subject?

Answer:
'OECD collection limitation principle'

Question:
What is an OECD core principle stating that personal data should be kept complete and current, and be relevant for the purpose?

Answer:
'OECD data quality principle'

Question:
What is an OECD core principle stating that subjects should be notified of the reason for the collection of personal data and should only be used for that purpose?

Answer:
'OECD purpose specification principle'

Security and Risk Management Domain

Question:
What is an OECD core principle stating that if data is to be used for any other purpose than stated, the subject must give consent or law must provide authority?

Answer:
'OECD use limitation principle'

Question:
What is an OECD core principle stating that safeguards should be put into place to protect collected data?

Answer:
'OECD security safeguards principle'

Question:
What is an OECD core principle stating that practices and policies regarding personal data should be openly communicated, and subjects should be able to easily determine what data has been collected and where it is stored?

Answer:
'OECD openness principle'

Question:
What is an OECD core principle stating that subjects must be able to find out if an organization has their personal data and be able to correct errors?

Answer:
'OECD individual participation principle'

Question:
What is an OECD core principle stating that organizations should be accountable for complying with measures that support all other privacy rules?

Answer:
'OECD accountability principle'

Question:
What is a special framework that has been developed for US and EU data transfer requirements?

Answer:
'Safe Harbor Privacy Principles, or Safe Harbor'

Question:
What is a Safe Harbor rule stating that individuals must be notified when personal data is to be collected?

Answer:
'Safe Harbor notice rule'

Question:
What is a Safe Harbor rule stating that individuals must be able to opt out of the collection?

Answer:
'Safe Harbor choice rule'

Security and Risk Management Domain

Question:
What is a Safe Harbor rule stating that transfer of data to third parties may happen only if the third party follows adequate data protection principles?

Answer:
'Safe Harbor onward transfer rule'

Question:
What is a Safe Harbor rule stating that reasonable effort must be made to prevent loss of collected data?

Answer:
'Safe Harbor security rule'

Question:
What is a Safe Harbor rule stating that collected data must be relevant and reliable for the purpose it was collected for?

Answer:
'Safe Harbor Data Integrity rule'

Question:
What is a Safe Harbor rule stating that individuals must be able to access the information held about them and correct errors?

Answer:
'Safe Harbor access rule'

Question:
What is a Safe Harbor rule stating that there must be an effective means of enforcing other Safe Harbor rules?

Answer:
'Safe Harbor enforcement rule'

Question:
What is an international agreement regarding the import and export of goods?

Answer:
'Wassenaar Arrangement'

Question:
What is a legal system used in European countries based on rules, where lower courts can ignore higher court decisions?

Answer:
'civil law legal system, or code law'

Question:
What is a legal system based on precedence using a judge and jury, where higher court decisions must be recognized by lower courts?

Answer:
'common law legal system'

Security and Risk Management Domain

Question:
What is a legal system in which a government law has been broken and guilt must be established beyond reasonable doubt for a guilty/not guilty verdict, with loss of freedom if convicted?

Answer:
'criminal legal system'

Question:
What is a legal system in which wrongs committed against an individual or company, and a prudent man, is used to reach a liable/not liable verdict; no loss of freedom results?

Answer:
'civil/tort legal system'

Question:
What is a legal system in which regulatory standards are defined by government agencies and are almost always applied to companies only?

Answer:
'administrative legal system'

Question:
What is a legal system based on traditions and customs of a specific region, usually mixed with another law, in which restitution is money or services; this is often found in China and India?

Answer:
'customary law legal system'

Question:
What is a legal system based on religious beliefs of a region, clerics have authority?

Answer:
'religious law legal system'

Question:
What is a legal system in which two or more of other law systems are mixed together?

Answer:
'mixed law legal system'

Question:
What is a work or invention that is the result of creativity and for which one may apply for a patent, copyright, or trademark?

Answer:
'intellectual property'

Question:
What is a law that allows individuals or companies to protect what is rightly theirs from illegal duplication or use?

Answer:
'intellectual property law'

Security and Risk Management Domain

Question:
What is a type of property covering inventions or patents, industrial designs and trademarks?

Answer:
'industrial property'

Question:
What is a type of property covering literary and artistic works?

Answer:
'copyright property'

Question:
What is something a company creates or owns that is crucial to its survival and profitability?

Answer:
'trade secret'

Question:
What protects the expression of an idea rather than the idea itself?

Answer:
'copyright'

Question:
What protects a name, symbol, word, sound, shape, color or any combination thereof?

Answer:
'trademark'

Question:
What provides ownership of an invention and prevents others from copying or using the invention without permission?

Answer:
'patent'

Question:
What occurs when protected works or data are duplicated or used without permission?

Answer:
'software piracy'

Question:
What is a type of software licensing in which there are no restrictions on the use or redistribution?

Answer:
'freeware'

Question:
What is a type of software licensing in which the software is free for a period, during which some features may be disabled; after the period expires, the user is asked to pay for the continued use?

Answer:
'shareware, or trialware'

Security and Risk Management Domain

19

Question:
What is a type of software licensing in which an upfront price is paid for a copy or a license?

Answer:
'commercial'

Question:
What is a type of software licensing in which the software is provided for academic purposes at a reduced price?

Answer:
'academic'

Question:
What is used to communicate the licensing requirements for software?

Answer:
'End User License Agreement, or EULA'

Question:
What is an organization that promotes the enforcement of software rights in order to combat piracy?

Answer:
'Federation Against Software Theft, or FAST'

Question:
What is an organization that promotes the enforcement of software rights in order to combat piracy?

Answer:
'Business Software Alliance'

Question:
What is a law that prohibits attempts to circumvent copyright protection mechanisms?

Answer:
'Digital Millennium Copyright Act, or DMCA'

Question:
What is Europe's version of DCMA?

Answer:
'Copyright Directive'

Question:
What is any data that can be used to uniquely identify, contact or locate an individual?

Answer:
'Personally Identifiable Information, or PII'

Question:
What is a governmental organization that defines PII as name, ID, IP, vehicle, license, face/fingerprint/handwriting, credit card, birthdate, birthplace or genetic info?

Answer:
'Office of Management and Budget, or OMB'

Security and Risk Management Domain

20

Question:
What is a law stating that federal agencies could collect PII only if they had a need to?

Answer:
'Federal Privacy Act of 1974'

Question:
What is a law stating that federal agencies must secure PII?

Answer:
'Federal Information Security Management Act of 2002, or FISMA'

Question:
What is a law that applies to DVA only due to their gross neglect?

Answer:
'Department of Veterans Affairs Information Security Protection Act'

Question:
What is a law specific to the healthcare industry and defines PHI?

Answer:
'Health Insurance Portability and Accountability Act (HIPPA)'

Question:
What is a law that enforces HIPPA rules?

Answer:
'Health Information Technology for Economic and Clinical Health, or HITECH'

Question:
What is a law that greatly extended the government's power, particularly with monitoring electronic communication at-will?

Answer:
'USA Patriot Act'

Question:
What is a law that requires banks to allow customers to opt out of information sharing?

Answer:
'Gramm-Leach-Bliley Act, or GLBA'

Question:
What is a Canadian law dealing with the collection of private data?

Answer:
'Personal Information Protection and Electronic Document, or PIPEDA'

Question:
What is not a law, but rather a standard to protect credit card data?

Answer:
'Payment Card Industry Data Security Standard, or PCI-DSS'

Security and Risk Management Domain

21

Question:
What is a law that specifies who can investigate data breaches and protects intellectual property?

Answer:
'Economic Espionage Act of 1996'

Question:
What is a policy that contains a high-level statement describing how security works within the organization?

Answer:
'security policy'

Question:
What is a policy that dictates how a security program will be constructed, sets the various goals and describes how enforcement will be implemented?

Answer:
'organizational security policy, or master security policy'

Question:
What is a policy that provides more detail around areas that need further explanation?

Answer:
'issues-specific policy, or a functional policy'

Question:
What is a policy that contains details that are specific to a system?

Answer:
'system-specific policy'

Question:
What are informative, regulatory and advisory?

Answer:
'categories of policies'

Question:
What is a policy category that informs employees on a broad range of topics in an unenforceable manner?

Answer:
'informative'

Question:
What is a policy category that addresses regulatory requirements for a specific industry such as GLBA, PCI or HIPAA?

Answer:
'regulatory'

Question:
What is a policy category that advises employees on enforceable rules governing actions and behaviors?

Answer:
'advisory'

Security and Risk Management Domain

Question:
What provides tools on how to meet a policy?

Answer:
'standards'

Question:
What contains recommendations and guides for employees when a specific standard does not really apply?

Answer:
'guidelines'

Question:
What provides the step-by-step instructions on how to implement policies?

Answer:
'procedures'

Question:
What is established when a control has been put in place to mitigate a risk, used to know if risk has decreased or increased?

Answer:
'baselines'

Question:
What is the process of identifying, assessing and reducing risks to an acceptable level?

Answer:
'risk management'

Question:
What is a business-wide NIST SP 800-53 tier?

Answer:
'organizational'

Question:
What is a NIST SP 800-53 tier specific to major business processes within an organization?

Answer:
'business process'

Question:
What is a NIST SP 800-53 tier specific to information systems within a process?

Answer:
'information systems'

Question:
What is a policy that addresses objectives, acceptable risk, identification, strategic, poles, controls and budgets, allocation and monitoring?

Answer:
'Information Systems Risk Management Policy, or ISRM'

Security and Risk Management Domain

Question:
What is a type of team that has a single leader, and one to many people?

Answer:
'risk management team'

Question:
What is the risk management component that defines the assumptions, constraints, priorities and the amount of risk the organization can tolerate?

Answer:
'frame component'

Question:
What is the risk management component that determines threats, vulnerabilities and attack vectors?

Answer:
'assess component'

Question:
What is the risk management component that matches the available resources against a prioritized list of risks?

Answer:
'respond component'

Question:
What is the risk management component that continuously watches the controls to assess their effectiveness against the risk each was designed to protect the organization from?

Answer:
'monitor component'

Question:
What is an activity that produces a prioritized list of likely threats?

Answer:
'threat modeling'

Question:
What are comprised of information, processes and people?

Answer:
'information systems'

Question:
What is an information data type in which data is persisted to some type of storage device; this data can be stolen, thereby compromising its confidentiality?

Answer:
'data-at-rest'

Security and Risk Management Domain

Question:
What is an information data type in which data is in-transit from one system to another across some type of network; it can be stolen (compromised confidentiality) or modified (compromised integrity)?

Answer:
'data-in-motion'

Question:
What is an information data type which is being retrieved and exists in-memory; it can be stolen by retrieving from memory dumps (compromised confidentiality) or deleted (compromised availability)?

Answer:
'data-in-use'

Question:
What is a block of code executing in-memory?

Answer:
'process'

Question:
What is an attack in which an attacker tricks a person into ignoring security policies, usually through email or text messaging?

Answer:
'social engineering attack'

Question:
What is an attack in which an attacker either blackmails an individual using information found on social networking sites, or by customizing an email with that information to appear to be more legitimate?

Answer:
'social network attack'

Question:
What is an attack in which an attacker uses weak passwords and/or infrequently changed passwords?

Answer:
'password attack'

Question:
What is a potential cause of an unwanted incident, which may result in harm to a system or organization?

Answer:
'threat'

Question:
What is a node/leaf tree that shows the path an attack can follow?

Answer:
'attack tree'

Security and Risk Management Domain

25

Question:
What is a single path in an attack tree?

Answer:
'attack chain'

Question:
What is the act of figuring out which vulnerabilities should be addressed and which can be accepted without mitigation?

Answer:
'reduction analysis'

Question:
What is a list of vulnerabilities and threats?

Answer:
'risk assessment'

Question:
What prioritizes the risk assessment list and assesses resources required to mitigate top threats?

Answer:
'risk analysis'

Question:
What is an output of risk analysis that shows costs for a single year?

Answer:
'cost/benefit comparison'

Question:
What is a risk team made up of all departments?

Answer:
'risk analysis team'

Question:
What is a type of value representing a currency value assigned to an asset?

Answer:
'quantitative value'

Question:
What is a type of value that represents an intangible loss for the organization if an asset was compromised, stolen or lost?

Answer:
'qualitative value'

Question:
What is a logic flaw in computers?

Answer:
'illogical processing'

Security and Risk Management Domain

Question:
What is a small flaw passed to another process, which can then amplify the flaw?

Answer:
'cascading error'

Question:
What is the loss an organization would incur if a threat agent exploited a vulnerability?

Answer:
'loss potential'

Question:
What is a loss that occurs indirectly after a vulnerability is exploited?

Answer:
'delayed loss'

Question:
What is a methodology describing how risk management should be carried out?

Answer:
'ISO 27005'

Question:
What is a risk management methodology that states the people involved with a system or process should be the only ones making the decisions on security?

Answer:
'Operationally Critical Threat Asset and Valuation, or OCTAVE'

Question:
What is a risk management methodology that focuses on IT systems instead of organizational strategy?

Answer:
'NIST SP 800-30'

Question:
What is a risk management methodology that stresses a qualitative measurement of risk instead of trying to actually calculate a risk value?

Answer:
'Facilitated Risk Analysis Process, or FRAP'

Question:
What is a risk management methodology that identifies functions, their failures and the causes of those failures for a single system?

Answer:
'Failure Mode and Effect Analysis, FMEA'

Question:
What is FMEA for complex systems, with an attack tree but with the root being a failure instead of a successful attack?

Answer:
'fault tree analysis'

Security and Risk Management Domain

Question:
What is a risk management methodology that focuses on an organization's overall health?

Answer:
'AS/NZS 4360'

Question:
What is a risk management methodology form the UK, and for which Siemens has an automated tool?

Answer:
'Central Computing and Telecommunications Agency Risk Analysis and Management Method, or CRAMM'

Question:
What takes the output of a risk assessment and performs either a qualitative or quantitative analysis on it?

Answer:
'risk analysis approaches'

Question:
What is an analysis performed on a risk assessment that delivers categorizations that are more subjective and general in nature?

Answer:
'quantitative risk analysis'

Question:
What is the currency value of an asset calculated during the risk assessment?

Answer:
'Asset Value, or AV'

Question:
What is the percentage of loss a threat could have?

Answer:
'Exposure Factor, or EF'

Question:
What is represented by the formula SLE = AV*EF?

Answer:
'Single Loss Expectancy, or SLE'

Question:
What is the number of times per year we can expect the threat to take place?

Answer:
'Annualized Rate of Occurrence, or ARO'

Question:
What is represented by the formula ALE = SLE*ARO?

Answer:
'Annual Loss Expectancy, or ALE'

Security and Risk Management Domain

Question:
What is an analysis performed on a risk assessment that produces numbers, and is a scientific or mathematical approach, often with the y-axis representing likelihood, and x-axis representing the impact level?

Answer:
'qualitative risk analysis'

Question:
What is an iterative approach to reaching anonymous consensus?

Answer:
'Delphi technique'

Question:
What represents the risk an organization takes on if they choose not to put any controls in place?

Answer:
'total risk'

Question:
What represents the remaining risk after controls are applied?

Answer:
'residual risk'

Question:
What is the result if insurance against a risk is taken out, so that if we encounter an instance, someone else pays for it?

Answer:
'transferring risk'

Question:
What is a term used to describe when we terminate an activity that is causing risk?

Answer:
'risk avoidance'

Question:
What occurs when we reduce the risk using countermeasures (or controls) until the level of risk is acceptable?

Answer:
'risk reduction'

Question:
What is the result of deciding to take the hit if we encounter an instance?

Answer:
'accepting risk'

Security and Risk Management Domain

Question:
What is an internal controls audit useful when outsourcing?

Answer:
'SAS 70'

Question:
What are frameworks employed to allow an organization to identify, reduce and monitor risk mitigation?

Answer:
'Risk Management Frameworks, or RMFs'

Question:
What is a framework that operates around a systems life-cycle and focuses on certification and accreditation?

Answer:
'NIST RMF, or SP 800-37'

Question:
What is a framework standard that acknowledges that there are things which we cannot control, focuses instead on managing the fallout and can be broadly applied to an entire organization?

Answer:
'ISO 31000'

Question:
What is a framework that attempts to integrate NIST, ISO 31000 and COBIT?

Answer:
'ISACA Risk IT'

Question:
What is a generic framework taking a top-down approach?

Answer:
'COSO Enterprise Risk Management–Integrated Framework'

Question:
What are a collection of security controls that together constitute a baseline?

Answer:
'common controls'

Question:
What is an existing control that needs to be modified?

Answer:
'hybrid control'

Question:
What is a new control that should be created?

Answer:
'system-specific control'

Security and Risk Management Domain

Question:
What describes how we can minimize the effects of a disaster or disruption and return to productivity?

Answer:
'Disaster Recovery, or DR'

Question:
What is a plan that goes into effect during a disaster or emergency?

Answer:
'Disaster Recovery Plan, or DRP'

Question:
What describes how an organization will return to full capacity?

Answer:
'Continuity Planning'

Question:
What results when both DR and continuity planning are combined?

Answer:
'Business Continuity Management, or BCM'

Question:
What is a plan that implements BCM?

Answer:
'Business Continuity Plan, or BCP'

Question:
What is a person who works with management to create a BCP committee?

Answer:
'business continuity coordinator'

Question:
What is a policy that defines BCM scope, mission, principles, guidelines and standards?

Answer:
'BCP policy'

Question:
What stands for Strengths, Weaknesses, Opportunities, Threats?

Answer:
'SWOT'

Question:
What occurs when everything within one's power has been done to prevent a disaster from happening?

Answer:
'due diligence'

Question:

Security and Risk Management Domain

Question:
What occurs when precautions have been taken that a reasonable and competent person would have implemented?

Answer:
'due care'

Question:
What is an action that identifies and classifies business and individual functions?

Answer:
'Business Impact Analysis, or BIA'

Question:
What defines how long an organization can survive without a system?

Answer:
'Maximum Tolerable Downtime, or MTD'

Question:
What is another name for MTD, or Maximum Tolerable Downtime?

Answer:
'Maximum Period Time of Disruption, or MPTD'

Question:
What is a plan that dictates who will step in until the executive returns or a permanent replacement can be found?

Answer:
'executive succession plan'

Question:
What is a personnel security control that ensures a single person cannot complete a critical task by himself?

Answer:
'separation of duties'

Question:
What is a personnel security control that ensures a single person cannot purposefully or accidentally cause a disastrous incident?

Answer:
'dual control'

Question:
What is a personnel security control in which separation of duties is usually put into place to prevent fraud?

Answer:
'split knowledge'

Question:
What is a personnel security control that prevents two people knowingly working together to from committing fraud?

Answer:
'collusion'

Security and Risk Management Domain

Question:
What is a personnel security control that moves employees around so that each does not have control over the same business function for too long?

Answer:
'rotation of duties'

Question:
What is a personnel security control that forces an employee to vacate a position so the organization can detect a change in potentially fraudulent activities?

Answer:
'mandatory vacation'

Question:
What are NDAs, background checks and behavioral testing?

Answer:
'good hiring practices'

Question:
What is an employee contract that addresses conflict of interests and protection of the organization's intellectual property?

Answer:
'Non-Disclosure Agreement, or NDA'

Question:
What is a policy for terminated employees that defines how to recover assets, disable access, and escort the employee from the premises?

Answer:
'termination policy'

Question:
What is a type of training that must happen during the hiring process?

Answer:
'security-awareness training'

Question:
What consists of a short orientation that focuses on how security pertains to corporate assets and financial goals and losses?

Answer:
'management security training'

Question:
What consists of a discussion of policies, procedures, standards and guidelines?

Answer:
'staff security training'

Security and Risk Management Domain

Question:
What is 'seclusion'?

Answer:
'seclusion' is achieved by storing something in an out-of-the-way manner.

Question:
What is 'isolation'?

Answer:
'isolation' is achieved when we keep something separate from others.

Question:
What is 'integrity'?

Answer:
'integrity' is achieved when information remains unaltered (and can be proven to be so) except by authorized parties, prevents both intentional and accidental modifications, and ensures consistency remains valid.

Question:
What is 'availability'?

Answer:
'availability' is achieved when usable access to a resource is always provided in a timely and uninterrupted manner.

Question:
What is 'AAA'?

Answer:
'AAA' is an abbreviation for authentication, authorization and auditing.

Question:
What is 'identification'?

Answer:
'identification' occurs when a subject claims a specific identity.

Question:
What is 'authentication'?

Answer:
'authentication' occurs when a subject proves they are who they claim to be.

Question:
What is 'authorization'?

Answer:
'authorization' is the act of deciding what object a subject can access and how it can be used.

Question:
What is 'auditing'?

Answer:
'auditing' is the act of recording the activities of a subject in a log.

Security and Risk Management Domain

Question:
What is 'accountability'?

Answer:
'accountability' occurs when logs are reviewed to check for compliance.

Question:
What is a 'vulnerability'?

Answer:
A 'vulnerability' is a weakness in a system that allows a threat to compromise security.

Question:
What is a 'threat'?

Answer:
A 'threat' is the danger that a vulnerability might be exploited.

Question:
What is an 'exploit'?

Answer:
An 'exploit' occurs when a vulnerability is taken advantage of by an attacker.

Question:
What is a 'threat agent'?

Answer:
A 'threat agent' is a person or process that exploits a vulnerability.

Question:
What is a 'risk'?

Answer:
A 'risk' is the likelihood that a threat agent will exploit a vulnerability combined with the damage that could result.

Question:
What is an 'exposure'?

Answer:
An 'exposure' is a single real-world instance of a vulnerability being exploited by a threat agent.

Question:
What is a 'control'?

Answer:
A 'control' mitigates a risk.

Question:
What is an 'administrative control'?

Answer:
An 'administrative control' is a type of management control that includes training, security policies and documentation, and managing risk.

Security and Risk Management Domain

Question:
What is a 'technical control'?

Answer:
A 'technical control' is a type of control comprised of software or hardware elements such as hashing or encryption, firewalls and enforcing authentication.

Question:
What is a 'logical control'?

Answer:
A 'logical control' is another name for a technical control.

Question:
What is a 'physical control'?

Answer:
A 'physical control' is a type of control comprised of external lighting, locked doors, fences, card keys and security guards.

Question:
What is 'defense-in-depth'?

Answer:
'defense-in-depth' occurs when we use multiple categories of controls in a layered approach.

Question:
What is a 'preventative control'?

Answer:
A 'preventative control' is a control that can avoid an incident.

Question:
What is a 'deterrent control'?

Answer:
A 'deterrent control' is a control that can discourage an attacker.

Question:
What is a 'detective control'?

Answer:
A 'detective control' is a control that can identify an intruder.

Question:
What is a 'corrective control'?

Answer:
A 'corrective control' is a control that can fix a component or system.

Question:
What is a 'recovery control'?

Answer:
A 'recovery control' is a control that can bring environments back to normal operation.

Security and Risk Management Domain

Question:
What is a 'compensating control'?

Answer:
A 'compensating control' is a control that can provide an alternative control if the first choice is unavailable.

Question:
What is a 'security framework'?

Answer:
A 'security framework' is an approach on how to recognize and deal with weaknesses.

Question:
What is the 'ISO 27000 series'?

Answer:
The 'ISO 27000 series' is the only framework geared specifically to security.

Question:
What is an 'ISMS'?

Answer:
An 'ISMS' is a set of policies, processes and systems to manage risk.

Question:
What is 'ISO 27001'?

Answer:
'ISO 27001' is a standard that sets forward an ISMS.

Question:
What is 'ISO 27002'?

Answer:
'ISO 27002' is a standard that provides a code of practice for implementing an ISMS.

Question:
What is an 'enterprise architecture'?

Answer:
An 'enterprise architecture' addresses the more general structure and behavior of an entire organization.

Question:
What is the 'Zachman Framework'?

Answer:
The 'Zachman Framework' is a 2-dimensional matrix with 5 different audiences on the Y-axis, and 6 different views on the X-axis.

Question:
What is the 'Open-Group Architecture Framework, or TOGAF'?

Answer:
The 'Open-Group Architecture Framework, or TOGAF' defines 4 types - Business, Data, Application and Technology - and is created by the Architecture Development Method (ADM).

Security and Risk Management Domain

Question:
What is the 'Department of Defense Architecture Framework, or DoDAF'?

Answer:
The 'Department of Defense Architecture Framework, or DoDAF' was created by the US military and ensures a common communication protocol as well as standard payloads.

Question:
What is the 'Ministry of Defence Architecture Framework, or MoDAF'?

Answer:
The 'Ministry of Defence Architecture Framework, or MoDAF' is the British version of DoDAF.

Question:
What is the 'Sherwood Applied Business Security Architecture, or SABSA'?

Answer:
The 'Sherwood Applied Business Security Architecture, or SABSA' is a framework similar to Zachman but focused on security; also, a methodology and process, not just a framework.

Question:
What is 'strategic alignment'?

Answer:
'strategic alignment' is achieved when the needs of the business are met as well as all legal or regulatory requirements.

Question:
What is 'business enablement'?

Answer:
'business enablement' is achieved when we acknowledge the importance of security while not losing sight of the reason for an organization's existence.

Question:
What is 'process enhancement'?

Answer:
'process enhancement' is achieved when security actually increases an existing process' efficiency.

Question:
What is 'security effectiveness'?

Answer:
'security effectiveness' ensures that ISMS controls have achieved the desired results.

Question:
What is the 'Control Objectives for Information and Related Technologies, or COBIT'?

Answer:
The 'Control Objectives for Information and Related Technologies, or COBIT' is a framework that ties private industry IT, business and stakeholder goals together and provides for IT governance.

Security and Risk Management Domain

Question:
What is 'NIST SP 800-53'?

Answer:
'NIST SP 800-53' is a framework that ties federal agency goals to FISMA.

Question:
What is the 'Committee of Sponsoring Organizations, or COSO'?

Answer:
The 'Committee of Sponsoring Organizations, or COSO' is a framework that provides corporate governance (COBIT is a subset for security).

Question:
What is 'ITIL'?

Answer:
'ITIL' is a process management tool that focuses on SLAs between IT and internal customers.

Question:
What is 'Six Sigma'?

Answer:
'Six Sigma' is a process management tool that measures process quality using statistical calculations by identifying defects.

Question:
What is the 'Capability Maturity Model Integration, or CMMI'?

Answer:
The 'Capability Maturity Model Integration, or CMMI' is a process management tool that determines the maturity of an organization's processes by assigning 1 of 6 levels.

Question:
What is the 'Process Life Cycle'?

Answer:
The 'Process Life Cycle' is a process in which the last step feeds into the first step iteratively.

Question:
What is the 'plan step'?

Answer:
The 'plan step' contains the following activities: identify changes needed, create architecture, select solutions, and get approval.

Question:
What is the 'implement step'?

Answer:
The 'implement step' contains the following activities: assign duties, create baselines, create blueprint, implement, enable monitoring, and define SLAs.

Security and Risk Management Domain

Question:
What is the 'operate step'?

Answer:
The 'operate step' contains the following activities: monitor, carry out tasks, and ensure SLAs.

Question:
What is the 'evaluate step'?

Answer:
The 'evaluate step' contains the following activities: review and identify changes for the next iteration.

Question:
What is 'computer crime law'?

Answer:
'computer crime law' is any activity that deals with a computer-based crime.

Question:
What is 'categories of computer crime law'?

Answer:
'categories of computer crime law' are the 3 following categories: computer assisted, computer-targeted and computer is incidental.

Question:
What is 'computer-assisted'?

Answer:
'computer-assisted' is a computer-crime category in which the computer is a tool.

Question:
What is 'computer-targeted'?

Answer:
'computer-targeted' is a computer-crime category in which the computer is the victim (and indirectly the computer's owner).

Question:
What is 'computer is incidental'?

Answer:
'computer is incidental' is a computer-crime category in which the computer was involved but was not the victim or did not play a significant role in the crime.

Question:
What is 'script kiddies'?

Answer:
'script kiddies' are unsophisticated individuals who use pre-built tools.

Question:
What is an 'Advanced Persistent Threat, or APT'?

Answer:
An 'Advanced Persistent Threat, or APT' are patient criminals who will spend weeks or months probing for weaknesses.

Security and Risk Management Domain

Question:
What is the 'foothold step'?

Answer:
The 'foothold step' is the first step in gaining access by using phishing or zero-day attacks.

Question:
What is the 'install step'?

Answer:
The 'install step' is the second step in gaining access by installing back doors on vulnerable machines.

Question:
What is the 'lateral step'?

Answer:
The 'lateral step' is the third step in gaining access by using lateral movement to other accounts or systems.

Question:
What is the 'gather step'?

Answer:
The 'gather step' is the fourth step in gaining access by gathering data from servers and preparing for exfiltration.

Question:
What is the 'exfiltrate step'?

Answer:
The 'exfiltrate step' is the fifth step in gaining access by exfiltrating the data via various means to a compromised machine hosted elsewhere.

Question:
What is the 'OECD'?

Answer:
The 'OECD' is an international organization providing guidelines dealing with data transferred between countries.

Question:
What is the 'OECD collection limitation principle'?

Answer:
The 'OECD collection limitation principle' is an OECD core principle stating that collection of personal data must be limited and lawful, and with the knowledge of the subject.

Question:
What is the 'OECD data quality principle'?

Answer:
The 'OECD data quality principle' is an OECD core principle stating that personal data should be kept complete and current, and be relevant for the purpose.

Security and Risk Management Domain

Question:
What is the 'OECD purpose specification principle'?

Answer:
The 'OECD purpose specification principle' is an OECD core principle stating that subjects should be notified of the reason for the collection of personal data and should only be used for that purpose.

Question:
What is the 'OECD use limitation principle'?

Answer:
The 'OECD use limitation principle' is an OECD core principle stating that if data is to be used for any other purpose than stated, the subject must give consent or law must provide authority.

Question:
What is the 'OECD security safeguards principle'?

Answer:
The 'OECD security safeguards principle' is an OECD core principle stating that safeguards should be put into place to protect collected data.

Question:
What is the 'OECD openness principle'?

Answer:
The 'OECD openness principle' is an OECD core principle stating that practices and policies with regard to personal data should be openly communicated, and subjects should be able to easily determine what data has been collected and where it is stored.

Question:
What is the 'OECD individual participation principle'?

Answer:
The 'OECD individual participation principle' is an OECD core principle stating that subjects must be able to find out if an organization has their personal data and be able to correct errors.

Question:
What is the 'OECD accountability principle'?

Answer:
The 'OECD accountability principle' is an OECD core principle stating that organizations should be accountable for complying with measures that support all other privacy rules.

Question:
What is the 'Safe Harbor Privacy Principles, or Safe Harbor'?

Answer:
The 'Safe Harbor Privacy Principles, or Safe Harbor' is a special framework that has been developed for US and EU data transfer requirements.

Question:
What is the 'Safe Harbor notice rule'?

Answer:
The 'Safe Harbor notice rule' is a Safe Harbor rule stating that individuals must be notified when personal data is to be collected.

Security and Risk Management Domain

Question:
What is the 'Safe Harbor choice rule'?

Answer:
The 'Safe Harbor choice rule' is a Safe Harbor rule stating that individuals must be able to opt out of the collection.

Question:
What is the 'Safe Harbor onward transfer rule'?

Answer:
The 'Safe Harbor onward transfer rule' is a Safe Harbor rule stating that transfer of data to third parties may happen only if the third party follows adequate data protection principles.

Question:
What is the 'Safe Harbor security rule'?

Answer:
The 'Safe Harbor security rule' is a Safe Harbor rule stating that reasonable effort must be made to prevent loss of collected data.

Question:
What is the 'Safe Harbor Data Integrity rule'?

Answer:
The 'Safe Harbor Data Integrity rule' is a Safe Harbor rule stating that collected data must be relevant and reliable for the purpose it was collected for.

Question:
What is the 'Safe Harbor access rule'?

Answer:
The 'Safe Harbor access rule' is a Safe Harbor rule stating that individuals must be able to access the information held about them and correct errors.

Question:
What is the 'Safe Harbor enforcement rule'?

Answer:
The 'Safe Harbor enforcement rule' is a Safe Harbor rule stating that there must be an effective means of enforcing other Safe Harbor rules.

Question:
What is the 'Wassenaar Arrangement'?

Answer:
The 'Wassenaar Arrangement' is an international agreement regarding the import and export of goods.

Question:
What is the 'civil law legal system, or code law'?

Answer:
The 'civil law legal system, or code law' is a legal system used in European countries based on rules, where lower courts can ignore higher court decisions.

Security and Risk Management Domain

Question:
What is the 'common law legal system'?

Answer:
The 'common law legal system' is a legal system based on precedence using a judge and jury, where higher court decisions must be recognized by lower courts.

Question:
What is the 'criminal legal system'?

Answer:
The 'criminal legal system' is a legal system in which a government law has been broken and guilt must be established beyond reasonable doubt for a guilty/not guilty verdict, with loss of freedom if convicted.

Question:
What is the 'civil/tort legal system'?

Answer:
The 'civil/tort legal system' is a legal system in which wrongs committed against an individual or company, and a prudent man, is used to reach a liable/not liable verdict; no loss of freedom results.

Question:
What is the 'administrative legal system'?

Answer:
The 'administrative legal system' is a legal system in which regulatory standards are defined by government agencies and are almost always applied to companies only.

Question:
What is the 'customary law legal system'?

Answer:
The 'customary law legal system' is a legal system based on traditions and customs of a specific region, usually mixed with another law, in which restitution is money or services; this is often found in China and India.

Question:
What is the 'religious law legal system'?

Answer:
The 'religious law legal system' is a legal system based on religious beliefs of a region, clerics have authority.

Question:
What is the 'mixed law legal system'?

Answer:
The 'mixed law legal system' is a legal system in which two or more of other law systems are mixed together.

Question:
What is 'intellectual property'?

Answer:
'intellectual property' is a work or invention that is the result of creativity and for which one may apply for a patent, copyright, or trademark.

Security and Risk Management Domain

Question:
What is the 'intellectual property law'?

Answer:
The 'intellectual property law' is a law that allows individuals or companies to protect what is rightly theirs from illegal duplication or use.

Question:
What is 'industrial property'?

Answer:
'industrial property' is a type of property covering inventions or patents, industrial designs and trademarks.

Question:
What is 'copyright property'?

Answer:
'copyright property' is a type of property covering literary and artistic works.

Question:
What is 'trade secret'?

Answer:
'trade secret' is something a company creates or owns that is crucial to its survival and profitability.

Question:
What is 'copyright'?

Answer:
'copyright' protects the expression of an idea rather than the idea itself.

Question:
What is 'trademark'?

Answer:
'trademark' protects a name, symbol, word, sound, shape, color or any combination thereof.

Question:
What is 'patent'?

Answer:
'patent' provides ownership of an invention and prevents others from copying or using the invention without permission.

Question:
What is 'software piracy'?

Answer:
'software piracy' occurs when protected works or data are duplicated or used without permission.

Question:
What is 'freeware'?

Answer:
'freeware' is a type of software licensing in which there are no restrictions on the use or redistribution.

Security and Risk Management Domain

Question:
What is 'shareware, or trialware'?

Answer:
'shareware, or trialware' is a type of software licensing in which the software is free for a period of time, during which some features may be disabled; after the period expires, the user is asked to pay for the continued use.

Question:
What is 'commercial'?

Answer:
'commercial' is a type of software licensing in which an upfront price is paid for a copy or a license.

Question:
What is 'academic'?

Answer:
'academic' is a type of software licensing in which the software is provided for academic purposes at a reduced price.

Question:
What is the 'End User License Agreement, or EULA'?

Answer:
The 'End User License Agreement, or EULA' is used to communicate the licensing requirements for software.

Question:
What is the 'Federation Against Software Theft, or FAST'?

Answer:
The 'Federation Against Software Theft, or FAST' is an organization that promotes the enforcement of software rights in order to combat piracy.

Question:
What is the 'Business Software Alliance'?

Answer:
The 'Business Software Alliance' is an organization that promotes the enforcement of software rights in order to combat piracy.

Question:
What is the 'Digital Millennium Copyright Act, or DMCA'?

Answer:
The 'Digital Millennium Copyright Act, or DMCA' is a law that prohibits attempts to circumvent copyright protection mechanisms.

Question:
What is the 'Copyright Directive'?

Answer:
The 'Copyright Directive' is Europe's version of DCMA.

Question:
What is 'Personally Identifiable Information, or PII'?

Answer:
'Personally Identifiable Information, or PII' is any data that can be used to uniquely identify, contact or locate an individual.

Security and Risk Management Domain

Question:
What is the 'Office of Management and Budget, or OMB'?

Answer:
The 'Office of Management and Budget, or OMB' is a governmental organization that defines PII as name, ID, IP, vehicle, license, face/fingerprint/handwriting, credit card, birthdate, birthplace or genetic info.

Question:
What is the 'Federal Privacy Act of 1974'?

Answer:
The 'Federal Privacy Act of 1974' is a law stating that federal agencies could collect PII only if they had a need to.

Question:
What is the 'Federal Information Security Management Act of 2002, or FISMA'?

Answer:
The 'Federal Information Security Management Act of 2002, or FISMA' is a law stating that federal agencies must secure PII.

Question:
What is the 'Department of Veterans Affairs Information Security Protection Act'?

Answer:
The 'Department of Veterans Affairs Information Security Protection Act' is a law that applies to DVA only due to their gross neglect.

Question:
What is the 'Health Insurance Portability and Accountability Act (HIPPA)'?

Answer:
The 'Health Insurance Portability and Accountability Act (HIPPA)' is a law specific to the healthcare industry and defines PHI.

Question:
What is the 'Health Information Technology for Economic and Clinical Health, or HITECH'?

Answer:
The 'Health Information Technology for Economic and Clinical Health, or HITECH' is a law that enforces HIPPA rules.

Question:
What is the 'USA Patriot Act'?

Answer:
The 'USA Patriot Act' is a law that greatly extended the government's power, particularly with monitoring electronic communication at-will.

Question:
What is the 'Gramm-Leach-Bliley Act, or GLBA'?

Answer:
The 'Gramm-Leach-Bliley Act, or GLBA' is a law that requires banks to allow customers to opt out of information sharing.

Security and Risk Management Domain

Question:
What is the 'Personal Information Protection and Electronic Document, or PIPEDA'?

Answer:
The 'Personal Information Protection and Electronic Document, or PIPEDA' is a Canadian law dealing with the collection of private data.

Question:
What is the 'Payment Card Industry Data Security Standard, or PCI-DSS'?

Answer:
The 'Payment Card Industry Data Security Standard, or PCI-DSS' is not a law, but rather a standard to protect credit card data.

Question:
What is the 'Economic Espionage Act of 1996'?

Answer:
The 'Economic Espionage Act of 1996' is a law that specifies who can investigate data breaches and protects intellectual property.

Question:
What is 'security policy'?

Answer:
'security policy' is a policy that contains a high-level statement describing how security works within the organization.

Question:
What is the 'organizational security policy, or master security policy'?

Answer:
The 'organizational security policy, or master security policy' is a policy that dictates how a security program will be constructed, sets the various goals and describes how enforcement will be implemented.

Question:
What is an 'issues-specific policy, or a functional policy'?

Answer:
An 'issues-specific policy, or a functional policy' is a policy that provides more detail around areas that need further explanation.

Question:
What is the 'system-specific policy'?

Answer:
The 'system-specific policy' is a policy that contains details that are specific to a system.

Question:
What is 'categories of policies'?

Answer:
'categories of policies' are informative, regulatory and advisory.

Question:
What is 'informative'?

Answer:
'informative' is a policy category that informs employees on a broad range of topics in an unenforceable manner.

Security and Risk Management Domain

Question:
What is 'regulatory'?

Answer:
'regulatory' is a policy category that addresses regulatory requirements for a specific industry such as GLBA, PCI or HIPAA.

Question:
What is 'advisory'?

Answer:
'advisory' is a policy category that advises employees on enforceable rules governing actions and behaviors.

Question:
What is 'standards'?

Answer:
'standards' provides tools on how to meet a policy.

Question:
What is 'guidelines'?

Answer:
'guidelines' contains recommendations and guides for employees when a specific standard does not really apply.

Question:
What is 'procedures'?

Answer:
'procedures' provides the step-by-step instructions on how to implement policies.

Question:
What is 'baselines'?

Answer:
'baselines' is established when a control has been put in place to mitigate a risk, used to know if risk has decreased or increased.

Question:
What is 'risk management'?

Answer:
'risk management' is the process of identifying, assessing and reducing risks to an acceptable level.

Question:
What is 'organizational'?

Answer:
'organizational' is a business-wide NIST SP 800-53 tier.

Question:
What is 'business process'?

Answer:
'business process' is a NIST SP 800-53 tier specific to major business processes within an organization.

Security and Risk Management Domain

51

Question:
What is 'information systems'?

Answer:
'information systems' is a NIST SP 800-53 tier specific to information systems within a process.

Question:
What is the 'Information Systems Risk Management Policy, or ISRM'?

Answer:
The 'Information Systems Risk Management Policy, or ISRM' is a policy that addresses objectives, acceptable risk, identification, strategic, poles, controls and budgets, allocation and monitoring.

Question:
What is the 'risk management team'?

Answer:
The 'risk management team' is a type of team that has a single leader, and one to many people.

Question:
What is the 'frame component'?

Answer:
The 'frame component' is the risk management component that defines the assumptions, constraints, priorities and the amount of risk the organization can tolerate.

Question:
What is the 'assess component'?

Answer:
The 'assess component' is the risk management component that determines threats, vulnerabilities and attack vectors.

Question:
What is the 'respond component'?

Answer:
The 'respond component' is the risk management component that matches the available resources against a prioritized list of risks.

Question:
What is the 'monitor component'?

Answer:
The 'monitor component' is the risk management component that continuously watches the controls to assess their effectiveness against the risk each was designed to protect the organization from.

Question:
What is 'threat modeling'?

Answer:
'threat modeling' is an activity that produces a prioritized list of likely threats.

Security and Risk Management Domain

Question:
What is 'information systems'?

Answer:
'information systems' are comprised of information, processes and people.

Question:
What is 'data-at-rest'?

Answer:
'data-at-rest' is an information data type in which data is persisted to some type of storage device; this data can be stolen, thereby compromising its confidentiality.

Question:
What is 'data-in-motion'?

Answer:
'data-in-motion' is an information data type in which data is in-transit from one system to another across some type of network; it can be stolen (compromised confidentiality) or modified (compromised integrity).

Question:
What is 'data-in-use'?

Answer:
'data-in-use' is an information data type which is being retrieved and exists in-memory; it can be stolen by retrieving from memory dumps (compromised confidentiality) or deleted (compromised availability).

Question:
What is a 'process'?

Answer:
A 'process' is a block of code executing in-memory.

Question:
What is a 'social engineering attack'?

Answer:
A 'social engineering attack' is an attack in which an attacker tricks a person into ignoring security policies, usually through email or text messaging.

Question:
What is a 'social network attack'?

Answer:
A 'social network attack' is an attack in which an attacker either blackmails an individual using information found on social networking sites, or by customizing an email with that information to appear to be more legitimate.

Question:
What is a 'password attack'?

Answer:
A 'password attack' is an attack in which an attacker uses weak passwords and/or infrequently changed passwords.

Security and Risk Management Domain

Question:
What is a 'threat'?

Answer:
A 'threat' is a potential cause of an unwanted incident, which may result in harm to a system or organization.

Question:
What is an 'attack tree'?

Answer:
An 'attack tree' is a node/leaf tree that shows the path an attack can follow.

Question:
What is an 'attack chain'?

Answer:
An 'attack chain' is a single path in an attack tree.

Question:
What is a 'reduction analysis'?

Answer:
A 'reduction analysis' is the act of figuring out which vulnerabilities should be addressed and which can be accepted without mitigation.

Question:
What is a 'risk assessment'?

Answer:
A 'risk assessment' is a list of vulnerabilities and threats.

Question:
What is a 'risk analysis'?

Answer:
A 'risk analysis' prioritizes the risk assessment list and assesses resources required to mitigate top threats.

Question:
What is a 'cost/benefit comparison'?

Answer:
A 'cost/benefit comparison' is an output of risk analysis that shows costs for a single year.

Question:
What is a 'risk analysis team'?

Answer:
A 'risk analysis team' is a risk team made up of all departments.

Question:
What is a 'quantitative value'?

Answer:
A 'quantitative value' is a type of value representing a currency value assigned to an asset.

Security and Risk Management Domain

Question:
What is a 'qualitative value'?

Answer:
A 'qualitative value' is a type of value that represents an intangible loss for the organization if an asset was compromised, stolen or lost.

Question:
What is 'illogical processing'?

Answer:
'illogical processing' is a logic flaw in computers.

Question:
What is a 'cascading error'?

Answer:
A 'cascading error' is a small flaw passed to another process, which can then amplify the flaw.

Question:
What is a 'loss potential'?

Answer:
A 'loss potential' is the loss an organization would incur if a threat agent exploited a vulnerability.

Question:
What is a 'delayed loss'?

Answer:
A 'delayed loss' is a loss that occurs indirectly after a vulnerability is exploited.

Question:
What is 'ISO 27005'?

Answer:
'ISO 27005' is a methodology describing how risk management should be carried out.

Question:
What is the 'Operationally Critical Threat Asset and Valuation, or OCTAVE'?

Answer:
The 'Operationally Critical Threat Asset and Valuation, or OCTAVE' is a risk management methodology that states the people involved with a system or process should be the only ones making the decisions on security.

Question:
What is 'NIST SP 800-30'?

Answer:
'NIST SP 800-30' is a risk management methodology that focuses on IT systems instead of organizational strategy.

Security and Risk Management Domain

Question:
What is the 'Facilitated Risk Analysis Process, or FRAP'?

Answer:
The 'Facilitated Risk Analysis Process, or FRAP' is a risk management methodology that stresses a qualitative measurement of risk instead of trying to actually calculate a risk value.

Question:
What is the 'Failure Mode and Effect Analysis, FMEA'?

Answer:
The 'Failure Mode and Effect Analysis, FMEA' is a risk management methodology that identifies functions, their failures and the causes of those failures for a single system.

Question:
What is a 'fault tree analysis'?

Answer:
A 'fault tree analysis' is FMEA for complex systems, with an attack tree but with the root being a failure instead of a successful attack.

Question:
What is the 'AS/NZS 4360'?

Answer:
The 'AS/NZS 4360' is a risk management methodology that focuses on an organization's overall health.

Question:
What is the 'Central Computing and Telecommunications Agency Risk Analysis and Management Method, or CRAMM'?

Answer:
The 'Central Computing and Telecommunications Agency Risk Analysis and Management Method, or CRAMM' is a risk management methodology form the UK, and for which Siemens has an automated tool.

Question:
What is 'risk analysis approaches'?

Answer:
'risk analysis approaches' takes the output of a risk assessment and performs either a qualitative or quantitative analysis on it.

Question:
What is 'quantitative risk analysis'?

Answer:
'quantitative risk analysis' is an analysis performed on a risk assessment that delivers categorizations that are more subjective and general in nature.

Question:
What is the 'Asset Value, or AV'?

Answer:
The 'Asset Value, or AV' is the currency value of an asset calculated during the risk assessment.

Security and Risk Management Domain

Question:
What is the 'Exposure Factor, or EF'?

Answer:
The 'Exposure Factor, or EF' is the percentage of loss a threat could have.

Question:
What is the 'Single Loss Expectancy, or SLE'?

Answer:
The 'Single Loss Expectancy, or SLE' is represented by the formula SLE = AV*EF.

Question:
What is the 'Annualized Rate of Occurrence, or ARO'?

Answer:
The 'Annualized Rate of Occurrence, or ARO' is the number of times per year we can expect the threat to take place.

Question:
What is the 'Annual Loss Expectancy, or ALE'?

Answer:
The 'Annual Loss Expectancy, or ALE' is represented by the formula ALE = SLE*ARO.

Question:
What is 'qualitative risk analysis'?

Answer:
'qualitative risk analysis' is an analysis performed on a risk assessment that produces numbers, and is a scientific or mathematical approach, often with the y-axis representing likelihood, and x-axis representing the impact level.

Question:
What is the 'Delphi technique'?

Answer:
The 'Delphi technique' is an iterative approach to reaching anonymous consensus.

Question:
What is 'total risk'?

Answer:
'total risk' represents the risk an organization takes on if they choose not to put any controls in place.

Question:
What is 'residual risk'?

Answer:
'residual risk' represents the remaining risk after controls are applied.

Question:
What is 'transferring risk'?

Answer:
'transferring risk' is the result if insurance against a risk is taken out, so that if we encounter an instance, someone else pays for it.

Security and Risk Management Domain

Question:
What is 'risk avoidance'?

Answer:
'risk avoidance' is a term used to describe when we terminate an activity that is causing risk.

Question:
What is 'risk reduction'?

Answer:
'risk reduction' occurs when we reduce the risk using countermeasures (or controls) until the level of risk is acceptable.

Question:
What is 'accepting risk'?

Answer:
'accepting risk' is the result of deciding to take the hit if we encounter an instance.

Question:
What is the 'SAS 70'?

Answer:
The 'SAS 70' is an internal controls audit useful when outsourcing.

Question:
What is the 'Risk Management Frameworks, or RMFs'?

Answer:
The 'Risk Management Frameworks, or RMFs' are frameworks employed to allow an organization to identify, reduce and monitor risk mitigation.

Question:
What is 'NIST RMF, or SP 800-37'?

Answer:
'NIST RMF, or SP 800-37' is a framework that operates around a systems life-cycle and focuses on certification and accreditation.

Question:
What is 'ISO 31000'?

Answer:
'ISO 31000' is a framework standard that acknowledges that there are things which we cannot control, focuses instead on managing the fallout and can be broadly applied to an entire organization.

Question:
What is 'ISACA Risk IT'?

Answer:
'ISACA Risk IT' is a framework that attempts to integrate NIST, ISO 31000 and COBIT.

Question:
What is the 'COSO Enterprise Risk Management–Integrated Framework'?

Answer:
The 'COSO Enterprise Risk Management–Integrated Framework' is a generic framework taking a top-down approach.

Security and Risk Management Domain

Question:
What is 'common controls'?

Answer:
'common controls' are a collection of security controls that together constitute a baseline.

Question:
What is a 'hybrid control'?

Answer:
A 'hybrid control' is an existing control that needs to be modified.

Question:
What is a 'system-specific control'?

Answer:
A 'system-specific control' is a new control that should be created.

Question:
What is 'Disaster Recovery, or DR'?

Answer:
'Disaster Recovery, or DR' describes how we can minimize the effects of a disaster or disruption and return to productivity.

Question:
What is the 'Disaster Recovery Plan, or DRP'?

Answer:
The 'Disaster Recovery Plan, or DRP' is a plan that goes into effect during a disaster or emergency.

Question:
What is 'Continuity Planning'?

Answer:
'Continuity Planning' describes how an organization will return to full capacity.

Question:
What is 'Business Continuity Management, or BCM'?

Answer:
'Business Continuity Management, or BCM' results when both DR and continuity planning are combined.

Question:
What is the 'Business Continuity Plan, or BCP'?

Answer:
The 'Business Continuity Plan, or BCP' is a plan that implements BCM.

Question:
What is the 'business continuity coordinator'?

Answer:
The 'business continuity coordinator' is a person who works with management to create a BCP committee.

Question:
What is the 'BCP policy'?

Security and Risk Management Domain

Answer:
The 'BCP policy' is a policy that defines BCM scope, mission, principles, guidelines and standards.

Question:
What is 'SWOT'?

Answer:
'SWOT' stands for Strengths, Weaknesses, Opportunities, Threats.

Question:
What is 'due diligence'?

Answer:
'due diligence' occurs when everything within one's power has been done to prevent a disaster from happening.

Question:
What is 'due care'?

Answer:
'due care' occurs when precautions have been taken that a reasonable and competent person would have implemented.

Question:
What is the 'Business Impact Analysis, or BIA'?

Answer:
The 'Business Impact Analysis, or BIA' is an action that identifies and classifies business and individual functions.

Question:
What is 'Maximum Tolerable Downtime, or MTD'?

Answer:
'Maximum Tolerable Downtime, or MTD' defines how long an organization can survive without a system.

Question:
What is 'Maximum Period Time of Disruption, or MPTD'?

Answer:
'Maximum Period Time of Disruption, or MPTD' is another name for MTD, or Maximum Tolerable Downtime.

Question:
What is the 'executive succession plan'?

Answer:
The 'executive succession plan' is a plan that dictates who will step in until the executive returns or a permanent replacement can be found.

Question:
What is 'separation of duties'?

Answer:
'separation of duties' is a personnel security control that ensures a single person cannot complete a critical task by himself.

Security and Risk Management Domain

Question:
What is 'dual control'?

Answer:
'dual control' is a personnel security control that ensures a single person cannot purposefully or accidentally cause a disastrous incident.

Question:
What is 'split knowledge'?

Answer:
'split knowledge' is a personnel security control in which separation of duties is usually put into place to prevent fraud.

Question:
What is 'collusion'?

Answer:
'collusion' is a personnel security control that prevents two people knowingly working together to from committing fraud.

Question:
What is 'rotation of duties'?

Answer:
'rotation of duties' is a personnel security control that moves employees around so that each does not have control over the same business function for too long.

Question:
What is 'mandatory vacation'?

Answer:
'mandatory vacation' is a personnel security control that forces an employee to vacate a position so the organization can detect a change in potentially fraudulent activities.

Question:
What is 'good hiring practices'?

Answer:
'good hiring practices' are NDAs, background checks and behavioral testing.

Question:
What is the 'Non-Disclosure Agreement, or NDA'?

Answer:
The 'Non-Disclosure Agreement, or NDA' is an employee contract that addresses conflict of interests and protection of the organization's intellectual property.

Question:
What is a 'termination policy'?

Answer:
A 'termination policy' is a policy for terminated employees that defines how to recover assets, disable access, and escort the employee from the premises.

Security and Risk Management Domain

61

Question:
What is 'security-awareness training'?

Answer:
'security-awareness training' is a type of training that must happen during the hiring process.

Question:
What is 'management security training'?

Answer:
'management security training' consists of a short orientation that focuses on how security pertains to corporate assets and financial goals and losses.

Question:
What is 'staff security training'?

Answer:
'staff security training' consists of a discussion of policies, procedures, standards and guidelines.

Question:
What is 'technical employee security training'?

Answer:
'technical employee security training' consists of an in-depth training on daily activities.

Question:
What is 'security governance'?

Answer:
'security governance' is a framework providing oversight, accountability and compliance for a security program.

Question:
What is 'ISO 27004'?

Answer:
'ISO 27004' is a standard that tells you how to measure the effectiveness of a security program.

Question:
What is 'NIST SP 800-55'?

Answer:
'NIST SP 800-55' is the government's version of ISO 27004.

Question:
What is the '(ISC)2 Code of Ethics'?

Answer:
The '(ISC)2 Code of Ethics' is a group of laws describing the ISC values.

Question:
What is the 'Computer Ethics Institute'?

Answer:
The 'Computer Ethics Institute' is a non-profit organization helping to advance technology by ethical means, and has created the Ten Commandments.

Security and Risk Management Domain

Question:
What is the 'Internet Architecture Board, or IAB'?

Answer:
The 'Internet Architecture Board, or IAB' is an organization that coordinates design, engineering and management for the Internet.

Question:
What is 'RFC 1087, or Ethics and the Internet'?

Answer:
'RFC 1087, or Ethics and the Internet' is a document that states what IAB considers to be unethical.

Security and Risk Management Domain

Quiz

Question:
What are 3 common methods to attack people?

Answer:
'social engineering attacks, social network attacks and password attacks'.

Question:
What are two components of reduction analysis?

Answer:
'reducing the number of attacks we have to consider and reducing the threat posed by attackers'.

Question:
What are the 3 categories of controls?

Answer:
'administrative, technical and physical'.

Question:
What are the 2 types of intellectual property?

Answer:
'industrial and copyright'.

Question:
What are the 3 NIST SP 800-53 tiers?

Answer:
'organizational, business process and information systems'.

Question:
What are the 4 components of the risk management process?

Answer:
'frame, assess, respond and monitor'.

Question:
What are the 3 information data types?

Answer:
'data-at-rest, data-in-motion and data-in-use'.

Question:
What are the 3 sources of human threats?

Answer:
'deliberate outsiders, deliberate insiders and accidental insiders'.

Security and Risk Management Domain

Question:
What are the 3 BCM Standards and Best Practices?

Answer:
'NIST SP 800-34, ISO 27031, ISO 22301'.

Question:
What are the 3 audiences for security training?

Answer:
'management, staff and technical employees'.

Question:
What are the 4 terms representing the (ISC)2 Code of Ethics?

Answer:
'protect, act, service, profession'.

Asset Security Domain

Definitions

Question:
What occurs when information is created, and has value for a time until it is no longer needed?

Answer:
'information life cycle'

Question:
What is an information life cycle stage that happens when information is created within or copied into a system?

Answer:
'acquisition stage'

Question:
What is an information life cycle stage that dictates information must remain available while still enforcing confidentiality and integrity?

Answer:
'use stage'

Question:
What is an information life cycle stage that moves authoritative source of information to a secondary storage point that is not optimized for reading?

Answer:
'archival stage'

Question:
What is a copy of information that exists to restore authoritative information that has been compromised or lost?

Answer:
'information backup'

Question:
What is an information life cycle stage that controls transfer and destruction of information?

Answer:
'disposal stage'

Question:
What is the act of classifying data by sensitivity, criticality, or both?

Answer:
'information classification'

Question:
What are increasing levels of security assigned to information?

Answer:
'classification levels'

Asset Security Domain

Question:
What is a method of information classification dealing with the level of loss incurred if the information were to be revealed to unauthorized sources?

Answer:
'sensitivity'

Question:
What is a method of information classification measuring the impact to an organization's business processes if the data were to be lost?

Answer:
'criticality'

Question:
What are confidential, private, sensitive or proprietary, and public?

Answer:
'common levels of information classification'

Question:
What are top secret, secret, confidential, sensitive but unclassified, and unclassified?

Answer:
'military levels of information classification'

Question:
What is a layer of security management responsibility that holds the vision and are ultimately responsible for the entire organization?

Answer:
'senior management'

Question:
What is a layer of security management responsibility that understands their own department and the roles of individuals?

Answer:
'functional management'

Question:
What is a layer of security management responsibility closest to the day-to-day operations?

Answer:
'operational managers and staff'

Question:
What are the 'c-suite' positions, such as CEO, CFO, etc.?

Answer:
'executive management positions'

Asset Security Domain

Question:
What is the executive who is the highest-ranking officer in the company and acts as the visionary?

Answer:
'CEO'

Question:
What is the executive responsible for the financial structure of a company?

Answer:
'CFO'

Question:
What is the executive who oversees information systems and technologies?

Answer:
'CIO'

Question:
What is the executive who is usually an attorney and ensures the company's data is kept safe?

Answer:
'CPO'

Question:
What is the executive who is responsible for understanding company risks and for mitigating those risks?

Answer:
'CSO'

Question:
What is the executive who is more of a technical role and reports to the CSO?

Answer:
'CISO'

Question:
What is a role that is usually a member of management, and make decisions regarding who can access their data and when?

Answer:
'data owner'

Question:
What is a role that is responsible for storing and keeping data safe?

Answer:
'data custodian'

Question:
What is a role that is responsible for one or more systems?

Answer:
'system owner'

Asset Security Domain

Question:
What is a role that implements and maintains security network devices and software?

Answer:
'security administrator'

Question:
What is a role that is responsible for access and assets for the people under the role's supervision?

Answer:
'supervisor'

Question:
What is a role that approves or rejects changes?

Answer:
'change control analyst'

Question:
What is a role that works with data owners, and is responsible for ensuring data is properly stored?

Answer:
'data analyst'

Question:
What is a role that uses data for work-related tasks?

Answer:
'user'

Question:
What is a role that makes sure all other roles are doing what they are supposed to be doing?

Answer:
'auditor'

Question:
What is a policy that dictates what, where, how and for how long data is stored?

Answer:
'retention policy'

Question:
What addresses the retained data issue of how classifications are labeled?

Answer:
'taxonomy'

Question:
What addresses the retained data issue of how classifications affect the archival of data?

Answer:
'classification'

Asset Security Domain

Question:
What addresses the retained data issue of adding attributes to make locating data easier?

Answer:
'normalization'

Question:
What addresses the retained data issue of making searches quicker by precomputing indexes?

Answer:
'indexing'

Question:
What is the process of producing electronically stored information (ESI) for a court or external attorney?

Answer:
'e-discovery'

Question:
What are the users who touch the privacy data on a daily basis?

Answer:
'data processors'

Question:
What occurs when data is not permanently erased from storage media?

Answer:
'data remanence'

Question:
What occurs when replacing 1's and 0's with random data?

Answer:
'overwriting'

Question:
What occurs when a powerful magnetic force is applied to magnetic media such as hard drives and tapes?

Answer:
'degaussing'

Question:
What occurs when we delete a key, rendering data unusable?

Answer:
'encryption'

Question:
What occurs when we destroy a data storage device by shredding it, exposing it to destructive chemicals, or incineration?

Answer:
'physical destruction'

Asset Security Domain

Question:
What is a publication containing 'Guide to Storage Encryption Technologies for End User Devices'?

Answer:
'NIST SP 800-111'

Question:
What is the type of data best secured using TLS or IPSec?

Answer:
'data in motion'

Question:
What is an attack that exploits information being leaked by a cryptosystem?

Answer:
'side-channel attack'

Question:
What is a type of control referring to any method of storing data?

Answer:
'media control'

Question:
What occurs when media has been properly erased or destroyed?

Answer:
'sanitized'

Question:
What is a term describing data escaping the confines of an organization's control?

Answer:
'data leakage'

Question:
What prevents unauthorized external parties from gaining access to sensitive data?

Answer:
'Data Leak Prevention, or DLP'

Question:
What is a term that means we no longer know the location of something?

Answer:
'loss'

Question:
What occurs when the confidentiality of something has been compromised?

Answer:
'leakage'

Asset Security Domain

Question:
What describes how sensitive a security tool is locating protected data?

Answer:
'sensitivity'

Question:
What describes how granular a security tool policy can be adjusted?

Answer:
'policies'

Question:
What describes how much integration effort must be undertaken to make a security tool work with existing infrastructure?

Answer:
'interoperability'

Question:
What can be discovered only by testing the product in your own environment?

Answer:
'accuracy'

Question:
What are paths that properly functioned prior to a security tool being installed?

Answer:
'existing paths'

Question:
What are paths representing invalid or malicious avenues that security tools should detect?

Answer:
'misuse paths'

Question:
What is a DLP tool that resides inside of a network appliance and examines all data in motion?

Answer:
'Network DLP, or NDLP'

Question:
What is a software-based DLP tool that is installed on devices themselves and applies to data at rest and in use?

Answer:
'Endpoint DLP, or EDLP'

Question:
What is a security solution that deploys NDLP and EDLP together, resulting in a costly but effective solution?

Answer:
'Hybrid DLP'

Asset Security Domain

Terms

Question:
What is the 'information life cycle'?

Answer:
The 'information life cycle' occurs when information is created, and has value for a time until it is no longer needed.

Question:
What is the 'acquisition stage'?

Answer:
The 'acquisition stage' is an information life cycle stage that happens when information is created within or copied into a system.

Question:
What is the 'use stage'?

Answer:
The 'use stage' is an information life cycle stage that dictates information must remain available while still enforcing confidentiality and integrity.

Question:
What is the 'archival stage'?

Answer:
The 'archival stage' is an information life cycle stage that moves authoritative source of information to a secondary storage point that is not optimized for reading.

Question:
What is 'information backup'?

Answer:
'information backup' is a copy of information that exists to restore authoritative information that has been compromised or lost.

Question:
What is the 'disposal stage'?

Answer:
The 'disposal stage' is an information life cycle stage that controls transfer and destruction of information.

Question:
What is 'information classification'?

Answer:
'information classification' is the act of classifying data by sensitivity, criticality, or both.

Question:
What is 'classification levels'?

Answer:
'classification levels' are increasing levels of security assigned to information.

Asset Security Domain

Question:
What is 'sensitivity'?

Answer:
'sensitivity' is a method of information classification dealing with the level of loss incurred if the information were to be revealed to unauthorized sources.

Question:
What is 'criticality'?

Answer:
'criticality' is a method of information classification measuring the impact to an organization's business processes if the data were to be lost.

Question:
What is 'common levels of information classification'?

Answer:
'common levels of information classification' are confidential, private, sensitive or proprietary, and public.

Question:
What is 'military levels of information classification'?

Answer:
'military levels of information classification' are top secret, secret, confidential, sensitive but unclassified, and unclassified.

Question:
What is 'senior management'?

Answer:
'senior management' is a layer of security management responsibility that holds the vision and are ultimately responsible for the entire organization.

Question:
What is 'functional management'?

Answer:
'functional management' is a layer of security management responsibility that understands their own department and the roles of individuals.

Question:
What is 'operational managers and staff'?

Answer:
'operational managers and staff' is a layer of security management responsibility closest to the day-to-day operations.

Question:
What is 'executive management positions'?

Answer:
'executive management positions' are the 'c-suite' positions, such as CEO, CFO, etc..

Asset Security Domain

Question:
What is the 'CEO'?

Answer:
The 'CEO' is the executive who is the highest-ranking officer in the company and acts as the visionary.

Question:
What is the 'CFO'?

Answer:
The 'CFO' is the executive responsible for the financial structure of a company.

Question:
What is the 'CIO'?

Answer:
The 'CIO' is the executive who oversees information systems and technologies.

Question:
What is the 'CPO'?

Answer:
The 'CPO' is the executive who is usually an attorney and ensures the company's data is kept safe.

Question:
What is the 'CSO'?

Answer:
The 'CSO' is the executive who is responsible for understanding company risks and for mitigating those risks.

Question:
What is the 'CISO'?

Answer:
The 'CISO' is the executive who is more of a technical role and reports to the CSO.

Question:
What is the 'data owner'?

Answer:
The 'data owner' is a role that is usually a member of management, and make decisions regarding who can access their data and when.

Question:
What is the 'data custodian'?

Answer:
The 'data custodian' is a role that is responsible for storing and keeping data safe.

Question:
What is the 'system owner'?

Answer:
The 'system owner' is a role that is responsible for one or more systems.

Asset Security Domain

Question:
What is the 'security administrator'?

Answer:
The 'security administrator' is a role that implements and maintains security network devices and software.

Question:
What is the 'supervisor'?

Answer:
The 'supervisor' is a role that is responsible for access and assets for the people under the role's supervision.

Question:
What is the 'change control analyst'?

Answer:
The 'change control analyst' is a role that approves or rejects changes.

Question:
What is the 'data analyst'?

Answer:
The 'data analyst' is a role that works with data owners, and is responsible for ensuring data is properly stored.

Question:
What is the 'user'?

Answer:
The 'user' is a role that uses data for work-related tasks.

Question:
What is the 'auditor'?

Answer:
The 'auditor' is a role that makes sure all other roles are doing what they are supposed to be doing.

Question:
What is a 'retention policy'?

Answer:
A 'retention policy' is a policy that dictates what, where, how and for how long data is stored.

Question:
What is 'taxonomy'?

Answer:
'taxonomy' addresses the retained data issue of how classifications are labeled.

Question:
What is 'classification'?

Answer:
'classification' addresses the retained data issue of how classifications affect the archival of data.

Asset Security Domain

Question:
What is 'normalization'?

Answer:
'normalization' addresses the retained data issue of adding attributes to make locating data easier.

Question:
What is 'indexing'?

Answer:
'indexing' addresses the retained data issue of making searches quicker by precomputing indexes.

Question:
What is 'e-discovery'?

Answer:
'e-discovery' is the process of producing electronically stored information (ESI) for a court or external attorney.

Question:
What is 'data processors'?

Answer:
'data processors' are the users who touch the privacy data on a daily basis.

Question:
What is 'data remanence'?

Answer:
'data remanence' occurs when data is not permanently erased from storage media.

Question:
What is 'overwriting'?

Answer:
'overwriting' occurs when replacing 1's and 0's with random data.

Question:
What is 'degaussing'?

Answer:
'degaussing' occurs when a powerful magnetic force is applied to magnetic media such as hard drives and tapes.

Question:
What is 'encryption'?

Answer:
'encryption' occurs when we delete a key, rendering data unusable.

Question:
What is 'physical destruction'?

Answer:
'physical destruction' occurs when we destroy a data storage device by shredding it, exposing it to destructive chemicals, or incineration.

Asset Security Domain

Question:
What is the 'NIST SP 800-111'?

Answer:
The 'NIST SP 800-111' is a publication containing 'Guide to Storage Encryption Technologies for End User Devices'.

Question:
What is 'data in motion'?

Answer:
'data in motion' is the type of data best secured using TLS or IPSec.

Question:
What is a 'side-channel attack'?

Answer:
A 'side-channel attack' is an attack that exploits information being leaked by a cryptosystem.

Question:
What is a 'media control'?

Answer:
A 'media control' is a type of control referring to any method of storing data.

Question:
What is 'sanitized'?

Answer:
'sanitized' occurs when media has been properly erased or destroyed.

Question:
What is 'data leakage'?

Answer:
'data leakage' is a term describing data escaping the confines of an organization's control.

Question:
What is 'Data Leak Prevention, or DLP'?

Answer:
'Data Leak Prevention, or DLP' prevents unauthorized external parties from gaining access to sensitive data.

Question:
What is a 'loss'?

Answer:
A 'loss' is a term that means we no longer know the location of something.

Question:
What is 'leakage'?

Answer:
'leakage' occurs when the confidentiality of something has been compromised.

Asset Security Domain

Question:
What is 'sensitivity'?

Answer:
'sensitivity' describes how sensitive a security tool is locating protected data.

Question:
What is 'policies'?

Answer:
'policies' describes how granular a security tool policy can be adjusted.

Question:
What is 'interoperability'?

Answer:
'interoperability' describes how much integration effort must be undertaken to make a security tool work with existing infrastructure.

Question:
What is 'accuracy'?

Answer:
'accuracy' can be discovered only by testing the product in your own environment.

Question:
What is 'existing paths'?

Answer:
'existing paths' are paths that properly functioned prior to a security tool being installed.

Question:
What is 'misuse paths'?

Answer:
'misuse paths' are paths representing invalid or malicious avenues that security tools should detect.

Question:
What is 'Network DLP, or NDLP'?

Answer:
'Network DLP, or NDLP' is a DLP tool that resides inside of a network appliance and examines all data in motion.

Question:
What is 'Endpoint DLP, or EDLP'?

Answer:
'Endpoint DLP, or EDLP' is a software-based DLP tool that is installed on devices themselves and applies to data at rest and in use.

Question:
What is 'Hybrid DLP'?

Answer:
'Hybrid DLP' is a security solution that deploys NDLP and EDLP together, resulting in a costly but effective solution.

Asset Security Domain

Quiz

Question:
What are the 8 attributes used for classification?

Answer:
'security, legal, age, value, useful, disclosure, lost, access'.

Question:
What are the 3 layers of responsibility in organizational security?

Answer:
'senior management, functional management, and operational managers'.

Question:
What are the 5 guidelines on data retention times?

Answer:
'permanent, 7 years, 5 years, 4 years, 3 years'.

Question:
What are the 8 steps of the electronic discovery reference model (EDRM)?

Answer:
'identification, preservation, collection, processing, review, analysis, production and presentation'.

Question:
What are the 4 counters for data remanence?

Answer:
'overwriting, degaussing, encryption and physical destruction'.

Question:
What are the 6 threats physical security counteracts?

Answer:
'environmental integrity, access, theft, interruption, damage, and compromised systems'.

Question:
What are the 9 attributes for proper management of media?

Answer:
'audit, access, backups, history, environment, integrity, inventory, disposal and labeling'.

Question:
What are the 7 losses due to data leakage?

Answer:
'investigation, contacting, fines, contract, expenses, direct damage and reputation'.

Asset Security Domain

Question:
What are the 3 steps to properly implement DLP?

Answer:
'inventory, classify, map'.

Question:
What are the 6 strategies to address leakage?

Answer:
'backups, life cycle, secure, culture, privacy and change'.

Question:
What are the 4 criteria to evaluate security products?

Answer:
'sensitivity, policies, interoperability and accuracy'.

Question:
What are the 2 aspects of security tool tuning?

Answer:
'existing paths and misuse paths'.

Question:
What are the drawbacks to EDLPs?

Answer:
'complexity, cost, updates and circumvention'.

Question:
What are the 11 precautions to protect mobile devices?

Answer:
'inventory, harden, BIOS, register, no check, no unattended, engrave, lock, back up, encrypt and remote wipe'.

Question:
What are the 8 precautions to protect paper records?

Answer:
'educate, minimize paper, tidy, lock, no take-homes, label, searches and shred'.

Question:
What are the 7 types of safes?

Answer:
'wall, floor, chest, depository, vault, passive relocking and thermal relocking'.

Question:
What are the 3 security guidelines for safes?

Answer:
'change combinations often, limited people who have access and a visible location'.

Security Engineering Domain

Definitions

Question:
What is the task of building security directly into the technology products we use every day?

Answer:
'security engineering'

Question:
What are the components of a system and how they interact?

Answer:
'system architecture'

Question:
What is a tool to understand a complex system?

Answer:
'architecture'

Question:
What represents the entire life cycle of a system from planning to retirement?

Answer:
'development'

Question:
What is a term that describes a computer, an application, a set of computers, and a network?

Answer:
'system'

Question:
What is the standard that outlines the specifications of a system architecture?

Answer:
'ISO 42010'

Question:
What describes a system made up of components, their relationships to each other and their environment, and the principles guiding its design and evolution?

Answer:
'architecture'

Question:
What are a collection of document types to document an architecture in a formal manner?

Answer:
'architecture descriptions, or AD'

Security Engineering Domain

Question:
What is an individual, team or organization with an interest in, or concern about, a system?

Answer:
'stakeholder'

Question:
What is an area of a system that a stakeholder is interested in?

Answer:
'concern'

Question:
What is a representation of the entire system from the perspective of a related set of concerns (functionality, performance, interoperability, security)?

Answer:
'view'

Question:
What is a specification of the conventions for creating and using a view?

Answer:
'viewpoint'

Question:
What is used to communicate decisions made by the architect (logical, physical, structural, behavioral, management, cost and security)?

Answer:
'architecture view'

Question:
What encompasses all aspects of a physical computer?

Answer:
'computer architecture'

Question:
What performs mathematical functions and logical operations on data it gets from computer memory?

Answer:
'algorithmic logic unit, or ALU'

Question:
What are the fast memory units which sit very close to the ALU?

Answer:
'registers'

Question:
What loads data from the main memory into the registers for the ALU?

Answer:
'control unit'

Security Engineering Domain

83

Question:
What is the collective name for the ALU, registers and control unit?

Answer:
'central processing unit, or CPU'

Question:
What is a list of very complex instructions for the ALU to execute?

Answer:
'operating system, or OS'

Question:
What holds variables and temporary results that the ALU will use?

Answer:
'general register'

Question:
What is a register that points to the next instruction to be executed?

Answer:
'program counter register'

Question:
What are registers that hold the stack pointer, program counter and the PWS?

Answer:
'special registers'

Question:
What holds different bits that reflect the execution mode the CPU should be operating in?

Answer:
'program status word, or PWS'

Question:
What is a list of pointers to addresses and data?

Answer:
'stack'

Question:
What points to where in the stack execution is currently going on?

Answer:
'stack pointer'

Question:
What is the mode which limits the functions that can be executed?

Answer:
'user mode'

Security Engineering Domain

Question:
What is another name for user mode?

Answer:
'problem state'

Question:
What is the mode allows unlimited execution and runs in Ring 0?

Answer:
'privilege mode'

Question:
What is another name for privilege or supervisor mode?

Answer:
'kernel mode'

Question:
What is another name for privilege or kernel mode?

Answer:
'supervisor mode'

Question:
What is a communications pathway used to send address pointers between the CPU and memory?

Answer:
'address bus'

Question:
What occurs when an instruction is sent from the CPU across the address bus, and contains the memory address where an instruction or data resides?

Answer:
'fetch request'

Question:
What is used to transfer data between the CPU and memory?

Answer:
'data bus'

Question:
What occurs when more than one CPU in a single computer is used?

Answer:
'multiprocessing'

Question:
What occurs when all processors are load-balanced, and are handed work as they become available?

Answer:
'symmetric mode'

Security Engineering Domain

Question:
What describes when processors may be completely dedicated to a specific task or application?

Answer:
'asymmetric mode'

Question:
What is a memory type that will lose contents if power is interrupted?

Answer:
'volatile'

Question:
What is a memory type that will not lose contents if power is interrupted?

Answer:
'non-Volatile'

Question:
What is a type of volatile memory?

Answer:
'random access memory, or RAM'

Question:
What is a type of memory that must be continuously refreshed to retain contents?

Answer:
'dynamic RAM, or DRAM'

Question:
What is a type of memory that does not have to be refreshed, is faster and is used for caches?

Answer:
'static RAM, or SRAM'

Question:
What is a type of memory that synchronizes itself with the CPU clock to make communication faster?

Answer:
'synchronous DRAM, or SDRAM'

Question:
What is a type of memory that can 'look ahead' and fetch the next block at the same time?

Answer:
'extended data out DRAM, or EDO DRAM'

Question:
What is a type of memory that can send 4 blocks in a 'burst' instead of just two blocks like EDO or BEDO?

Answer:
'burst EDO RAM, or BEDO RAM'

Security Engineering Domain

Question:
What is a type of memory that can execute two instructions per clock cycle?
Answer:
'double data rate SDRAM, or DDR SDRAM'

Question:
What occurs when memory is physically segmented so that only certain processes can access the memory?

Answer:
'hardware segmentation'

Question:
What is a type of non-volatile memory?

Answer:
'read-only memory, or ROM'

Question:
What is a type of non-volatile memory that can be reprogrammed one time?

Answer:
'programmable read-only memory, or PROM'

Question:
What is a type of non-volatile memory that can be reprogrammed any number of times by using a UV light to erase the previous contents?

Answer:
'erasable programmable read-only memory, or EPROM'

Question:
What is a type of non-volatile memory that allows for erasing electrically, but only a single byte at a time?

Answer:
'electrically erasable programmable read-only memory, or EEPROM'

Question:
What is a type of non-volatile memory that is a solid-state device, and uses voltage to indicate the existence of a value?

Answer:
'flash memory'

Question:
What is content stored in ROM?

Answer:
'firmware'

Question:
What is memory used for high-speed writing and reading activities?

Answer:
'cache memory'

Security Engineering Domain

Question:
What is memory built directly into processors and controllers?

Answer:
'levels 1 and 2'

Question:
What is memory used anywhere else than in processors and controllers?

Answer:
'level 3'

Question:
What contains physical memory address locations?

Answer:
'absolute address'

Question:
What is used by software and maps to an absolute memory location, resulting in increased security?

Answer:
'logical address'

Question:
What is an address that is an offset to, or relative to, an absolute or logical address?

Answer:
'relative address'

Question:
What is a variable passed from one process to another?

Answer:
'parameter'

Question:
What wraps a parameter value?

Answer:
'buffer'

Question:
What results when the size of a buffer is exceeded?

Answer:
'buffer overflow'

Question:
What prevents the same memory address from being used each time?

Answer:
'address space layout randomization, or ASLR'

Security Engineering Domain

88

Question:
What prevents execution of code in certain memory segments?

Answer:
'data execution prevention, or DEP'

Question:
What occurs when badly-written code forgets to release allocated memory?

Answer:
'memory leaks'

Question:
What is a background process that ensures all allocated memory is freed up?

Answer:
'garbage collector'

Question:
What is the software on top of which applications will run?

Answer:
'operating systems'

Question:
What is a term describing the portion of an application that has been initialized and loaded for execution?

Answer:
'process'

Question:
What is a term describing the ability to load multiple applications into memory at the same time?

Answer:
'multiprogramming'

Question:
What is a term describing the ability to deal with requests from multiple applications simultaneously?

Answer:
'multitasking'

Question:
What is the term describing applications having to volunteer CPU time for some other application to use in early OSs ?

Answer:
'cooperative multitasking'

Question:
What is the term describing CPUs that multitask no matter what the application wants to do?

Answer:
'preemptive multitasking'

Security Engineering Domain

Question:
What is the process state in which the process has not yet sent any instructions to the CPU?

Answer:
'ready'

Question:
What is the process state in which the CPU is executing the process' instructions?

Answer:
'running'

Question:
What is the process state in which a process is waiting for some kind of input, such as a keystroke?

Answer:
'blocked'

Question:
What is used by the OS to keep track of each process?

Answer:
'process table'

Question:
What occurs when a process is loaded into the CPU for a short period of time and executed?

Answer:
'time slice'

Question:
What is an event that causes the OS to consider executing a process ahead of its schedule time slice?

Answer:
'interrupt'

Question:
What is a flag assigned to an event that doesn't necessarily have to be taken care of immediately?

Answer:
'maskable'

Question:
What is a flag assigned to an event that makes the CPU stop whatever was going on and take care of a that event?

Answer:
'non-maskable'

Question:
What is a background process using a non-maskable interrupt that will perform a warm boot if the OS ever hangs?

Answer:
'watchdog timer'

Security Engineering Domain

Question:
What contains some of the process' instruction sets, and shares the process' memory space and resource?

Answer:
'thread'

Question:
What is a term describing a process that creates more than one thread?

Answer:
'multithreaded'

Question:
What occurs when two threads within a process are both waiting for the other to release a common resource?

Answer:
'software deadlock'

Question:
What occurs when we make sure that misbehaving processes do not affect other processes?

Answer:
'process isolation'

Question:
What is achieved when we make sure that a process does not expose its inner workings by only communicating through a well-defined interface - this is also called data hiding?

Answer:
'encapsulation'

Question:
What is used when the OS must manage access to resources that are shared between multiple processes (such as multiple processes all reading from the same file)?

Answer:
'time multiplexing'

Question:
What occurs when each process has its own unique ID assigned by the OS?

Answer:
'naming distinctions'

Question:
What is used by the OS so that physical memory is not exposed directly – instead it is mapped through a virtual address, allowing the OS to play memory cop?

Answer:
'virtual memory mapping'

Security Engineering Domain

91

Question:
What is used to prevent a subject from accessing an object directly?

Answer:
'abstraction layer'

Question:
What is achieved when details are hidden?

Answer:
'abstraction'

Question:
What is a term describing a division of the computer's memory into subsections?

Answer:
'memory segment'

Question:
What is a layer that abstracts memory locations away from any process wishing to use the memory?

Answer:
'memory manager'

Question:
What is a responsibility of the memory manager and happens when memory contents are swapped from RAM to the hard drive, but is hidden from the process?

Answer:
'relocation'

Question:
What is a responsibility of the memory manager and is achieved when processes can only access their memory segments?

Answer:
'protection'

Question:
What is a responsibility of the memory manager and ensures CIA is enforced with shared memory by allowing different levels of access to interact with the same memory?

Answer:
'sharing'

Question:
What is a responsibility of the memory manager which segments memory types and provide an addressing scheme, thereby allowing multiple processes to access the same shared DLL?

Answer:
'local organization'

Security Engineering Domain

Question:
What is a responsibility of the memory manager which segments the physical memory for use by the applications and OS processes?

Answer:
'physical organization'

Question:
What is a shared set of functions that processes can reuse?

Answer:
'dynamic link library, or DLL'

Question:
What is a register that points to the beginning memory address for a segment?

Answer:
'base register'

Question:
What is a register that points to the ending memory address for a segment?

Answer:
'limit register'

Question:
What is a memory management term describing both volatile and non-volatile storage collectively?

Answer:
'virtual memory'

Question:
What is a memory management term describing non-volatile storage only?

Answer:
'secondary storage'

Question:
What occurs when a portion of volatile memory is copied to non-volatile storage, thereby freeing up volatile memory for use?

Answer:
'swapping'

Question:
What is the name of the non-volatile storage used during swapping?

Answer:
'swap space'

Question:
What are units used to describe the swap space?

Answer:
'pages'

Security Engineering Domain

Question:
What is the term describing when memory pages are loaded back into volatile memory?

Answer:
'virtual memory paging'

Question:
What is a device exposing data in fixed-block sizes, with each block having a unique address?

Answer:
'block device'

Question:
What is a device using a stream of characters only?

Answer:
'character device'

Question:
What is very low-level software that knows all of the specifics about a device?

Answer:
'device driver'

Question:
What occurs when a process has direct access to a physical memory address?

Answer:
'direct memory access, or DMA'

Question:
What is an I/O service method in which the CPU polls the device to see if it is ready?

Answer:
'programmable I/O'

Question:
What is an I/O service method in which the device sends an interrupt to the CPU when it is ready?

Answer:
'interrupt-Driven I/O'

Question:
What is an I/O service method in which the process and the device share memory without bothering the CPU?

Answer:
'I/O Using DMA'

Question:
What is an I/O service method in which the CPU gives the process the physical memory address to the device?

Answer:
'pre-mapped I/O'

Security Engineering Domain

Question:
What is an I/O service method which is the same as pre-mapped I/O, but uses logical memory addresses?

Answer:
'fully mapped I/O'

Question:
What is a language that both the OS and CPU understand?

Answer:
'instruction set'

Question:
What is comprised of everything that makes up the CPU?

Answer:
'microarchitecture'

Question:
What is a term used to describe layers within an OS?

Answer:
'rings'

Question:
What is the OS layer in which the kernel runs?

Answer:
'ring 0'

Question:
What is the OS layer in which user processes normally run?

Answer:
'ring 3'

Question:
What is the term used to describe the gatekeeper between two processes?

Answer:
'application programming interface, or API'

Question:
What is the mode represented by processes running in ring 0?

Answer:
'kernel mode'

Question:
What is the mode represented by processes running in rings 1,2 or 3?

Answer:
'user mode'

Security Engineering Domain

Question:
What is a collection of resources a process has access to, with the larger the ring, the larger the domain?

Answer:
'domain'

Question:
What occurs when a call is made from a user mode process into a kernel mode process?

Answer:
'kernel mode transition'

Question:
What is another name for encapsulation?

Answer:
'data hiding'

Question:
What is the OS architecture in which everything is in kernel mode?

Answer:
'monolithic'

Question:
What is the OS architecture which contains rings, but the OS still runs in kernel mode?

Answer:
'layered'

Question:
What is the OS architecture in which a medium-sized kernel is in kernel mode?

Answer:
'microkernel'

Question:
What is the OS architecture in which a very small kernel and executive services run in kernel mode?

Answer:
'hybrid microkernel'

Question:
What is a term describing the creation of a virtual environment in which software runs?

Answer:
'virtualization'

Question:
What is the term used to describe running a virtualized instance of an operating system?

Answer:
'virtual machine'

Security Engineering Domain

Question:
What is the term used to describe sharing physical resources among multiple guests in a virtualized environment?

Answer:
'hypervisor'

Question:
What is something that defines how sensitive information and resources should be managed and protected?

Answer:
'security policy'

Question:
What is a tool used by the US government to evaluate how well computer systems meet security criteria?

Answer:
'Trusted Computer System Evaluation Criteria'

Question:
What is a term that represents all hardware, software and firmware in a system coupled that enforces security (basically the kernel)?

Answer:
'Trusted Computer Base, or TCB'

Question:
What is a term used to describe a user or process communicating with the TCB?

Answer:
'trusted path'

Question:
What is a term used when someone or some process is working on the trusted path exclusively?

Answer:
'trusted shell'

Question:
What is a domain in the TCB that refers to Ring 0 only?

Answer:
'execution domain'

Question:
What is an imaginary wall between the TCB and everything outside of the TCB where great scrutiny occurs?

Answer:
'security perimeter'

Question:
What is an abstract machine that deals with subjects and objects crossing the security perimeter?

Answer:
'reference monitor'

Security Engineering Domain

Question:
What is the TCB plus the actual implementation of the reference monitor?

Answer:
'security kernel'

Question:
What are policies that prevent flow from a high security level to a lower security level?

Answer:
'multilevel security policies'

Question:
What are patterns that implement reference monitors within the security kernel?

Answer:
'security models'

Question:
What are the word 'simple' means 'read', the word 'star' or the symbol '*' means 'write'?

Answer:
'security model rules'

Question:
What is the security model that ensures confidentiality by enforcing no read up, no write down and read/write at the same level only?

Answer:
'Bell-Lampedusa Model'

Question:
What is the rule meaning 'no read up'?

Answer:
'simple security rule'

Question:
What is the rule meaning 'no write down'?

Answer:
'* property rule'

Question:
What is the rule meaning 'read/write at same level only'?

Answer:
'strong * property rule'

Question:
What is the security model that ensures integrity by enforcing no read down and no write up?

Answer:
'Biba Model'

Security Engineering Domain

Question:
What is the rule meaning 'no write up'?

Answer:
'* integrity axiom rule'

Question:
What is the rule meaning ''no read down'?

Answer:
'simple integrity axiom rule'

Question:
What is the term meaning that a subject cannot invoke a service higher up?

Answer:
'invocation property'

Question:
What is the security model that ensures integrity by enforcing the access triple, separation of duties and auditing?

Answer:
'Clark-Wilson Model'

Question:
What represents subjects attempting to access a UDI within the Clark-Wilson model?

Answer:
'users'

Question:
What represents read, write and modify within the Clark-Wilson model?

Answer:
'transformation procedures, or TPs'

Question:
What represents things that can be manipulated only by TPs within the Clark-Wilson model?

Answer:
'constrained data items, or CDIs'

Question:
What represents things that can be manipulated by users via primitive read and write operations within the Clark-Wilson model?

Answer:
'unconstrained data items, or UDIs'

Question:
What represents processes that check the consistency of CDIs with the real world within the Clark-Wilson model?

Answer:
'integrity verification procedures, or IVPs'

Security Engineering Domain

Question:
What represents a User employing a TP to modify a CDI within the Clark-Wilson model?

Answer:
'access triple'

Question:
What represents the result of an access triple that has been verified by an IVP within the Clark-Wilson model?

Answer:
'well-formed transaction'

Question:
What is a security model that ensures commands and activities at one level are not visible to other levels and actions at a lower security level?

Answer:
'noninterference model'

Question:
What is a security model that allows for dynamically changing access controls that prevent conflicts of interest?

Answer:
'Brewer and Nash Model, or the Chinese Wall model'

Question:
What is a security model that shows how subjects and objects should be created and deleted, and how to assign access rights?

Answer:
'Graham-Denning Model'

Question:
What is a security model that shows how a finite set of procedures can be used to edit the access rights of a subject?

Answer:
'Harrison-Ruzzo-Ullman Model'

Question:
What describes sending or receiving information in an unauthorized manner?

Answer:
'covert channel'

Question:
What describes communicating through a shared storage system - this does not have to be files containing data – it could simply be the presence or absence of some system feature?

Answer:
'covert storage channel'

Question:
What describes communicating through the presence or absence of a system resource in a timed fashion?

Answer:
'covert timing channel'

Security Engineering Domain

100

Question:
What describes the determination of the level of protection required and provided by a system?

Answer:
'assurance evaluation'

Question:
What allows user submission of requirements, vendor claims of meeting those requirements, and independent verification of the claims, and is codified in ISO 15408?

Answer:
'common criteria'

Question:
What is the result of a Common Criteria analysis?

Answer:
'Evaluation Assurance Level, or EAL'

Question:
What is the common criteria EAL level representing a functionally tested system?

Answer:
'EAL1'

Question:
What is the common criteria EAL level representing a structurally tested system?

Answer:
'EAL2'

Question:
What is the common criteria EAL level representing a methodically tested and checked system?

Answer:
'EAL3'

Question:
What is the common criteria EAL level representing a methodically designed, tested and reviewed system?

Answer:
'EAL4'

Question:
What is the common criteria EAL level representing a semi formally designed and tested system?

Answer:
'EAL5'

Question:
What is the common criteria EAL level representing a semi formally verified designed and tested system?

Answer:
'EAL6'

Security Engineering Domain

101

Question:
What is the common criteria EAL level representing a formally verified design and tested system based on a mathematical model that can be proven?

Answer:
'EAL7'

Question:
What is the common criteria term for a description of a needed security solution?

Answer:
'protection profile'

Question:
What is a list of threats a common criteria product must address?

Answer:
'security problem description'

Question:
What is a list of functionality a common criteria product must provide to address the threats?

Answer:
'security objectives'

Question:
What is a list of very specific common criteria requirements, detailed enough to be implemented and verified?

Answer:
'security requirements'

Question:
What is the proposed common criteria product that meets a protection profile?

Answer:
'target of Evaluation, or TOE'

Question:
What is the common criteria vendor's own explanation of what a target of evaluation does and how it does it?

Answer:
'security target'

Question:
What is a list of common criteria security functions a security target must provide?

Answer:
'security functional requirements'

Security Engineering Domain

Question:
What is a list of items the common criteria vendor did during product development and evaluation to ensure compliance with security functional requirements?

Answer:
'security assurance requirements'

Question:
What is a term for security functional requirements and security assurance requirements that are packaged for reuse?

Answer:
'packages'

Question:
What is the term used to describe the technical review of security mechanisms to evaluate their effectiveness?

Answer:
'certification'

Question:
What is the term used to describe management's formal acceptance of the certification's findings?

Answer:
'accreditation'

Question:
What is a system built on top of open standards, interfaces and protocols that have published specifications?

Answer:
'open system'

Question:
What is a system that does not follow industry standards and therefore does not as easily communicate well with other systems?

Answer:
'closed system'

Question:
What is the name of system that contains multiple computer nodes connected by a network, all working together to accomplish a specific task?

Answer:
'distributed system'

Question:
What is the term for the use of shared, remote servers, usually based on virtual machines?

Answer:
'cloud computing'

Security Engineering Domain

Question:
What is an offering in which the vendor provides the server with the appropriate operating system installed and gives you administrative access?

Answer:
'Infrastructure as a Service, or IaaS'

Question:
What is an offering in which the vendor provides a server with the appropriate software installed for you to build on top of, but you don't get administrative access?

Answer:
'Platform as a Service, or PaaS'

Question:
What is an offering in which the vendor gives you an account for a specific web-based application, but you don't have access to the servers running the application?

Answer:
'Software as a Service, or SaaS'

Question:
What is the term used to describe taking multiple computers and having them all work on the same task simultaneously?

Answer:
'parallel computing'

Question:
What occurs when a CPU operates on multiple bits simultaneously; all CPUs handling bytes can do this?

Answer:
'bit-level parallelism'

Question:
What occurs when multiple CPUs execute multiple instructions simultaneously; almost all computing devices these days have this feature?

Answer:
'instruction-level parallelism'

Question:
What occurs when a program is divided into multiple threads, all operating simultaneously?

Answer:
'task-level parallelism'

Question:
What occurs when data is distributed among multiple nodes and processed in parallel?

Answer:
'data-level parallelism'

Security Engineering Domain

104

Question:
What occurs when combining data for a user from separate sources that results in a view the user should not have access to?

Answer:
'aggregation'

Question:
What is the intended result of aggregation?

Answer:
'inference'

Question:
What is a counter-measure in which only the content is examined when determining access?

Answer:
'content-dependent access control'

Question:
What is a counter-measure in which the system keeps track of previous requests by this user and recognizes that the danger exists for that user to infer sensitive information from their latest request?

Answer:
'context-dependent access control'

Question:
What is a method to mitigate inference attacks by hiding specific information that could be used in an attack?

Answer:
'cell suppression'

Question:
What is a method to mitigate inference attacks by dividing a database into multiple parts?

Answer:
'partitioning'

Question:
What occurs when we insert bogus information in hopes of confusing an attacker?

Answer:
'noise and perturbation'

Question:
What are antivirus, encrypt data, include in policies, manage all connected devices, enable remote policies, enable encrypt/idle lock/screen lock/authentication and remote wipe?

Answer:
'11 guidelines for securing mobile devices'

Question:
What is a computer controlling a physical device?

Answer:
'cyber-physical systems'

Security Engineering Domain

105

Question:
What is a mechanical or electrical device that has a computer embedded into it?

Answer:
'embedded system'

Question:
What is the global network of connected embedded systems that are connected to the Internet and are uniquely addressable?

Answer:
'Internet of Things, or IoT'

Question:
What is a security measure for which IoT devices usually have a very poor implementation of?

Answer:
'authentication'

Question:
What is a security measure that IoT devices seldom include due to limited processing power?

Answer:
'encryption'

Question:
What is an automatic measure that many IoT vendors do not implement?

Answer:
'updates'

Question:
What are systems where software is used to control physical devices in industrial processes?

Answer:
'industrial control system, or ICS'

Question:
What are applying risk management, using IDS/IPS, disabling ports, implementing least privilege, using encryption, proper patch management and monitoring audit logs?

Answer:
'7 guidelines for ICS provided by NIST SP 800-82'

Question:
What are programmable computers connected to physical devices using standard interfaces such as RS-232, and are normally network-enabled?

Answer:
'programmable logic controller, or PLC'

Security Engineering Domain

Question:
What is a small network of PLCs connected to physical devices, all orchestrated by higher-level controllers?

Answer:
'distributed control system, or DCS'

Question:
What is DCS over long distances?

Answer:
'supervisory control and data acquisition, or SCADA'

Question:
What are remote terminal units or PLCs that connect directly to physical components?

Answer:
'endpoints'

Question:
What are data acquisition servers that collect data from endpoints?

Answer:
'backends'

Question:
What are human-machine interfaces that display data from endpoints and allow the user to issue commands?

Answer:
'user stations'

Question:
What are non-malicious methods put in by developers to gain privileged access after deployment?

Answer:
'maintenance hooks, or back doors'

Question:
What is an attack in-between 'can I access' and 'access'?

Answer:
'time-of-check/time-of-use attack, or asynchronous attack'

Question:
What is reversing the order of execution to gain access?

Answer:
'race condition'

Question:
What does not split steps but makes them one, and applies software locks at the OS level on the requested resource?

Answer:
'countermeasure to TOC/TOU attacks'

Security Engineering Domain

Question:
What is the act of storing or transmitting data in a form that only the intended audience can read?

Answer:
'cryptography'

Question:
What is one of the first examples of cryptography?

Answer:
'at bash'

Question:
What is used when each character is replaced by a different character?

Answer:
'substitution cipher'

Question:
What is a cipher using a single alphabet?

Answer:
'monoalphabetic substitution cipher'

Question:
What is a cipher using more than one alphabet?

Answer:
'polyalphabetic substitution cipher'

Question:
What is a message written on a sheet of papyrus wrapped around a stick of a certain thickness?

Answer:
'scytale cipher'

Question:
What is a device that substitutes letters using multiple rotors within the machine; an example is the Enigma?

Answer:
'rotor cipher machine'

Question:
What is one of the earliest successful encryption projects that introduced mathematics?

Answer:
'Lucifer'

Question:
What is the science of studying and breaking encryption as well as reverse-engineering algorithms and keys?

Answer:
'cryptanalysis'

Security Engineering Domain

Question:
What is the study of both cryptanalysis and cryptography?

Answer:
'cryptology'

Question:
What is human-readable data before encryption?

Answer:
'plaintext'

Question:
What is plaintext that has been encrypted into a form that appears to be random and is unreadable?

Answer:
'ciphertext'

Question:
What provides encryption and decryption services and contains algorithms, keys, software and protocols?

Answer:
'cryptosystem'

Question:
What is a secret value used by the algorithm to encrypt and decrypt plaintext?

Answer:
'key'

Question:
What is a set of usually well-known rules?

Answer:
'algorithm, or cipher'

Question:
What is the number of possible values a key can have?

Answer:
'key space'

Question:
What states that the only secrecy involved with a cryptographic system should be the key, and the algorithm should be publicly known?

Answer:
'Kerckhoff's Principle'

Question:
What controls how hard it is to discover the secret (algorithm or key)?

Answer:
'strength of the cryptosystem'

Security Engineering Domain

109

Question:
What is an attack that tries every possible key until the resulting plaintext is meaningful?

Answer:
'brute-force method'

Question:
What is the amount of work required to break a cryptosystem?

Answer:
'work factor'

Question:
What is achieved when only authorized entities can read the data?

Answer:
'confidentiality'

Question:
What proves the data has not been altered?

Answer:
'integrity'

Question:
What verifies the identity of the creator of the information?

Answer:
'authentication'

Question:
What occurs after authentication?

Answer:
'authorization'

Question:
What occurs when the sender cannot deny sending the message?

Answer:
'nonrepudiation'

Question:
What is the perfect encryption scheme and is unbreakable if properly implemented?

Answer:
'one-Time Pad'

Question:
What is a mathematical operation that returns 0 if the bits are the same and 1 if they are different?

Answer:
'XOR'

Security Engineering Domain

Question:
What is the term used for numbers generated by computers, given that computers cannot generate a truly random number?

Answer:
'pseudorandom numbers'

Question:
What is a cipher that uses a key based on things in the physical world?

Answer:
'running key cipher'

Question:
What is a message within a message?

Answer:
'concealment cipher, or null cipher'

Question:
What is the art of hiding a message in another type of media such that it is not detected?

Answer:
'steganography'

Question:
What is attempting to hide messages within electronic files, programs or protocols?

Answer:
'digital steganography'

Question:
What is a signal, data stream or file that contains a hidden message?

Answer:
'carrier'

Question:
What is a medium in which a message is hidden?

Answer:
'stegomedium'

Question:
What is the term for a concealed message?

Answer:
'payload'

Question:
What is a concealment method that modifies bits that do not impact the overall container?

Answer:
'least significant bit, or LSB'

Security Engineering Domain

111

Question:
What includes a very tiny image of the actual message in a much larger image?

Answer:
'microdot'

Question:
What is an algorithm that uses a single key for both encryption and decryption when both the sender and the receiver must have that key?

Answer:
'symmetric encryption algorithm'

Question:
What is a cipher that replaces bits, blocks or characters with different values of equal length?

Answer:
'substitution ciphers'

Question:
What is a cipher that puts the bits, blocks or characters in a different order?

Answer:
'transposition ciphers'

Question:
What looks for common occurrences of the same value?

Answer:
'frequency analysis'

Question:
What is a key derived from a master key?

Answer:
'subkey'

Question:
What is used to generate keys made from random values?

Answer:
'Key Derivation Function, or KDF'

Question:
What uses a private and public key for encryption, where only the owner has the private key?

Answer:
'asymmetric encryption algorithm'

Question:
What is a formula of $n(n-1)/2$ where n is the number of individuals involved?

Answer:
'number of keys formula'

Security Engineering Domain

Question:
What are Data encryption standard (DES), Triple-DES (3DES), Blowfish, International data encryption algorithm (IDEA), RC4, RC5, and RC6 and the Advanced Encryption Standard (AES)?

Answer:
'examples of symmetric algorithms'

Question:
What is a set of keys consisting of both a private and public key?

Answer:
'public key pair'

Question:
What is an asymmetric cryptosystem using a public key pair?

Answer:
'public key system'

Question:
What is the term for encrypting a message with a private key?

Answer:
'open message format'

Question:
What is the act of encrypting and decrypting a message with a public key pair?

Answer:
'digital envelope'

Question:
What is a type of cipher that divides data into blocks of bits?

Answer:
'block cipher'

Question:
What is a block cipher mode in which a 64-bit block of plaintext is encrypted with a key, producing a 64-bit block of ciphertext, and uses padding?

Answer:
'Electronic Code Book mode, or ECB'

Question:
What is a block cipher mode that is the same as ECB but uses chaining?

Answer:
'Cipher Block Chaining mode, or CBC'

Question:
What is a block cipher mode which uses a keystream to encrypt blocks?

Answer:
'Cipher Feedback mode, or CFB'

Security Engineering Domain

Question:
What is a block cipher mode just like CFB but does not use chaining?

Answer:
'Output Feedback mode, or OFB'

Question:
What is a block cipher mode just like OFB but increments the IV for each block?

Answer:
'Counter mode, or CTR'

Question:
What is another term for substitution?

Answer:
'confusion'

Question:
What is another term for transposition?

Answer:
'diffusion'

Question:
What occurs when a slight change to the input of an encryption algorithm causes significant change in the output?

Answer:
'avalanche effect'

Question:
What is a cipher that views the data as a single stream of bits?

Answer:
'stream cipher'

Question:
What generates a keystream to be XOR'd with plaintext?

Answer:
'keystream generator'

Question:
What uses keystreams to encrypt each bit, one at a time?

Answer:
'synchronous algorithm'

Question:
What uses previously generated ciphertext to encrypt the next plaintext value, called chaining?

Answer:
'asynchronous algorithm'

Security Engineering Domain

Question:
What is used with the key to reduce the chance of a repeating pattern?

Answer:
'initialization vector, or IV'

Question:
What is a technique that reduces the size of the data before encryption?

Answer:
'compression'

Question:
What is a technique that expands the plaintext to correspond to key sizes?

Answer:
'expansion'

Question:
What is a technique that adds data to the plaintext before encryption?

Answer:
'padding'

Question:
What is a technique that uses a subkey instead of the entire key, thereby reducing exposure of the key?

Answer:
'key mixing'

Question:
What is a single letter abbreviation representing the word size in bits of 16, 32 or 64 bits?

Answer:
''w' when using shorthand notation'

Question:
What is a single letter abbreviation representing the number of rounds of computation of 0 to 255?

Answer:
''r' when using shorthand notation'

Question:
What is a single letter abbreviation representing the key size, in bytes?

Answer:
''b' when using shorthand notation'

Question:
What is a symmetric block cipher using 64-bits blocks with 8-bits of parity, and uses 16 rounds of transposition and substitution?

Answer:
'Data Encryption Algorithm, or DEA'

Security Engineering Domain

Question:
What is a symmetric block cipher using 48 rounds of computation with each pass using a different key?

Answer:
'Triple-DES, or 3DES'

Question:
What is a symmetric block cipher using 64-bit blocks, uses 8 rounds of computation with a 128-bit key size and is faster than DES?

Answer:
'International Data Encryption Algorithm, or IDEA'

Question:
What is a symmetric block cipher using 64-bit blocks, uses 16 rounds of computation with a 32 to 448 bit key size?

Answer:
'Blowfish'

Question:
What is a symmetric stream cipher, is used for SSL and was poorly implemented in 802.11 WEP?

Answer:
'RC4'

Question:
What is a symmetric block cipher using 32, 64 or 128 bit blocks, with keys up to 2,048 bits, and 255 rounds of computation?

Answer:
'RC5'

Question:
What is a type of function that is easy to create, but almost impossible to reverse?

Answer:
'one-way function'

Question:
What is a way to reverse a one-way function if you possess the secret key?

Answer:
'trapdoor'

Question:
What occurs when two parties independently calculate the secret key?

Answer:
'key agreement'

Question:
What occurs when two parties exchange the secret key?

Answer:
'key exchange'

Security Engineering Domain

Question:
What is a statement that we should only reveal the minimum of a security exchange and no more, and in practice means that the owner of a private key does not reveal how he got it or where it is stored?

Answer:
'Zero Knowledge Proof'

Question:
What is represented by an encryption algorithm using a private key that offers nonrepudiation?

Answer:
'digital signature'

Question:
What was the first asymmetric algorithm focused on distributing symmetric keys only, using discrete logarithms on a finite field?

Answer:
'Diffie-Hellman Algorithm'

Question:
What was an attempt at improving the Diffie-Hellman algorithm but wasn't much of a success?

Answer:
'MQV'

Question:
What was the algorithm that successfully solved the problems with Diffie-Hellman, and provides authentication and confidentiality based on large prime numbers?

Answer:
'RAS'

Question:
What is an algorithm very similar to Diffie-Hellman but slower?

Answer:
'El Gamal'

Question:
What is an algorithm using discrete logarithms on an elliptic curve, which is most efficient because it uses shorter keys and is often found on mobile devices?

Answer:
'Elliptic Curve Cryptosystems, or ECC'

Question:
What is an algorithm based the knapsack problem, which were found to be insecure?

Answer:
'Knapsack'

Security Engineering Domain

117

Question:
What occurs when a system secret key is used, so we only know what system sent the message, not what user?

Answer:
'data origin authentication, or system authentication'

Question:
What is a publicly known algorithm that accepts a string of any length and produces a string of a fixed length without the use of a key?

Answer:
'one-way hash'

Question:
What happens when the same hash result is calculated from different plaintext values?

Answer:
'collision'

Question:
What is used in an algorithm to apply a secret key to a hash, resulting in integrity?

Answer:
'Message Authentication Code, or MAC'

Question:
What is used to concatenate a message with a secret key, which is then hashed and sent with the message?

Answer:
'HMAC'

Question:
What uses CBC to encrypt a message, with the final block being used as the MAC?

Answer:
'Cipher Block Chaining Message Authentication Code, or CBC-MAC'

Question:
What is the same as CBC-MAC but uses AES or 3DES to create the symmetric key with subkeys?

Answer:
'Cipher-Based Message Authentication Code, or CMAC'

Question:
What is the output of a hashing function?

Answer:
'digest value, message digest or hash'

Question:
What is a hashing algorithm that produces a 128-bit hash and is considered to be insecure?

Answer:
'MD4'

Security Engineering Domain

Question:
What is a hashing algorithm that produces a 128-bit hash, is considered to be secure but is susceptible to collisions?

Answer:
'MD5'

Question:
What is a hashing algorithm that is used for DSS, creates a 160-bit hash and then runs that through an asymmetric algorithm?

Answer:
'SHA'

Question:
What is a hashing algorithm based on SHA but is vulnerable to collisions?

Answer:
'SHA-1'

Question:
What is a hashing algorithm based on SHA and is considered to be secure for any use?

Answer:
'SHA-2, examples being SHA-224, SHA-256, SHA-384, SHA-512'

Question:
What is a hashing algorithm that is an alternative to SHA-2, but is not derived from SHA-2?

Answer:
'SHA-3'

Question:
What is a hash attack that creates a message which collides with an existing hash using brute force?

Answer:
'birthday attack'

Question:
What is a hash value that has been encrypted with a private key, resulting in integrity, authenticity and nonrepudiation?

Answer:
'digital signature'

Question:
What is a standard that implements digital signatures using SHA and one of DSA, RSA or ECC algorithms?

Answer:
'Digital Signature Standard, or DSS'

Question:
What is an ISO framework using public key cryptography and X.509?

Answer:
'Public Key Infrastructure, or PKI'

Security Engineering Domain

119

Question:
What is an organization who creates a digital certificate on behalf of an individual and digitally signs it?

Answer:
'Certificate Authority, or CA'

Question:
What is an organization who verifies digital certificates?

Answer:
'Registration Authority, or RA'

Question:
What occurs when one CA agrees to trust all certificates issues by another CA?

Answer:
'cross certification'

Question:
What is a list of revoked certificates that a CA maintains?

Answer:
'Certificate Revocation List, or CRL'

Question:
What is used when a provider proactively notifies the browser that a certificate is no longer valid?

Answer:
'Online Certificate Status Protocol, or OCSP'

Question:
What is used to associate a public key with data sufficient to verify an owner's identity via X509?

Answer:
'certificate'

Question:
What is a standard that dictates the various fields contained within a digital certificate, and is used by both SSL and TLS?

Answer:
'x.509'

Question:
What is a microchip that may be installed on motherboards to execute dedicated security functions using RSA and SHA-1?

Answer:
'Trusted Platform Module, or TPM'

Question:
What is the organization that created TPM?

Answer:
'Trusted Computer Group, or TCG'

Security Engineering Domain

Question:
What occurs when TPM encrypts the contents of a hard drive?

Answer:
'binding'

Question:
What is a public/private key that is installed by the manufacturer in TPM and cannot be modified?

Answer:
'Endorsement Key, or EK'

Question:
What is the master key used to secure the TMP keys stored in versatile memory?

Answer:
'Storage Root Key, or SRK'

Question:
What is a key linked to the TPM's identity by the manufacturer, and ensures the integrity of the EK?

Answer:
'Attestation Identity Key, or AIK'

Question:
What stores hashes when sealing a TPM system?

Answer:
'Platform Configuration Registers, or PCR'

Question:
What is the term for keys used to encrypt a TPM system's storage media?

Answer:
'storage keys'

Question:
What is a cryptography attack that focuses on gathering information?

Answer:
'passive attack'

Question:
What is a cryptography attack in which the attacker is actively engaged instead of simply gathering data?

Answer:
'active attack'

Question:
What is a cryptography attack in which the result of one attack may result in the use a different attack next?

Answer:
'adaptive attack'

Security Engineering Domain

Question:
What is a cryptography attack in which the attacker figures out the encryption key using brute force against the cipher text?

Answer:
'Ciphertext-Only Attack'

Question:
What is a cryptography attack in which the attacker compares portions of known plaintext to the resulting ciphertext?

Answer:
'Known-Plaintext Attack'

Question:
What is a cryptography attack in which the attacker chooses the plaintext to encrypt and receives the resulting ciphertext?

Answer:
'Chosen-Plaintext Attack'

Question:
What is a cryptography attack in which the attacker chooses the ciphertext to decrypt and receives the results?

Answer:
'Chosen-Ciphertext Attack'

Question:
What is a type of chosen-plaintext attack, with the attacker analyzing the differences in the resulting ciphertext?

Answer:
'Differential Cryptanalysis'

Question:
What is similar to differential cryptanalysis, but the plaintext blocks do not need to be chosen, just known?

Answer:
'Linear Cryptanalysis'

Question:
What is a cryptography attack in which the attacker figures out something about the key based on changes in the environment during encryption and/or decryption?

Answer:
'Side-Channel Attack'

Question:
What is a cryptography attack in which the attacker captures some data and sends it back to the same system?

Answer:
'Replay Attack'

Question:
What is an analytical cryptography attack which exploits any mathematical weakness found?

Answer:
'algebraic attack'

Security Engineering Domain

Question:
What is an analytical cryptography attack that looks for structural weaknesses in the algorithm?

Answer:
'analytic attack'

Question:
What is an analytical cryptography attack that looks for values that will be statistically used more than others?

Answer:
'statistical attack'

Question:
What is a cryptographic attack which tricks people into revealing the key?

Answer:
'Social Engineering Attack'

Question:
What is cryptographic attack which works both the encryption and decryption ends of a cryptographic system simultaneously?

Answer:
'Meet-in-the-Middle Attack'

Question:
What are physical threats such as floods, storms, earthquakes, fires and other acts of God?

Answer:
'natural environment'

Question:
What are physical threats such as interruption of power, communication, water, gas and cooling?

Answer:
'supply system'

Question:
What are physical threats such as unauthorized access, disgruntled employees, theft or vandalism?

Answer:
'manmade'

Question:
What are physical threats such as riots, strikes, terrorist attacks and civil disobedience?

Answer:
'politically motivated'

Question:
What occurs when physical controls work together in layers?

Answer:
'layered defense strategy'

Security Engineering Domain

Question:
What is a CIA attribute that occurs when physical security is applied to the data and business processes?

Answer:
'confidentiality, as applied to physical security'

Question:
What is a CIA attribute that occurs when physical security is applied to the company resources?

Answer:
'availability, as applied to physical security'

Question:
What is a CIA attribute that occurs when physical security is applied to the assets and the environment?

Answer:
'integrity, as applied to physical security'

Question:
What is addressed by fences, warning signs and security guards?

Answer:
'deterrence, as applied to site planning'

Question:
What is addressed by locks, security guards and barriers?

Answer:
'delaying mechanisms, as applied to site planning'

Question:
What is addressed by smoke or motion detectors and closed-circuit TV?

Answer:
'detection, as applied to site planning'

Question:
What is addressed by security guards who must respond to incidents and assess damage?

Answer:
'incident assessment, as applied to site planning'

Question:
What is addressed by fire suppression and notification of law enforcement?

Answer:
'response procedures, as applied to site planning'

Question:
What are mitigated by using pre-employment background checks, separation of duties, and rotation of duties?

Answer:
'internal threats'

Security Engineering Domain

Question:
What are mitigated by using security officers?

Answer:
'external threats'

Question:
What is an approach to monitoring the effectiveness of a security program based on metrics?

Answer:
'performance-based approach'

Question:
What is the term for preventing access using physical barriers such as locks and fences?

Answer:
'target hardening'

Question:
What is the belief that a physical environment can reduce both crime and the fear of crime?

Answer:
'Crime Prevention Through Environmental Design, or CPTED'

Question:
What is the process of guiding people entering or exiting a location by the muted placement of doors, fences, lighting or landscaping?

Answer:
'Natural Access Control'

Question:
What are posts outside of entryways that prevent vehicles from driving into a building?

Answer:
'bollard'

Question:
What are areas that can be labelled public, controlled, restricted or sensitive?

Answer:
'security zones'

Question:
What is a method for making criminals feel uncomfortable and guests to feel safe by ensuring that all actions will be observed by people in the area?

Answer:
'natural surveillance'

Security Engineering Domain

125

Question:
What creates physical designs that extend the area of a building's area of influence, and enhances the feeling of ownership by legitimate occupants?

Answer:
'natural territory reinforcement'

Question:
What is a role that understands physical security constraints and understands how to stay in compliance?

Answer:
'facility safety officer'

Question:
What is a construction material consisting of untreated lumber that is susceptible to fire?

Answer:
'light-frame construction'

Question:
What is a construction material consisting of heavy untreated lumber that is 50% less susceptible to fire as light-frame lumber?

Answer:
'heavy-timber construction'

Question:
What is a construction material consisting of metal that will not burn but can collapse under high temperature?

Answer:
'incombustible material'

Question:
What is a construction material usually consisting of steel rods encased in concrete?

Answer:
'fire-resistant material'

Question:
What are large doors designed for heavy traffic?

Answer:
'personnel doors'

Question:
What are heavy steel doors designed for security and not aesthetics?

Answer:
'industrial doors'

Question:
What are large doors that normally roll up into the ceiling?

Answer:
'vehicle access doors'

Security Engineering Domain

Question:
What are made by sandwiching wood and steel veneers?

Answer:
'bullet-resistant doors'

Question:
What are extremely dense doors designed to withstand explosive force and lock securely?

Answer:
'vault doors'

Question:
What are hollow and should only be used internally - not used to separate security zones?

Answer:
'hollow or solid core doors'

Question:
What is a safety feature that on power interruption defaults to being locked?

Answer:
'fail-secure'

Question:
What are windows that provide no extra protection?

Answer:
'standard windows'

Question:
What are windows made using glass that is heated and suddenly cooled, resulting in a stronger build?

Answer:
'tempered windows'

Question:
What are windows that are constructed of plastic instead of glass, making them even stronger?

Answer:
'acrylic windows'

Question:
What are windows that contain a mesh of wires embedded between two sheets of glass, making them more shatter-resistant?

Answer:
'wired windows'

Question:
What are windows in which a plastic layer is inserted between two glass panels, making them more shatter- resistant?

Answer:
'laminated windows'

Security Engineering Domain

Question:
What are windows that provide extra security by tinting and slightly increases the strength of glass?

Answer:
'solar window film windows'

Question:
What are windows that have a transparent film applied to the glass to specifically increase strength?

Answer:
'security film windows'

Question:
What are thin walls that do not reach all the way into the structural ceiling?

Answer:
'internal compartments'

Question:
What is a device that monitors humidity?

Answer:
'hygrometer'

Question:
What is installed software that periodically 'phones home' and allows the tracking and possible recovery of a device?

Answer:
'tracing software'

Question:
What occurs when the voltage in a power source fluctuates to a level where equipment starts to malfunction?

Answer:
'voltage instability'

Question:
What occurs when all power is no longer accessible?

Answer:
'outage'

Question:
What is a device that provides a short term power supply?

Answer:
'uninterruptible power supply, or UPS'

Question:
What is a device that converts electrical output from DC to AC?

Answer:
'inverter'

Security Engineering Domain

Question:
What is a UPS device that delivers power with no detectable drop in voltage if an outage occurs?

Answer:
'online UPS'

Question:
What is a UPS device that delivers power with a momentary delay while power is switched over from source to the batteries?

Answer:
'standby UPS'

Question:
What is a method of protecting power supply by drawing the power from a secondary power substation?

Answer:
'redundant line feed'

Question:
What is a method of protecting power supply by drawing the power from a gas-powered electrical generator?

Answer:
'onsite generator'

Question:
What is a type of power interference resulting from electrical motors?

Answer:
'electromagnetic interference, or EMI'

Question:
What is a type of power interference resulting from fluorescent lighting?

Answer:
'radio interference, or RFI'

Question:
What is power free from voltage fluctuation?

Answer:
'clean power'

Question:
What is power line interference resulting from EMI or RFI?

Answer:
'line noise'

Question:
What is the initial surge of current required to start a load?

Answer:
'in-rush current'

Security Engineering Domain

Question:
What is a momentary disruption of clean power due to a high voltage?

Answer:
'spike'

Question:
What is a momentary disruption of clean power due to a low voltage?

Answer:
'sag/dip'

Question:
What is a momentary disruption of clean power due to a power outage?

Answer:
'fault'

Question:
What is a prolonged disruption of clean power due to a high voltage?

Answer:
'surge'

Question:
What is a prolonged disruption of clean power due to a low voltage?

Answer:
'brownout'

Question:
What is a prolonged disruption of clean power due to a power outage?

Answer:
'blackout'

Question:
What is a device that ensures clean power?

Answer:
'voltage regulator or line conditioner'

Question:
What occurs through both proper construction and employee training?

Answer:
'fire prevention'

Question:
What occurs by detecting the environmental changes due to fires?

Answer:
'fire detection'

Security Engineering Domain

130

Question:
What is a device that detects a change in light intensity?

Answer:
'photoelectric device'

Question:
What is a photoelectric device that detects when smoke obstructs the light source?

Answer:
'smoke-activated detector'

Question:
What is a device that detects when there is a rise in temperature?

Answer:
'heat activated detector'

Question:
What is a device that detects when the temperature reaches a specific value?

Answer:
'fixed temperature detector'

Question:
What is a device that detects a change in temperature over time?

Answer:
'rate-of-rise detector'

Question:
What is an automated system that engages when a fire is detected and acts to extinguish the fire?

Answer:
'fire suppression agent'

Question:
What is a chemical suppression agent that acts by robbing the fire of heat?

Answer:
'water'

Question:
What is a chemical suppression agent that is mixed with water and robs the fire of both heat and oxygen?

Answer:
'foam'

Security Engineering Domain

Question:
What is a gas chemical suppression agent that robs the fire of oxygen?

Answer:
'carbon dioxide'

Question:
What is a chemical suppression agent that acts by suppressing the chemical reaction?

Answer:
'gases'

Question:
What is a gas suppression agent that is no longer used as it affected the ozone layer?

Answer:
'halon'

Question:
What is a gas suppression agent that replaced halon?

Answer:
'FM-200'

Question:
What is a gas suppression agent that acts in different ways according to the chemical?

Answer:
'dry powder'

Question:
What are dry powder suppression agents that prevent chemical reactions?

Answer:
'sodium bicarbonate, potassium bicarbonate and calcium bicarbonate'

Question:
What is a dry powder suppression agent that robs the fire of oxygen?

Answer:
'monoammonium phosphate'

Question:
What is a suppression agent, normally containing potassium acetate, that robs the fire of heat and oxygen?

Answer:
'wet chemical'

Question:
What is a class of fire that is the most common and results from the ignition of wood, paper or laminates?

Answer:
'Class A'

Security Engineering Domain

Question:
What is a class of fire in which some type of liquid ignites?

Answer:
'Class B'

Question:
What is a class of fire found in electrical equipment or wires?

Answer:
'Class C'

Question:
What is a class of fire occurring by the ignition of combustible metals such as magnesium, sodium or potassium?

Answer:
'Class D'

Question:
What is a class of fire most commonly found in commercial kitchens?

Answer:
'Class K'

Question:
What is a type of water sprinkler in which pressurized water is always in the pipe leading to the sprinkler head, and is activated when elevated temperatures are detected?

Answer:
'wet pipe sprinkler'

Question:
What is a type of water sprinkler the same as a wet pipe, but the pipe leading to the sprinkler head contains air pressure, keeping the water in a central storage tank until elevated temperatures are detected?

Answer:
'dry pipe sprinkler'

Question:
What is a type of water sprinkler which is the same as a dry pipe, but before the sprinkler head can be activated, a thermal-fusible link on the sprinkler head must melt?

Answer:
'precaution sprinkler'

Question:
What is a type of water sprinkler that allows a massive amount of water to be released instead of 'sprinkled'?

Answer:
'deluge sprinkler'

Security Engineering Domain

133

Question:
What is cabling that should be used in overhead and under-floor spaces due to non-toxic fumes produced when burning?

Answer:
'plenum-rated cabling'

Security Engineering Domain

Terms

Question:
What is 'security engineering'?

Answer:
'security engineering' is the task of building security directly into the technology products we use every day.

Question:
What is 'system architecture'?

Answer:
'system architecture' are the components of a system and how they interact.

Question:
What is 'architecture'?

Answer:
'architecture' is a tool to understand a complex system.

Question:
What is 'development'?

Answer:
'development' represents the entire life cycle of a system from planning to retirement.

Question:
What is 'system'?

Answer:
'system' is a term that describes a computer, an application, a set of computers, and a network.

Question:
What is 'ISO 42010'?

Answer:
'ISO 42010' is the standard that outlines the specifications of a system architecture.

Question:
What is 'architecture'?

Answer:
'architecture' describes a system made up of components, their relationships to each other and their environment, and the principles guiding its design and evolution.

Question:
What is 'architecture descriptions, or AD'?

Answer:
'architecture descriptions, or AD' are a collection of document types to document an architecture in a formal manner.

Security Engineering Domain

Question:
What is the 'stakeholder'?

Answer:
The 'stakeholder' is an individual, team or organization with an interest in, or concern about, a system.

Question:
What is a 'concern'?

Answer:
A 'concern' is an area of a system that a stakeholder is interested in.

Question:
What is a 'view'?

Answer:
A 'view' is a representation of the entire system from the perspective of a related set of concerns (functionality, performance, interoperability, security).

Question:
What is a 'viewpoint'?

Answer:
A 'viewpoint' is a specification of the conventions for creating and using a view.

Question:
What is an 'architecture view'?

Answer:
An 'architecture view' is used to communicate decisions made by the architect (logical, physical, structural, behavioral, management, cost and security).

Question:
What is a 'computer architecture'?

Answer:
A 'computer architecture' encompasses all aspects of a physical computer.

Question:
What is an 'algorithmic logic unit, or ALU'?

Answer:
An 'algorithmic logic unit, or ALU' performs mathematical functions and logical operations on data it gets from computer memory.

Question:
What is 'registers'?

Answer:
'registers' are the fast memory units which sit very close to the ALU.

Question:
What is the 'control unit'?

Answer:
The 'control unit' loads data from the main memory into the registers for the ALU.

Security Engineering Domain

Question:
What is the 'central processing unit, or CPU'?

Answer:
The 'central processing unit, or CPU' is the collective name for the ALU, registers and control unit.

Question:
What is the 'operating system, or OS'?

Answer:
The 'operating system, or OS' is a list of very complex instructions for the ALU to execute.

Question:
What is the 'general register'?

Answer:
The 'general register' holds variables and temporary results that the ALU will use.

Question:
What is the 'program counter register'?

Answer:
The 'program counter register' is a register that points to the next instruction to be executed.

Question:
What is 'special registers'?

Answer:
'special registers' are registers that hold the stack pointer, program counter and the PWS.

Question:
What is the 'program status word, or PWS'?

Answer:
The 'program status word, or PWS' holds different bits that reflect the execution mode the CPU should be operating in.

Question:
What is the 'stack'?

Answer:
The 'stack' is a list of pointers to addresses and data.

Question:
What is the 'stack pointer'?

Answer:
The 'stack pointer' points to where in the stack execution is currently going on.

Question:
What is 'user mode'?

Answer:
'user mode' is the mode which limits the functions that can be executed.

Security Engineering Domain

Question:
What is 'problem state'?

Answer:
'problem state' is another name for user mode.

Question:
What is 'privilege mode'?

Answer:
'privilege mode' is the mode allows unlimited execution and runs in Ring 0.

Question:
What is 'kernel mode'?

Answer:
'kernel mode' is another name for privilege or supervisor mode.

Question:
What is 'supervisor mode'?

Answer:
'supervisor mode' is another name for privilege or kernel mode.

Question:
What is the 'address bus'?

Answer:
The 'address bus' is a communications pathway used to send address pointers between the CPU and memory.

Question:
What is a 'fetch request'?

Answer:
A 'fetch request' occurs when an instruction is sent from the CPU across the address bus, and contains the memory address where an instruction or data resides.

Question:
What is the 'data bus'?

Answer:
The 'data bus' is used to transfer data between the CPU and memory.

Question:
What is 'multiprocessing'?

Answer:
'multiprocessing' occurs when more than one CPU in a single computer is used.

Question:
What is 'symmetric mode'?

Answer:
'symmetric mode' occurs when all processors are load-balanced, and are handed work as they become available.

Security Engineering Domain

Question:
What is 'asymmetric mode'?

Answer:
'asymmetric mode' describes when processors may be completely dedicated to a specific task or application.

Question:
What is 'volatile'?

Answer:
'volatile' is a memory type that will lose contents if power is interrupted.

Question:
What is 'non-Volatile'?

Answer:
'non-Volatile' is a memory type that will not lose contents if power is interrupted.

Question:
What is 'random access memory, or RAM'?

Answer:
'random access memory, or RAM' is a type of volatile memory.

Question:
What is 'dynamic RAM, or DRAM'?

Answer:
'dynamic RAM, or DRAM' is a type of memory that must be continuously refreshed to retain contents.

Question:
What is 'static RAM, or SRAM'?

Answer:
'static RAM, or SRAM' is a type of memory that does not have to be refreshed, is faster and is used for caches.

Question:
What is 'synchronous DRAM, or SDRAM'?

Answer:
'synchronous DRAM, or SDRAM' is a type of memory that synchronizes itself with the CPU clock to make communication faster.

Question:
What is 'extended data out DRAM, or EDO DRAM'?

Answer:
'extended data out DRAM, or EDO DRAM' is a type of memory that can 'look ahead' and fetch the next block at the same time.

Question:
What is 'burst EDO RAM, or BEDO RAM'?

Answer:
'burst EDO RAM, or BEDO RAM' is a type of memory that can send 4 blocks in a 'burst' instead of just two blocks like EDO or BEDO.

Security Engineering Domain

Question:
What is 'double data rate SDRAM, or DDR SDRAM'?

Answer:
'double data rate SDRAM, or DDR SDRAM' is a type of memory that can execute two instructions per clock cycle.

Question:
What is 'hardware segmentation'?

Answer:
'hardware segmentation' occurs when memory is physically segmented so that only certain processes can access the memory.

Question:
What is 'read-only memory, or ROM'?

Answer:
'read-only memory, or ROM' is a type of non-volatile memory.

Question:
What is 'programmable read-only memory, or PROM'?

Answer:
'programmable read-only memory, or PROM' is a type of non-volatile memory that can be reprogrammed one time.

Question:
What is 'erasable programmable read-only memory, or EPROM'?

Answer:
'erasable programmable read-only memory, or EPROM' is a type of non-volatile memory that can be reprogrammed any number of times by using a UV light to erase the previous contents.

Question:
What is 'electrically erasable programmable read-only memory, or EEPROM'?

Answer:
'electrically erasable programmable read-only memory, or EEPROM' is a type of non-volatile memory that allows for erasing electrically, but only a single byte at a time.

Question:
What is 'flash memory'?

Answer:
'flash memory' is a type of non-volatile memory that is a solid-state device, and uses voltage to indicate the existence of a value.

Question:
What is 'firmware'?

Answer:
'firmware' is content stored in ROM.

Question:
What is 'cache memory'?

Answer:
'cache memory' is memory used for high-speed writing and reading activities.

Security Engineering Domain

Question:
What is 'levels 1 and 2'?

Answer:
'levels 1 and 2' is memory built directly into processors and controllers.

Question:
What is 'level 3'?

Answer:
'level 3' is memory used anywhere else than in processors and controllers.

Question:
What is an 'absolute address'?

Answer:
An 'absolute address' contains physical memory address locations.

Question:
What is a 'logical address'?

Answer:
A 'logical address' is used by software and maps to an absolute memory location, resulting in increased security.

Question:
What is a 'relative address'?

Answer:
A 'relative address' is an address that is an offset to, or relative to, an absolute or logical address.

Question:
What is a 'parameter'?

Answer:
A 'parameter' is a variable passed from one process to another.

Question:
What is a 'buffer'?

Answer:
A 'buffer' wraps a parameter value.

Question:
What is a 'buffer overflow'?

Answer:
A 'buffer overflow' results when the size of a buffer is exceeded.

Question:
What is 'address space layout randomization, or ASLR'?

Answer:
'address space layout randomization, or ASLR' prevents the same memory address from being used each time.

Security Engineering Domain

Question:
What is 'data execution prevention, or DEP'?

Answer:
'data execution prevention, or DEP' prevents execution of code in certain memory segments.

Question:
What is 'memory leaks'?

Answer:
'memory leaks' occurs when badly-written code forgets to release allocated memory.

Question:
What is the 'garbage collector'?

Answer:
The 'garbage collector' is a background process that ensures all allocated memory is freed up.

Question:
What is 'operating systems'?

Answer:
'operating systems' is the software on top of which applications will run.

Question:
What is a 'process'?

Answer:
A 'process' is a term describing the portion of an application that has been initialized and loaded for execution.

Question:
What is 'multiprogramming'?

Answer:
'multiprogramming' is a term describing the ability to load multiple applications into memory at the same time.

Question:
What is 'multitasking'?

Answer:
'multitasking' is a term describing the ability to deal with requests from multiple applications simultaneously.

Question:
What is 'cooperative multitasking'?

Answer:
'cooperative multitasking' is the term describing applications having to volunteer CPU time for some other application to use in early OSs.

Question:
What is 'preemptive multitasking'?

Answer:
'preemptive multitasking' is the term describing CPUs that multitask no matter what the application wants to do.

Security Engineering Domain

Question:
What is 'ready'?

Answer:
'ready' is the process state in which the process has not yet sent any instructions to the CPU.

Question:
What is 'running'?

Answer:
'running' is the process state in which the CPU is executing the process' instructions.

Question:
What is 'blocked'?

Answer:
'blocked' is the process state in which a process is waiting for some kind of input, such as a keystroke.

Question:
What is a 'process table'?

Answer:
A 'process table' is used by the OS to keep track of each process.

Question:
What is a 'time slice'?

Answer:
A 'time slice' occurs when a process is loaded into the CPU for a short period of time and executed.

Question:
What is an 'interrupt'?

Answer:
An 'interrupt' is an event that causes the OS to consider executing a process ahead of its schedule time slice.

Question:
What is 'maskable'?

Answer:
'maskable' is a flag assigned to an event that doesn't necessarily have to be taken care of immediately.

Question:
What is 'non-maskable'?

Answer:
'non-maskable' is a flag assigned to an event that makes the CPU stop whatever was going on and take care of a that event.

Question:
What is a 'watchdog timer'?

Answer:
A 'watchdog timer' is a background process using a non-maskable interrupt that will perform a warm boot if the OS ever hangs.

Security Engineering Domain

Question:
What is a 'thread'?

Answer:
A 'thread' contains some of the process' instruction sets, and shares the process' memory space and resource.

Question:
What is 'multithreaded'?

Answer:
'multithreaded' is a term describing a process that creates more than one thread.

Question:
What is a 'software deadlock'?

Answer:
A 'software deadlock' occurs when two threads within a process are both waiting for the other to release a common resource.

Question:
What is 'process isolation'?

Answer:
'process isolation' occurs when we make sure that misbehaving processes do not affect other processes.

Question:
What is 'encapsulation'?

Answer:
'encapsulation' is achieved when we make sure that a process does not expose its inner workings by only communicating through a well-defined interface - this is also called data hiding.

Question:
What is 'time multiplexing'?

Answer:
'time multiplexing' is used when the OS must manage access to resources that are shared between multiple processes (such as multiple processes all reading from the same file).

Question:
What is 'naming distinctions'?

Answer:
'naming distinctions' occurs when each process has its own unique ID assigned by the OS.

Question:
What is 'virtual memory mapping'?

Answer:
'virtual memory mapping' is used by the OS so that physical memory is not exposed directly – instead it is mapped through a virtual address, allowing the OS to play memory cop.

Security Engineering Domain

Question:
What is an 'abstraction layer'?

Answer:
An 'abstraction layer' is used to prevent a subject from accessing an object directly.

Question:
What is 'abstraction'?

Answer:
'abstraction' is achieved when details are hidden.

Question:
What is a 'memory segment'?

Answer:
A 'memory segment' is a term describing a division of the computer's memory into subsections.

Question:
What is the 'memory manager'?

Answer:
The 'memory manager' is a layer that abstracts memory locations away from any process wishing to use the memory.

Question:
What is 'relocation'?

Answer:
'relocation' is a responsibility of the memory manager and happens when memory contents are swapped from RAM to the hard drive, but is hidden from the process.

Question:
What is 'protection'?

Answer:
'protection' is a responsibility of the memory manager and is achieved when processes can only access their memory segments.

Question:
What is 'sharing'?

Answer:
'sharing' is a responsibility of the memory manager and ensures CIA is enforced with shared memory by allowing different levels of access to interact with the same memory.

Question:
What is the 'local organization'?

Answer:
The 'local organization' is a responsibility of the memory manager which segments memory types and provide an addressing scheme, thereby allowing multiple processes to access the same shared DLL.

Security Engineering Domain

Question:
What is the 'physical organization'?

Answer:
The 'physical organization' is a responsibility of the memory manager which segments the physical memory for use by the applications and OS processes.

Question:
What is a 'dynamic link library, or DLL'?

Answer:
A 'dynamic link library, or DLL' is a shared set of functions that processes can reuse.

Question:
What is the 'base register'?

Answer:
The 'base register' is a register that points to the beginning memory address for a segment.

Question:
What is the 'limit register'?

Answer:
The 'limit register' is a register that points to the ending memory address for a segment.

Question:
What is 'virtual memory'?

Answer:
'virtual memory' is a memory management term describing both volatile and non-volatile storage collectively.

Question:
What is 'secondary storage'?

Answer:
'secondary storage' is a memory management term describing non-volatile storage only.

Question:
What is 'swapping'?

Answer:
'swapping' occurs when a portion of volatile memory is copied to non-volatile storage, thereby freeing up volatile memory for use.

Question:
What is the 'swap space'?

Answer:
The 'swap space' is the name of the non-volatile storage used during swapping.

Question:
What is 'pages'?

Answer:
'pages' are units used to describe the swap space.

Security Engineering Domain

Question:
What is 'virtual memory paging'?

Answer:
'virtual memory paging' is the term describing when memory pages are loaded back into volatile memory.

Question:
What is a 'block device'?

Answer:
A 'block device' is a device exposing data in fixed-block sizes, with each block having a unique address.

Question:
What is a 'character device'?

Answer:
A 'character device' is a device using a stream of characters only.

Question:
What is a 'device driver'?

Answer:
A 'device driver' is very low-level software that knows all of the specifics about a device.

Question:
What is 'direct memory access, or DMA'?

Answer:
'direct memory access, or DMA' occurs when a process has direct access to a physical memory address.

Question:
What is 'programmable I/O'?

Answer:
'programmable I/O' is an I/O service method in which the CPU polls the device to see if it is ready.

Question:
What is 'interrupt-Driven I/O'?

Answer:
'interrupt-Driven I/O' is an I/O service method in which the device sends an interrupt to the CPU when it is ready.

Question:
What is 'I/O Using DMA'?

Answer:
'I/O Using DMA' is an I/O service method in which the process and the device share memory without bothering the CPU.

Question:
What is 'pre-mapped I/O'?

Answer:
'pre-mapped I/O' is an I/O service method in which the CPU gives the process the physical memory address to the device.

Security Engineering Domain

Question:
What is 'fully mapped I/O'?

Answer:
'fully mapped I/O' is an I/O service method which is the same as pre-mapped I/O, but uses logical memory addresses.

Question:
What is an 'instruction set'?

Answer:
An 'instruction set' is a language that both the OS and CPU understand.

Question:
What is the 'microarchitecture'?

Answer:
The 'microarchitecture' is comprised of everything that makes up the CPU.

Question:
What is 'rings'?

Answer:
'rings' is a term used to describe layers within an OS.

Question:
What is 'ring 0'?

Answer:
'ring 0' is the OS layer in which the kernel runs.

Question:
What is 'ring 3'?

Answer:
'ring 3' is the OS layer in which user processes normally run.

Question:
What is an 'application programming interface, or API'?

Answer:
An 'application programming interface, or API' is the term used to describe the gatekeeper between two processes.

Question:
What is 'kernel mode'?

Answer:
'kernel mode' is the mode represented by processes running in ring 0.

Question:
What is 'user mode'?

Answer:
'user mode' is the mode represented by processes running in rings 1,2 or 3.

Security Engineering Domain

Question:
What is the 'domain'?

Answer:
The 'domain' is a collection of resources a process has access to, with the larger the ring, the larger the domain.

Question:
What is 'kernel mode transition'?

Answer:
'kernel mode transition' occurs when a call is made from a user mode process into a kernel mode process.

Question:
What is 'data hiding'?

Answer:
'data hiding' is another name for encapsulation.

Question:
What is 'monolithic'?

Answer:
'monolithic' is the OS architecture in which everything is in kernel mode.

Question:
What is 'layered'?

Answer:
'layered' is the OS architecture which contains rings, but the OS still runs in kernel mode.

Question:
What is 'microkernel'?

Answer:
'microkernel' is the OS architecture in which a medium-sized kernel is in kernel mode.

Question:
What is 'hybrid microkernel'?

Answer:
'hybrid microkernel' is the OS architecture in which a very small kernel and executive services run in kernel mode.

Question:
What is 'virtualization'?

Answer:
'virtualization' is a term describing the creation of a virtual environment in which software runs.

Question:
What is a 'virtual machine'?

Answer:
A 'virtual machine' is the term used to describe running a virtualized instance of an operating system.

Security Engineering Domain

Question:
What is a 'hypervisor'?

Answer:
A 'hypervisor' is the term used to describe sharing physical resources among multiple guests in a virtualized environment.

Question:
What is a 'security policy'?

Answer:
A 'security policy' is something that defines how sensitive information and resources should be managed and protected.

Question:
What is the 'Trusted Computer System Evaluation Criteria'?

Answer:
The 'Trusted Computer System Evaluation Criteria' is a tool used by the US government to evaluate how well computer systems meet security criteria.

Question:
What is the 'Trusted Computer Base, or TCB'?

Answer:
The 'Trusted Computer Base, or TCB' is a term that represents all hardware, software and firmware in a system coupled that enforces security (basically the kernel).

Question:
What is a 'trusted path'?

Answer:
A 'trusted path' is a term used to describe a user or process communicating with the TCB.

Question:
What is a 'trusted shell'?

Answer:
A 'trusted shell' is a term used when someone or some process is working on the trusted path exclusively.

Question:
What is an 'execution domain'?

Answer:
An 'execution domain' is a domain in the TCB that refers to Ring 0 only.

Question:
What is a 'security perimeter'?

Answer:
A 'security perimeter' is an imaginary wall between the TCB and everything outside of the TCB where great scrutiny occurs.

Question:
What is the 'reference monitor'?

Answer:
The 'reference monitor' is an abstract machine that deals with subjects and objects crossing the security perimeter.

Security Engineering Domain

Question:
What is the 'security kernel'?

Answer:
The 'security kernel' is the TCB plus the actual implementation of the reference monitor.

Question:
What is 'multilevel security policies'?

Answer:
'multilevel security policies' are policies that prevent flow from a high security level to a lower security level.

Question:
What is 'security models'?

Answer:
'security models' are patterns that implement reference monitors within the security kernel.

Question:
What is 'security model rules'?

Answer:
'security model rules' are the word 'simple' means 'read', the word 'star' or the symbol '*' means 'write'.

Question:
What is the 'Bell-Lampedusa Model'?

Answer:
The 'Bell-LaPadula Model' is the security model that ensures confidentiality by enforcing no read up, no write down and read/write at the same level only.

Question:
What is the 'simple security rule'?

Answer:
The 'simple security rule' is the rule meaning 'no read up'.

Question:
What is the '* property rule'?

Answer:
The '* property rule' is the rule meaning 'no write down'.

Question:
What is the 'strong * property rule'?

Answer:
The 'strong * property rule' is the rule meaning 'read/write at same level only'.

Question:
What is the 'Biba Model'?

Answer:
The 'Biba Model' is the security model that ensures integrity by enforcing no read down and no write up.

Security Engineering Domain

151

Question:
What is the '* integrity axiom rule'?

Answer:
The '* integrity axiom rule' is the rule meaning 'no write up'.

Question:
What is the 'simple integrity axiom rule'?

Answer:
The 'simple integrity axiom rule' is the rule meaning "no read down'.

Question:
What is the 'invocation property'?

Answer:
The 'invocation property' is the term meaning that a subject cannot invoke a service higher up.

Question:
What is the 'Clark-Wilson Model'?

Answer:
The 'Clark-Wilson Model' is the security model that ensures integrity by enforcing the access triple, separation of duties and auditing.

Question:
What is 'users'?

Answer:
'users' represents subjects attempting to access a UDI within the Clark-Wilson model.

Question:
What is 'transformation procedures, or TPs'?

Answer:
'transformation procedures, or TPs' represents read, write and modify within the Clark-Wilson model.

Question:
What is 'constrained data items, or CDIs'?

Answer:
'constrained data items, or CDIs' represents things that can be manipulated only by TPs within the Clark-Wilson model.

Question:
What is 'unconstrained data items, or UDIs'?

Answer:
'unconstrained data items, or UDIs' represents things that can be manipulated by users via primitive read and write operations within the Clark-Wilson model.

Security Engineering Domain

Question:
What is 'integrity verification procedures, or IVPs'?

Answer:
'integrity verification procedures, or IVPs' represents processes that check the consistency of CDIs with the real world within the Clark-Wilson model.

Question:
What is an 'access triple'?

Answer:
An 'access triple' represents a User employing a TP to modify a CDI within the Clark-Wilson model.

Question:
What is a 'well-formed transaction'?

Answer:
A 'well-formed transaction' represents the result of an access triple that has been verified by an IVP within the Clark-Wilson model.

Question:
What is the 'noninterference model'?

Answer:
The 'noninterference model' is a security model that ensures commands and activities at one level are not visible to other levels and actions at a lower security level.

Question:
What is the 'Brewer and Nash Model, or the Chinese Wall model'?

Answer:
The 'Brewer and Nash Model, or the Chinese Wall model' is a security model that allows for dynamically changing access controls that prevent conflicts of interest.

Question:
What is the 'Graham-Denning Model'?

Answer:
The 'Graham-Denning Model' is a security model that shows how subjects and objects should be created and deleted, and how to assign access rights.

Question:
What is the 'Harrison-Ruzzo-Ullman Model'?

Answer:
The 'Harrison-Ruzzo-Ullman Model' is a security model that shows how a finite set of procedures can be used to edit the access rights of a subject.

Question:
What is a 'covert channel'?

Answer:
A 'covert channel' describes sending or receiving information in an unauthorized manner.

Security Engineering Domain

Question:
What is a 'covert storage channel'?

Answer:
A 'covert storage channel' describes communicating through a shared storage system - this does not have to be files containing data – it could simply be the presence or absence of some system feature.

Question:
What is a 'covert timing channel'?

Answer:
A 'covert timing channel' describes communicating through the presence or absence of a system resource in a timed fashion.

Question:
What is 'assurance evaluation'?

Answer:
'assurance evaluation' describes the determination of the level of protection required and provided by a system.

Question:
What is 'common criteria'?

Answer:
'common criteria' allows user submission of requirements, vendor claims of meeting those requirements, and independent verification of the claims, and is codified in ISO 15408.

Question:
What is the 'Evaluation Assurance Level, or EAL'?

Answer:
The 'Evaluation Assurance Level, or EAL' is the result of a Common Criteria analysis.

Question:
What is 'EAL1'?

Answer:
'EAL1' is the common criteria EAL level representing a functionally tested system.

Question:
What is 'EAL2'?

Answer:
'EAL2' is the common criteria EAL level representing a structurally tested system.

Question:
What is 'EAL3'?

Answer:
'EAL3' is the common criteria EAL level representing a methodically tested and checked system.

Question:
What is 'EAL4'?

Answer:
'EAL4' is the common criteria EAL level representing a methodically designed, tested and reviewed system.

Security Engineering Domain

Question:
What is 'EAL5'?

Answer:
'EAL5' is the common criteria EAL level representing a semi formally designed and tested system.

Question:
What is 'EAL6'?

Answer:
'EAL6' is the common criteria EAL level representing a semi formally verified designed and tested system.

Question:
What is 'EAL7'?

Answer:
'EAL7' is the common criteria EAL level representing a formally verified design and tested system based on a mathematical model that can be proven.

Question:
What is a 'protection profile'?

Answer:
A 'protection profile' is the common criteria term for a description of a needed security solution.

Question:
What is a 'security problem description'?

Answer:
A 'security problem description' is a list of threats a common criteria product must address.

Question:
What is 'security objectives'?

Answer:
'security objectives' is a list of functionality a common criteria product must provide to address the threats.

Question:
What is 'security requirements'?

Answer:
'security requirements' is a list of very specific common criteria requirements, detailed enough to be implemented and verified.

Question:
What is the 'target of Evaluation, or TOE'?

Answer:
The 'target of Evaluation, or TOE' is the proposed common criteria product that meets a protection profile.

Security Engineering Domain

Question:
What is a 'security target'?

Answer:
A 'security target' is the common criteria vendor's own explanation of what a target of evaluation does and how it does it.

Question:
What is 'security functional requirements'?

Answer:
'security functional requirements' is a list of common criteria security functions a security target must provide.

Question:
What is 'security assurance requirements'?

Answer:
'security assurance requirements' is a list of items the common criteria vendor did during product development and evaluation to ensure compliance with security functional requirements.

Question:
What is 'packages'?

Answer:
'packages' is a term for security functional requirements and security assurance requirements that are packaged for reuse.

Question:
What is a 'certification'?

Answer:
A 'certification' is the term used to describe the technical review of security mechanisms to evaluate their effectiveness.

Question:
What is an 'accreditation'?

Answer:
An 'accreditation' is the term used to describe management's formal acceptance of the certification's findings.

Question:
What is an 'open system'?

Answer:
An 'open system' is a system built on top of open standards, interfaces and protocols that have published specifications.

Question:
What is a 'closed system'?

Answer:
A 'closed system' is a system that does not follow industry standards and therefore does not as easily communicate well with other systems.

Security Engineering Domain

Question:
What is a 'distributed system'?

Answer:
A 'distributed system' is the name of system that contains multiple computer nodes connected by a network, all working together to accomplish a specific task.

Question:
What is 'cloud computing'?

Answer:
'cloud computing' is the term for the use of shared, remote servers, usually based on virtual machines.

Question:
What is 'Infrastructure as a Service, or IaaS'?

Answer:
'Infrastructure as a Service, or IaaS' is an offering in which the vendor provides the server with the appropriate operating system installed and gives you administrative access.

Question:
What is 'Platform as a Service, or PaaS'?

Answer:
'Platform as a Service, or PaaS' is an offering in which the vendor provides a server with the appropriate software installed for you to build on top of, but you don't get administrative access.

Question:
What is 'Software as a Service, or SaaS'?

Answer:
'Software as a Service, or SaaS' is an offering in which the vendor gives you an account for a specific web-based application, but you don't have access to the servers running the application.

Question:
What is 'parallel computing'?

Answer:
'parallel computing' is the term used to describe taking multiple computers and having them all work on the same task simultaneously.

Question:
What is 'bit-level parallelism'?

Answer:
'bit-level parallelism' occurs when a CPU operates on multiple bits simultaneously; all CPUs handling bytes can do this.

Question:
What is 'instruction-level parallelism'?

Answer:
'instruction-level parallelism' occurs when multiple CPUs execute multiple instructions simultaneously; almost all computing devices these days have this feature.

Security Engineering Domain

Question:
What is 'task-level parallelism'?

Answer:
'task-level parallelism' occurs when a program is divided into multiple threads, all operating simultaneously.

Question:
What is 'data-level parallelism'?

Answer:
'data-level parallelism' occurs when data is distributed among multiple nodes and processed in parallel.

Question:
What is 'aggregation'?

Answer:
'aggregation' occurs when combining data for a user from separate sources that results in a view the user should not have access to.

Question:
What is 'inference'?

Answer:
'inference' is the intended result of aggregation.

Question:
What is a 'content-dependent access control'?

Answer:
A 'content-dependent access control' is a counter-measure in which only the content is examined when determining access.

Question:
What is a 'context-dependent access control'?

Answer:
A 'context-dependent access control' is a counter-measure in which the system keeps track of previous requests by this user and recognizes that the danger exists for that user to infer sensitive information from their latest request.

Question:
What is 'cell suppression'?

Answer:
'cell suppression' is a method to mitigate inference attacks by hiding specific information that could be used in an attack.

Question:
What is 'partitioning'?

Answer:
'partitioning' is a method to mitigate inference attacks by dividing a database into multiple parts.

Question:
What is 'noise and perturbation'?

Answer:
'noise and perturbation' occurs when we insert bogus information in hopes of confusing an attacker.

Security Engineering Domain

Question:
What is the '11 guidelines for securing mobile devices'?

Answer:
The '11 guidelines for securing mobile devices' are antivirus, encrypt data, include in policies, manage all connected devices, enable remote policies, enable encrypt/idle lock/screen lock/authentication and remote wipe.

Question:
What is 'cyber-physical systems'?

Answer:
'cyber-physical systems' is a computer controlling a physical device.

Question:
What is an 'embedded system'?

Answer:
An 'embedded system' is a mechanical or electrical device that has a computer embedded into it.

Question:
What is the 'Internet of Things, or IoT'?

Answer:
The 'Internet of Things, or IoT' is the global network of connected embedded systems that are connected to the Internet and are uniquely addressable.

Question:
What is 'authentication'?

Answer:
'authentication' is a security measure for which IoT devices usually have a very poor implementation of.

Question:
What is 'encryption'?

Answer:
'encryption' is a security measure that IoT devices seldom include due to limited processing power.

Question:
What is 'updates'?

Answer:
'updates' is an automatic measure that many IoT vendors do not implement.

Question:
What is an 'industrial control system, or ICS'?

Answer:
An 'industrial control system, or ICS' are systems where software is used to control physical devices in industrial processes.

Security Engineering Domain

Question:
What is the '7 guidelines for ICS provided by NIST SP 800-82'?

Answer:
The '7 guidelines for ICS provided by NIST SP 800-82' are applying risk management, using IDS/IPS, disabling ports, implementing least privilege, using encryption, proper patch management and monitoring audit logs.

Question:
What is a 'programmable logic controller, or PLC'?

Answer:
A 'programmable logic controller, or PLC' are programmable computers connected to physical devices using standard interfaces such as RS-232, and are normally network-enabled.

Question:
What is a 'distributed control system, or DCS'?

Answer:
A 'distributed control system, or DCS' is a small network of PLCs connected to physical devices, all orchestrated by higher-level controllers.

Question:
What is a 'supervisory control and data acquisition, or SCADA'?

Answer:
A 'supervisory control and data acquisition, or SCADA' is DCS over long distances.

Question:
What is 'endpoints'?

Answer:
'endpoints' are remote terminal units or PLCs that connect directly to physical components.

Question:
What is 'backends'?

Answer:
'backends' are data acquisition servers that collect data from endpoints.

Question:
What is 'user stations'?

Answer:
'user stations' are human-machine interfaces that display data from endpoints and allow the user to issue commands.

Question:
What is 'maintenance hooks, or backdoors'?

Answer:
'maintenance hooks, or backdoors' are non-malicious methods put in by developers to gain privileged access after deployment.

Security Engineering Domain

Question:
What is a 'time-of-check/time-of-use attack, or asynchronous attack'?

Answer:
A 'time-of-check/time-of-use attack, or asynchronous attack' is an attack in-between 'can I access' and 'access'.

Question:
What is a 'race condition'?

Answer:
A 'race condition' is reversing the order of execution to gain access.

Question:
What is a 'countermeasure to TOC/TOU attacks'?

Answer:
A 'countermeasure to TOC/TOU attacks' does not split steps but makes them one, and applies software locks at the OS level on the requested resource.

Question:
What is 'cryptography'?

Answer:
'cryptography' is the act of storing or transmitting data in a form that only the intended audience can read.

Question:
What is 'atbash'?

Answer:
'atbash' is one of the first examples of cryptography.

Question:
What is a 'substitution cipher'?

Answer:
A 'substitution cipher' is used when each character is replaced by a different character.

Question:
What is a 'monoalphabetic substitution cipher'?

Answer:
A 'monoalphabetic substitution cipher' is a cipher using a single alphabet.

Question:
What is a 'polyalphabetic substitution cipher'?

Answer:
A 'polyalphabetic substitution cipher' is a cipher using more than one alphabet.

Question:
What is a 'scytale cipher'?

Answer:
A 'scytale cipher' is a message written on a sheet of papyrus wrapped around a stick of a certain thickness.

Security Engineering Domain

Question:
What is a 'rotor cipher machine'?

Answer:
A 'rotor cipher machine' is a device that substitutes letters using multiple rotors within the machine; an example is the Enigma.

Question:
What is 'Lucifer'?

Answer:
'Lucifer' is one of the earliest successful encryption projects that introduced mathematics.

Question:
What is 'cryptanalysis'?

Answer:
'cryptanalysis' is the science of studying and breaking encryption as well as reverse-engineering algorithms and keys.

Question:
What is 'cryptology'?

Answer:
'cryptology' is the study of both cryptanalysis and cryptography.

Question:
What is 'plaintext'?

Answer:
'plaintext' is human-readable data before encryption.

Question:
What is 'ciphertext'?

Answer:
'ciphertext' is plaintext that has been encrypted into a form that appears to be random and is unreadable.

Question:
What is a 'cryptosystem'?

Answer:
A 'cryptosystem' provides encryption and decryption services and contains algorithms, keys, software and protocols.

Question:
What is a 'key'?

Answer:
A 'key' is a secret value used by the algorithm to encrypt and decrypt plaintext.

Question:
What is an 'algorithm, or cipher'?

Answer:
An 'algorithm, or cipher' is a set of usually well-known rules.

Security Engineering Domain

Question:
What is a 'key space'?

Answer:
A 'keyspace' is the number of possible values a key can have.

Question:
What is 'Kerckhoff's Principle'?

Answer:
'Kerckhoff's Principle' states that the only secrecy involved with a cryptographic system should be the key, and the algorithm should be publicly known.

Question:
What is 'strength of the cryptosystem'?

Answer:
'strength of the cryptosystem' controls how hard it is to discover the secret (algorithm or key).

Question:
What is a 'brute-force method'?

Answer:
A 'brute-force method' is an attack that tries every possible key until the resulting plaintext is meaningful.

Question:
What is a 'work factor'?

Answer:
A 'work factor' is the amount of work required to break a cryptosystem.

Question:
What is 'confidentiality'?

Answer:
'confidentiality' is achieved when only authorized entities can read the data.

Question:
What is 'integrity'?

Answer:
'integrity' proves the data has not been altered.

Question:
What is 'authentication'?

Answer:
'authentication' verifies the identity of the creator of the information.

Question:
What is 'authorization'?

Answer:
'authorization' occurs after authentication.

Security Engineering Domain

Question:
What is 'nonrepudiation'?

Answer:
'nonrepudiation' occurs when the sender cannot deny sending the message.

Question:
What is a 'one-Time Pad'?

Answer:
A 'one-Time Pad' is the perfect encryption scheme and is unbreakable if properly implemented.

Question:
What is 'XOR'?

Answer:
'XOR' is a mathematical operation that returns 0 if the bits are the same and 1 if they are different.

Question:
What is 'pseudorandom numbers'?

Answer:
'pseudorandom numbers' is the term used for numbers generated by computers, given that computers cannot generate a truly random number.

Question:
What is a 'running key cipher'?

Answer:
A 'running key cipher' is a cipher that uses a key based on things in the physical world.

Question:
What is a 'concealment cipher, or null cipher'?

Answer:
A 'concealment cipher, or null cipher' is a message within a message.

Question:
What is 'steganography'?

Answer:
'steganography' is the art of hiding a message in another type of media such that it is not detected.

Question:
What is 'digital steganography'?

Answer:
'digital steganography' is attempting to hide messages within electronic files, programs or protocols.

Question:
What is a 'carrier'?

Answer:
A 'carrier' is a signal, data stream or file that contains a hidden message.

Security Engineering Domain

Question:
What is a 'stegomedium'?

Answer:
A 'stegomedium' is a medium in which a message is hidden.

Question:
What is a 'payload'?

Answer:
A 'payload' is the term for a concealed message.

Question:
What is the 'least significant bit, or LSB'?

Answer:
The 'least significant bit, or LSB' is a concealment method that modifies bits that do not impact the overall container.

Question:
What is a 'microdot'?

Answer:
A 'microdot' includes a very tiny image of the actual message in a much larger image.

Question:
What is a 'symmetric encryption algorithm'?

Answer:
A 'symmetric encryption algorithm' is an algorithm that uses a single key for both encryption and decryption when both the sender and the receiver must have that key.

Question:
What is 'substitution ciphers'?

Answer:
'substitution ciphers' is a cipher that replaces bits, blocks or characters with different values of equal length.

Question:
What is 'transposition ciphers'?

Answer:
'transposition ciphers' is a cipher that puts the bits, blocks or characters in a different order.

Question:
What is 'frequency analysis'?

Answer:
'frequency analysis' looks for common occurrences of the same value.

Security Engineering Domain

Question:
What is a 'subkey'?

Answer:
A 'subkey' is a key derived from a master key.

Question:
What is the 'Key Derivation Function, or KDF'?

Answer:
The 'Key Derivation Function, or KDF' is used to generate keys made from random values.

Question:
What is an 'asymmetric encryption algorithm'?

Answer:
An 'asymmetric encryption algorithm' uses a private and public key for encryption, where only the owner has the private key.

Question:
What is the 'number of keys formula'?

Answer:
The 'number of keys formula' is a formula of $n(n-1)/2$ where n is the number of individuals involved.

Question:
What is 'examples of symmetric algorithms'?

Answer:
'examples of symmetric algorithms' are Data encryption standard (DES), Triple-DES (3DES), Blowfish, International data encryption algorithm (IDEA), RC4, RC5, and RC6 and the Advanced Encryption Standard (AES).

Question:
What is a 'public key pair'?

Answer:
A 'public key pair' is a set of keys consisting of both a private and public key.

Question:
What is a 'public key system'?

Answer:
A 'public key system' is an asymmetric cryptosystem using a public key pair.

Question:
What is an 'open message format'?

Answer:
An 'open message format' is the term for encrypting a message with a private key.

Question:
What is a 'digital envelope'?

Answer:
A 'digital envelope' is the act of encrypting and decrypting a message with a public key pair.

Security Engineering Domain

Question:
What is a 'block cipher'?

Answer:
A 'block cipher' is a type of cipher that divides data into blocks of bits.

Question:
What is the 'Electronic Code Book mode, or ECB'?

Answer:
The 'Electronic Code Book mode, or ECB' is a block cipher mode in which a 64-bit block of plaintext is encrypted with a key, producing a 64-bit block of ciphertext, and uses padding.

Question:
What is the 'Cipher Block Chaining mode, or CBC'?

Answer:
The 'Cipher Block Chaining mode, or CBC' is a block cipher mode that is the same as ECB but uses chaining.

Question:
What is the 'Cipher Feedback mode, or CFB'?

Answer:
The 'Cipher Feedback mode, or CFB' is a block cipher mode which uses a keystream to encrypt blocks.

Question:
What is the 'Output Feedback mode, or OFB'?

Answer:
The 'Output Feedback mode, or OFB' is a block cipher mode just like CFB but does not use chaining.

Question:
What is the 'Counter mode, or CTR'?

Answer:
The 'Counter mode, or CTR' is a block cipher mode just like OFB but increments the IV for each block.

Question:
What is 'confusion'?

Answer:
'confusion' is another term for substitution.

Question:
What is 'diffusion'?

Answer:
'diffusion' is another term for transposition.

Question:
What is the 'avalanche effect'?

Answer:
The 'avalanche effect' occurs when a slight change to the input of an encryption algorithm causes significant change in the output.

Security Engineering Domain

Question:
What is a 'stream cipher'?

Answer:
A 'stream cipher' is a cipher that views the data as a single stream of bits.

Question:
What is a 'keystream generator'?

Answer:
A 'keystream generator' generates a keystream to be XOR'd with plaintext.

Question:
What is a 'synchronous algorithm'?

Answer:
A 'synchronous algorithm' uses keystreams to encrypt each bit, one at a time.

Question:
What is an 'asynchronous algorithm'?

Answer:
An 'asynchronous algorithm' uses previously generated ciphertext to encrypt the next plaintext value, called chaining.

Question:
What is an 'initialization vector, or IV'?

Answer:
An 'initialization vector, or IV' is used with the key to reduce the chance of a repeating pattern.

Question:
What is 'compression'?

Answer:
'compression' is a technique that reduces the size of the data before encryption.

Question:
What is 'expansion'?

Answer:
'expansion' is a technique that expands the plaintext to correspond to key sizes.

Question:
What is 'padding'?

Answer:
'padding' is a technique that adds data to the plaintext before encryption.

Question:
What is 'key mixing'?

Answer:
'key mixing' is a technique that uses a subkey instead of the entire key, thereby reducing exposure of the key.

Security Engineering Domain

Question:
What is ''w' when using shorthand notation'?

Answer:
''w' when using shorthand notation' is a single letter abbreviation representing the word size in bits of 16, 32 or 64 bits.

Question:
What is ''r' when using shorthand notation'?

Answer:
''r' when using shorthand notation' is a single letter abbreviation representing the number of rounds of computation of 0 to 255.

Question:
What is ''b' when using shorthand notation'?

Answer:
''b' when using shorthand notation' is a single letter abbreviation representing the key size, in bytes.

Question:
What is the 'Data Encryption Algorithm, or DEA'?

Answer:
The 'Data Encryption Algorithm, or DEA' is a symmetric block cipher using 64-bits blocks with 8-bits of parity, and uses 16 rounds of transposition and substitution.

Question:
What is 'Triple-DES, or 3DES'?

Answer:
'Triple-DES, or 3DES' is a symmetric block cipher using 48 rounds of computation with each pass using a different key.

Question:
What is the 'International Data Encryption Algorithm, or IDEA'?

Answer:
The 'International Data Encryption Algorithm, or IDEA' is a symmetric block cipher using 64-bit blocks, uses 8 rounds of computation with a 128-bit key size and is faster than DES.

Question:
What is 'Blowfish'?

Answer:
'Blowfish' is a symmetric block cipher using 64-bit blocks, uses 16 rounds of computation with a 32 to 448 bit key size.

Question:
What is 'RC4'?

Answer:
'RC4' is a symmetric stream cipher, is used for SSL and was poorly implemented in 802.11 WEP.

Question:
What is 'RC5'?

Answer:
'RC5' is a symmetric block cipher using 32, 64 or 128 bit blocks, with keys up to 2,048 bits, and 255 rounds of computation.

Security Engineering Domain

Question:
What is a 'one-way function'?

Answer:
A 'one-way function' is a type of function that is easy to create, but almost impossible to reverse.

Question:
What is a 'trapdoor'?

Answer:
A 'trapdoor' is a way to reverse a one-way function if you possess the secret key.

Question:
What is a 'key agreement'?

Answer:
A 'key agreement' occurs when two parties independently calculate the secret key.

Question:
What is a 'key exchange'?

Answer:
A 'key exchange' occurs when two parties exchange the secret key.

Question:
What is the 'Zero Knowledge Proof'?

Answer:
The 'Zero Knowledge Proof' is a statement that we should only reveal the minimum of a security exchange and no more, and in practice means that the owner of a private key does not reveal how he got it or where it is stored.

Question:
What is a 'digital signature'?

Answer:
A 'digital signature' is represented by an encryption algorithm using a private key that offers nonrepudiation.

Question:
What is the 'Diffie-Hellman Algorithm'?

Answer:
The 'Diffie-Hellman Algorithm' was the first asymmetric algorithm focused on distributing symmetric keys only, using discrete logarithms on a finite field.

Question:
What is 'MQV'?

Answer:
'MQV' was an attempt at improving the Diffie-Hellman algorithm but wasn't much of a success.

Security Engineering Domain

170

Question:
What is 'RAS'?

Answer:
'RAS' was the algorithm that successfully solved the problems with Diffie-Hellman, and provides authentication and confidentiality based on large prime numbers.

Question:
What is 'El Gamal'?

Answer:
'El Gamal' is an algorithm very similar to Diffie-Hellman but slower.

Question:
What is the 'Elliptic Curve Cryptosystems, or ECC'?

Answer:
The 'Elliptic Curve Cryptosystems, or ECC' is an algorithm using discrete logarithms on an elliptic curve, which is most efficient because it uses shorter keys and is often found on mobile devices.

Question:
What is 'Knapsack'?

Answer:
'Knapsack' is an algorithm based the knapsack problem, which were found to be insecure.

Question:
What is a 'data origin authentication, or system authentication'?

Answer:
A 'data origin authentication, or system authentication' occurs when a system secret key is used, so we only know what system sent the message, not what user.

Question:
What is a 'one-way hash'?

Answer:
A 'one-way hash' is a publicly known algorithm that accepts a string of any length and produces a string of a fixed length without the use of a key.

Question:
What is a 'collision'?

Answer:
A 'collision' happens when the same hash result is calculated from different plaintext values.

Question:
What is a 'Message Authentication Code, or MAC'?

Answer:
A 'Message Authentication Code, or MAC' is used in an algorithm to apply a secret key to a hash, resulting in integrity.

Security Engineering Domain

171

Question:
What is an 'HMAC'?

Answer:
An 'HMAC' is used to concatenate a message with a secret key, which is then hashed and sent with the message.

Question:
What is a 'Cipher Block Chaining Message Authentication Code, or CBC-MAC'?

Answer:
A 'Cipher Block Chaining Message Authentication Code, or CBC-MAC' uses CBC to encrypt a message, with the final block being used as the MAC.

Question:
What is a 'Cipher-Based Message Authentication Code, or CMAC'?

Answer:
A 'Cipher-Based Message Authentication Code, or CMAC' is the same as CBC-MAC but uses AES or 3DES to create the symmetric key with subkeys.

Question:
What is a 'digest value, message digest or hash'?

Answer:
A 'digest value, message digest or hash' is the output of a hashing function.

Question:
What is 'MD4'?

Answer:
'MD4' is a hashing algorithm that produces a 128-bit hash and is considered to be insecure.

Question:
What is 'MD5'?

Answer:
'MD5' is a hashing algorithm that produces a 128-bit hash, is considered to be secure but is susceptible to collisions.

Question:
What is 'SHA'?

Answer:
'SHA' is a hashing algorithm that is used for DSS, creates a 160-bit hash and then runs that through an asymmetric algorithm.

Question:
What is 'SHA-1'?

Answer:
'SHA-1' is a hashing algorithm based on SHA but is vulnerable to collisions.

Security Engineering Domain

Question:
What is 'SHA-2, examples being SHA-224, SHA-256, SHA-384, SHA-512'?

Answer:
'SHA-2, examples being SHA-224, SHA-256, SHA-384, SHA-512' is a hashing algorithm based on SHA and is considered to be secure for any use.

Question:
What is 'SHA-3'?

Answer:
'SHA-3' is a hashing algorithm that is an alternative to SHA-2, but is not derived from SHA-2.

Question:
What is a 'birthday attack'?

Answer:
A 'birthday attack' is a hash attack that creates a message which collides with an existing hash using brute force.

Question:
What is a 'digital signature'?

Answer:
A 'digital signature' is a hash value that has been encrypted with a private key, resulting in integrity, authenticity and nonrepudiation.

Question:
What is the 'Digital Signature Standard, or DSS'?

Answer:
The 'Digital Signature Standard, or DSS' is a standard that implements digital signatures using SHA and one of DSA, RSA or ECC algorithms.

Question:
What is 'Public Key Infrastructure, or PKI'?

Answer:
'Public Key Infrastructure, or PKI' is an ISO framework using public key cryptography and X.509.

Question:
What is a 'Certificate Authority, or CA'?

Answer:
A 'Certificate Authority, or CA' is an organization who creates a digital certificate on behalf of an individual and digitally signs it.

Question:
What is a 'Registration Authority, or RA'?

Answer:
A 'Registration Authority, or RA' is an organization who verifies digital certificates.

Security Engineering Domain

Question:
What is a 'cross certification'?

Answer:
A 'cross certification' occurs when one CA agrees to trust all certificates issues by another CA.

Question:
What is a 'Certificate Revocation List, or CRL'?

Answer:
A 'Certificate Revocation List, or CRL' is a list of revoked certificates that a CA maintains.

Question:
What is the 'Online Certificate Status Protocol, or OCSP'?

Answer:
The 'Online Certificate Status Protocol, or OCSP' is used when a provider proactively notifies the browser that a certificate is no longer valid.

Question:
What is a 'certificate'?

Answer:
A 'certificate' is used to associate a public key with data sufficient to verify an owner's identity via X509.

Question:
What is 'x.509'?

Answer:
'x.509' is a standard that dictates the various fields contained within a digital certificate, and is used by both SSL and TLS.

Question:
What is the 'Trusted Platform Module, or TPM'?

Answer:
The 'Trusted Platform Module, or TPM' is a microchip that may be installed on motherboards to execute dedicated security functions using RSA and SHA-1.

Question:
What is the 'Trusted Computer Group, or TCG'?

Answer:
The 'Trusted Computer Group, or TCG' is the organization that created TPM.

Question:
What is 'binding'?

Answer:
'binding' occurs when TPM encrypts the contents of a hard drive.

Question:
What is the 'Endorsement Key, or EK'?

Answer:
The 'Endorsement Key, or EK' is a public/private key that is installed by the manufacturer in TPM and cannot be modified.

Security Engineering Domain

Question:
What is the 'Storage Root Key, or SRK'?

Answer:
The 'Storage Root Key, or SRK' is the master key used to secure the TMP keys stored in versatile memory.

Question:
What is the 'Attestation Identity Key, or AIK'?

Answer:
The 'Attestation Identity Key, or AIK' is a key linked to the TPM's identity by the manufacturer, and ensures the integrity of the EK.

Question:
What is 'Platform Configuration Registers, or PCR'?

Answer:
'Platform Configuration Registers, or PCR' stores hashes when sealing a TPM system.

Question:
What is 'storage keys'?

Answer:
'storage keys' is the term for keys used to encrypt a TPM system's storage media.

Question:
What is a 'passive attack'?

Answer:
A 'passive attack' is a cryptography attack that focuses on gathering information.

Question:
What is an 'active attack'?

Answer:
An 'active attack' is a cryptography attack in which the attacker is actively engaged instead of simply gathering data.

Question:
What is an 'adaptive attack'?

Answer:
An 'adaptive attack' is a cryptography attack in which the result of one attack may result in the use a different attack next.

Question:
What is a 'Ciphertext-Only Attack'?

Answer:
A 'Ciphertext-Only Attack' is a cryptography attack in which the attacker figures out the encryption key using brute force against the cipher text.

Security Engineering Domain

Question:
What is a 'Known-Plaintext Attack'?

Answer:
A 'Known-Plaintext Attack' is a cryptography attack in which the attacker compares portions of known plaintext to the resulting ciphertext.

Question:
What is a 'Chosen-Plaintext Attack'?

Answer:
A 'Chosen-Plaintext Attack' is a cryptography attack in which the attacker chooses the plaintext to encrypt and receives the resulting ciphertext.

Question:
What is a 'Chosen-Ciphertext Attack'?

Answer:
A 'Chosen-Ciphertext Attack' is a cryptography attack in which the attacker chooses the ciphertext to decrypt and receives the results.

Question:
What is 'Differential Cryptanalysis'?

Answer:
'Differential Cryptanalysis' is a type of chosen-plaintext attack, with the attacker analyzing the differences in the resulting ciphertext.

Question:
What is 'Linear Cryptanalysis'?

Answer:
'Linear Cryptanalysis' is similar to differential cryptanalysis, but the plaintext blocks do not need to be chosen, just known.

Question:
What is a 'Side-Channel Attack'?

Answer:
A 'Side-Channel Attack' is a cryptography attack in which the attacker figures out something about the key based on changes in the environment during encryption and/or decryption.

Question:
What is a 'Replay Attack'?

Answer:
A 'Replay Attack' is a cryptography attack in which the attacker captures some data and sends it back to the same system.

Question:
What is an 'algebraic attack'?

Answer:
An 'algebraic attack' is an analytical cryptography attack which exploits any mathematical weakness found.

Security Engineering Domain

Question:
What is an 'analytic attack'?

Answer:
An 'analytic attack' is an analytical cryptography attack that looks for structural weaknesses in the algorithm.

Question:
What is a 'statistical attack'?

Answer:
A 'statistical attack' is an analytical cryptography attack that looks for values that will be statistically used more than others.

Question:
What is a 'Social Engineering Attack'?

Answer:
A 'Social Engineering Attack' is a cryptographic attack which tricks people into revealing the key.

Question:
What is a 'Meet-in-the-Middle Attack'?

Answer:
A 'Meet-in-the-Middle Attack' is cryptographic attack which works both the encryption and decryption ends of a cryptographic system simultaneously.

Question:
What is 'natural environment'?

Answer:
'natural environment' are physical threats such as floods, storms, earthquakes, fires and other acts of God.

Question:
What is a 'supply system'?

Answer:
A 'supply system' are physical threats such as interruption of power, communication, water, gas and cooling.

Question:
What is 'manmade'?

Answer:
'manmade' are physical threats such as unauthorized access, disgruntled employees, theft or vandalism.

Question:
What is 'politically motivated'?

Answer:
'politically motivated' are physical threats such as riots, strikes, terrorist attacks and civil disobedience.

Question:
What is a 'layered defense strategy'?

Answer:
A 'layered defense strategy' occurs when physical controls work together in layers.

Security Engineering Domain

Question:
What is 'confidentiality, as applied to physical security'?

Answer:
'confidentiality, as applied to physical security' is a CIA attribute that occurs when physical security is applied to the data and business processes.

Question:
What is 'availability, as applied to physical security'?

Answer:
'availability, as applied to physical security' is a CIA attribute that occurs when physical security is applied to the company resources.

Question:
What is 'integrity, as applied to physical security'?

Answer:
'integrity, as applied to physical security' is a CIA attribute that occurs when physical security is applied to the assets and the environment.

Question:
What is a 'deterrence, as applied to site planning'?

Answer:
A 'deterrence, as applied to site planning' is addressed by fences, warning signs and security guards.

Question:
What is 'delaying mechanisms, as applied to site planning'?

Answer:
'delaying mechanisms, as applied to site planning' is addressed by locks, security guards and barriers.

Question:
What is 'detection, as applied to site planning'?

Answer:
'detection, as applied to site planning' is addressed by smoke or motion detectors and closed-circuit TV.

Question:
What is an 'incident assessment, as applied to site planning'?

Answer:
An 'incident assessment, as applied to site planning' is addressed by security guards who must respond to incidents and assess damage.

Question:
What is 'response procedures, as applied to site planning'?

Answer:
'response procedures, as applied to site planning' is addressed by fire suppression and notification of law enforcement.

Security Engineering Domain

Question:
What is 'internal threats'?

Answer:
'internal threats' are mitigated by using pre-employment background checks, separation of duties, and rotation of duties.

Question:
What is 'external threats'?

Answer:
'external threats' are mitigated by using security officers.

Question:
What is a 'performance-based approach'?

Answer:
A 'performance-based approach' is an approach to monitoring the effectiveness of a security program based on metrics.

Question:
What is 'target hardening'?

Answer:
'target hardening' is the term for preventing access using physical barriers such as locks and fences.

Question:
What is the 'Crime Prevention Through Environmental Design, or CPTED'?

Answer:
The 'Crime Prevention Through Environmental Design, or CPTED' is the belief that a physical environment can reduce both crime and the fear of crime.

Question:
What is 'Natural Access Control'?

Answer:
'Natural Access Control' is the process of guiding people entering or exiting a location by the muted placement of doors, fences, lighting or landscaping.

Question:
What is a 'bollard'?

Answer:
A 'bollard' are posts outside of entryways that prevent vehicles from driving into a building.

Question:
What is 'security zones'?

Answer:
'security zones' are areas that can be labelled public, controlled, restricted or sensitive.

Security Engineering Domain

Question:
What is 'natural surveillance'?

Answer:
'natural surveillance' is a method for making criminals feel uncomfortable and guests to feel safe by ensuring that all actions will be observed by people in the area.

Question:
What is 'natural territory reinforcement'?

Answer:
'natural territory reinforcement' creates physical designs that extend the area of a building's area of influence, and enhances the feeling of ownership by legitimate occupants.

Question:
What is a 'facility safety officer'?

Answer:
A 'facility safety officer' is a role that understands physical security constraints and understands how to stay in compliance.

Question:
What is 'light-frame construction'?

Answer:
'light-frame construction' is a construction material consisting of untreated lumber that is susceptible to fire.

Question:
What is 'heavy-timber construction'?

Answer:
'heavy-timber construction' is a construction material consisting of heavy untreated lumber that is 50% less susceptible to fire as light-frame lumber.

Question:
What is 'incombustible material'?

Answer:
'incombustible material' is a construction material consisting of metal that will not burn but can collapse under high temperature.

Question:
What is 'fire-resistant material'?

Answer:
'fire-resistant material' is a construction material usually consisting of steel rods encased in concrete.

Question:
What is 'personnel doors'?

Answer:
'personnel doors' are large doors designed for heavy traffic.

Security Engineering Domain

180

Question:
What is 'industrial doors'?

Answer:
'industrial doors' are heavy steel doors designed for security and not aesthetics.

Question:
What is 'vehicle access doors'?

Answer:
'vehicle access doors' are large doors that normally roll up into the ceiling.

Question:
What is 'bullet-resistant doors'?

Answer:
'bullet-resistant doors' are made by sandwiching wood and steel veneers.

Question:
What is 'vault doors'?

Answer:
'vault doors' are extremely dense doors designed to withstand explosive force and lock securely.

Question:
What is 'hollow or solid core doors'?

Answer:
'hollow or solid core doors' are hollow and should only be used internally - not used to separate security zones.

Question:
What is 'fail-secure'?

Answer:
'fail-secure' is a safety feature that on power interruption defaults to being locked.

Question:
What is 'standard windows'?

Answer:
'standard windows' are windows that provide no extra protection.

Question:
What is 'tempered windows'?

Answer:
'tempered windows' are windows made using glass that is heated and suddenly cooled, resulting in a stronger build.

Question:
What is 'acrylic windows'?

Answer:
'acrylic windows' are windows that are constructed of plastic instead of glass, making them even stronger.

Security Engineering Domain

Question:
What is 'wired windows'?

Answer:
'wired windows' are windows that contain a mesh of wires embedded between two sheets of glass, making them more shatter-resistant.

Question:
What is 'laminated windows'?

Answer:
'laminated windows' are windows in which a plastic layer is inserted between two glass panels, making them more shatter-resistant.

Question:
What is 'solar window film windows'?

Answer:
'solar window film windows' are windows that provide extra security by tinting and slightly increases the strength of glass.

Question:
What is 'security film windows'?

Answer:
'security film windows' are windows that have a transparent film applied to the glass to specifically increase strength.

Question:
What is 'internal compartments'?

Answer:
'internal compartments' are thin walls that do not reach all the way into the structural ceiling.

Question:
What is a 'hygrometer'?

Answer:
A 'hygrometer' is a device that monitors humidity.

Question:
What is 'tracing software'?

Answer:
'tracing software' is installed software that periodically 'phones home' and allows the tracking and possible recovery of a device.

Question:
What is 'voltage instability'?

Answer:
'voltage instability' occurs when the voltage in a power source fluctuates to a level where equipment starts to malfunction.

Question:
What is an 'outage'?

Answer:
An 'outage' occurs when all power is no longer accessible.

Security Engineering Domain

Question:
What is an 'uninterruptible power supply, or UPS'?

Answer:
An 'uninterruptible power supply, or UPS' is a device that provides a short term power supply.

Question:
What is an 'inverter'?

Answer:
An 'inverter' is a device that converts electrical output from DC to AC.

Question:
What is an 'online UPS'?

Answer:
An 'online UPS' is a UPS device that delivers power with no detectable drop in voltage if an outage occurs.

Question:
What is a 'standby UPS'?

Answer:
A 'standby UPS' is a UPS device that delivers power with a momentary delay while power is switched over from source to the batteries.

Question:
What is a 'redundant line feed'?

Answer:
A 'redundant line feed' is a method of protecting power supply by drawing the power from a secondary power substation.

Question:
What is an 'onsite generator'?

Answer:
An 'onsite generator' is a method of protecting power supply by drawing the power from a gas-powered electrical generator.

Question:
What is 'electromagnetic interference, or EMI'?

Answer:
'electromagnetic interference, or EMI' is a type of power interference resulting from electrical motors.

Question:
What is 'radio interference, or RFI'?

Answer:
'radio interference, or RFI' is a type of power interference resulting from fluorescent lighting.

Question:
What is 'clean power'?

Answer:
'clean power' is power free from voltage fluctuation.

Security Engineering Domain

Question:
What is 'line noise'?

Answer:
'line noise' is power line interference resulting from EMI or RFI.

Question:
What is an 'in-rush current'?

Answer:
An 'in-rush current' is the initial surge of current required to start a load.

Question:
What is a 'spike'?

Answer:
A 'spike' is a momentary disruption of clean power due to a high voltage.

Question:
What is a 'sag/dip'?

Answer:
A 'sag/dip' is a momentary disruption of clean power due to a low voltage.

Question:
What is a 'fault'?

Answer:
A 'fault' is a momentary disruption of clean power due to a power outage.

Question:
What is a 'surge'?

Answer:
A 'surge' is a prolonged disruption of clean power due to a high voltage.

Question:
What is a 'brownout'?

Answer:
A 'brownout' is a prolonged disruption of clean power due to a low voltage.

Question:
What is a 'blackout'?

Answer:
A 'blackout' is a prolonged disruption of clean power due to a power outage.

Question:
What is a 'voltage regulator or line conditioner'?

Answer:
A 'voltage regulator or line conditioner' is a device that ensures clean power.

Security Engineering Domain

184

Question:
What is 'fire prevention'?

Answer:
'fire prevention' occurs through both proper construction and employee training.

Question:
What is 'fire detection'?

Answer:
'fire detection' occurs by detecting the environmental changes due to fires.

Question:
What is a 'photoelectric device'?

Answer:
A 'photoelectric device' is a device that detects a change in light intensity.

Question:
What is a 'smoke-activated detector'?

Answer:
A 'smoke-activated detector' is a photoelectric device that detects when smoke obstructs the light source.

Question:
What is a 'heat activated detector'?

Answer:
A 'heat activated detector' is a device that detects when there is a rise in temperature.

Question:
What is a 'fixed temperature detector'?

Answer:
A 'fixed temperature detector' is a device that detects when the temperature reaches a specific value.

Question:
What is a 'rate-of-rise detector'?

Answer:
A 'rate-of-rise detector' is a device that detects a change in temperature over time.

Question:
What is a 'fire suppression agent'?

Answer:
A 'fire suppression agent' is an automated system that engages when a fire is detected and acts to extinguish the fire.

Question:
What is 'water'?

Answer:
'water' is a chemical suppression agent that acts by robbing the fire of heat.

Security Engineering Domain

Question:
What is 'foam'?

Answer:
'foam' is a chemical suppression agent that is mixed with water and robs the fire of both heat and oxygen.

Question:
What is 'carbon dioxide'?

Answer:
'carbon dioxide' is a gas chemical suppression agent that robs the fire of oxygen.

Question:
What is 'gases'?

Answer:
'gases' is a chemical suppression agent that acts by suppressing the chemical reaction.

Question:
What is 'halon'?

Answer:
'halon' is a gas suppression agent that is no longer used as it affected the ozone layer.

Question:
What is 'FM-200'?

Answer:
'FM-200' is a gas suppression agent that replaced halon.

Question:
What is 'dry powder'?

Answer:
'dry powder' is a gas suppression agent that acts in different ways according to the chemical.

Question:
What is 'sodium bicarbonate, potassium bicarbonate and calcium bicarbonate'?

Answer:
'sodium bicarbonate, potassium bicarbonate and calcium bicarbonate' are dry powder suppression agents that prevent chemical reactions.

Question:
What is 'monoammonium phosphate'?

Answer:
'monoammonium phosphate' is a dry powder suppression agent that robs the fire of oxygen.

Question:
What is a 'wet chemical'?

Answer:
A 'wet chemical' is a suppression agent, normally containing potassium acetate, that robs the fire of heat and oxygen.

Security Engineering Domain

Question:
What is 'Class A'?

Answer:
'Class A' is a class of fire that is the most common and results from the ignition of wood, paper or laminates.

Question:
What is 'Class B'?

Answer:
'Class B' is a class of fire in which some type of liquid ignites.

Question:
What is 'Class C'?

Answer:
'Class C' is a class of fire found in electrical equipment or wires.

Question:
What is 'Class D'?

Answer:
'Class D' is a class of fire occurring by the ignition of combustible metals such as magnesium, sodium or potassium.

Question:
What is 'Class K'?

Answer:
'Class K' is a class of fire most commonly found in commercial kitchens.

Question:
What is a 'wet pipe sprinkler'?

Answer:
A 'wet pipe sprinkler' is a type of water sprinkler in which pressurized water is always in the pipe leading to the sprinkler head, and is activated when elevated temperatures are detected.

Question:
What is a 'dry pipe sprinkler'?

Answer:
A 'dry pipe sprinkler' is a type of water sprinkler the same as a wet pipe, but the pipe leading to the sprinkler head contains air pressure, keeping the water in a central storage tank until elevated temperatures are detected.

Question:
What is a 'precaution sprinkler'?

Answer:
A 'precaution sprinkler' is a type of water sprinkler which is the same as a dry pipe, but before the sprinkler head can be activated, a thermal-fusible link on the sprinkler head must melt.

Security Engineering Domain

Question:
What is a 'deluge sprinkler'?

Answer:
A 'deluge sprinkler' is a type of water sprinkler that allows a massive amount of water to be released instead of 'sprinkled'.

Question:
What is 'plenum-rated cabling'?

Answer:
'plenum-rated cabling' is cabling that should be used in overhead and under-floor spaces due to non-toxic fumes produced when burning.

Security Engineering Domain

Quiz

Question:
What are the 5 factors affecting the strength of a cryptosystem?

Answer:
'algorithm, secrecy of the key, length of the key, Initialization vectors and how well the first four work together'.

Question:
What are the 2 language generations susceptible to buffer overflows?

Answer:
'2nd generation languages such as assembly, and 3rd generation languages such as C or C++'.

Question:
What are the 3 process states?

Answer:
'ready, running, and blocked'.

Question:
What are the 12 advantages of using virtualization?

Answer:
'optimized resources, legacy apps, sandboxes, limited systems, illusion, hot standbys, debugging, inject faults, migrations, packages, restore state and testing'.

Question:
What are the 3 requirements for a secure kernel?

Answer:
'tamperproof reference monitor, invoked for every access and small enough to be tested'.

Question:
What are the 8 guidelines for secure web sites?

Answer:
'KISS, sanitize input, sanitize output, encrypt, fail secure, simple user-facing security, no security through obscurity and firewall'.

Question:
What are the 3 countermeasures to backdoors?

Answer:
'using IDS, encrypting files and monitoring audit logs'.

Question:
What are the 4 ways to increase work factor?

Answer:
'use an algorithm without flaws, use a large key size or large keyspace, use the entire keyspace as randomly as possible and protect the key'.

Security Engineering Domain

Question:
What are the 5 requirements for an unbreakable message?

Answer:
'used one time only, as long as the message, securely delivered to the recipient, protected at both ends, and made up of truly random values'.

Question:
What are the 2 types of ciphers?

Answer:
'block and stream'.

Question:
What are the top 5 examples of asymmetric algorithms?

Answer:
'RSA, Elliptic Curve cryptosystem or ECC, Diffie-Hellman, El Gamal and the Digital Signature Algorithm or DSA'.

Question:
What type of encryption algorithm is fastest - symmetric or asymmetric?

Answer:
'Symmetric'.

Question:
What type of encryption algorithm can handle large amounts of data - symmetric or asymmetric?

Answer:
'Symmetric'.

Question:
What type of encryption algorithm scales the best - symmetric or asymmetric?

Answer:
'Asymmetric'.

Question:
What type of encryption algorithm has the best key management - symmetric or asymmetric?

Answer:
'Asymmetric'.

Question:
What type of encryption algorithm provides authentication - symmetric or asymmetric?

Answer:
'Asymmetric'.

Question:
What type of encryption algorithm provides integrity - symmetric or asymmetric?

Answer:
'Asymmetric'.

Security Engineering Domain

Question:
What type of encryption algorithm provides confidentiality - symmetric or asymmetric?

Answer:
'Symmetric'.

Question:
What type of encryption algorithm provides non-repudiation - symmetric or asymmetric?

Answer:
'Asymmetric'.

Question:
What block cipher modes use initialization vectors?

Answer:
'All but ECB'.

Question:
What block cipher mode is the fastest?

Answer:
'ECB'.

Question:
What block cipher mode is the slowest?

Answer:
'OFB'.

Question:
What block cipher modes provide the most random values?

Answer:
'CBC, CFB, and OFB'.

Question:
What block cipher modes provide parallel processing?

Answer:
'ECB and CTR'.

Question:
What block cipher modes use chaining?

Answer:
'CBC and CFB'.

Question:
What block cipher modes are the most susceptible to error propagation?

Answer:
'CBC and CFB'.

Security Engineering Domain

Question:
What block cipher modes support the longest data length?

Answer:
'CBC, OFB and CTR'.

Question:
What block cipher mode does not support pre-processing?

Answer:
'ECB'.

Question:
What type of cipher is the fastest - block or stream?

Answer:
'Stream'.

Question:
What type of cipher provides the most random values - block or stream?

Answer:
'Block'.

Question:
What type of cipher is best for files - block or stream?

Answer:
'Block'.

Question:
What type of cipher is the most susceptible to error propagation - block or stream?

Answer:
'Stream'.

Question:
What type of cipher uses the most memory - block or stream?

Answer:
'Block'.

Question:
What type of cipher is the most complex - block or stream?

Answer:
'Block'.

Question:
What type of cipher is the most secure - block or stream?

Answer:
'Block'.

Security Engineering Domain

Question:
What type of cipher supports symmetric algorithms - block or stream?

Answer:
'Both'.

Question:
What type of cipher only supports asymmetric algorithms - block or stream?

Answer:
'Stream'.

Question:
What is so much better about symmetric encryption than asymmetric encryption?

Answer:
'Symmetric is so blazingly fast'.

Question:
If symmetric algorithms are so much faster, then why do we even have asymmetric algorithms?

Answer:
'Because managing keys with symmetric is such a pain.'.

Question:
If you encrypt a message with your own private key, what security services are being provided to the recipient?

Answer:
'Authenticity and Nonrepudiation – only you could have sent the message if it can be decrypted with your public key.'.

Question:
If you encrypt a message with the recipient's public key, what security services are being provided?

Answer:
'Confidentiality – only the recipient can decrypt the message with their private key.'.

Question:
Why don't we just encrypt the symmetric key with another symmetric key?

Answer:
'How would you get the second symmetric key to the recipient? We only compounded the problem.'.

Question:
If a sender encrypts data with your private key, what security services are being provided?

Answer:
'None, and by the way you need to generate a new pair of keys because someone has stolen it!'.

Question:
If you encrypt a message with your own public key, what security services are being provided?

Answer:
'None – who can read it but you (only you have your own private key)?'.

Security Engineering Domain

Question:
What is a session key?

Answer:
'The session key is a symmetric key that is generated for one conversation and then tossed. How long is a conversation? That is up to you, but anywhere from seconds to days – and conceivably decades.'.

Question:
How many different names can you think of for a symmetric key?

Answer:
'Secret key, private key, shared key and session key.'.

Question:
What are the 4 Strong cipher attributes?

Answer:
'hardware, non-repeating, keystream/key relationship and unbiased'.

Question:
What are 4 strong encryption algorithm techniques?

Answer:
'compression, expansion, padding and key mixing'.

Question:
What encryption algorithm was originally called Lucifer?

Answer:
'The Data Encryption Standard, or DES'.

Question:
What is the only symmetric algorithm to use a stream cipher?

Answer:
'RC4'.

Question:
What is the symmetric algorithm that uses only a 128-bit block?

Answer:
'AES'.

Question:
What symmetric algorithms use 64-bit blocks?

Answer:
'All but AES'.

Question:
What is the symmetric algorithm that was a stop-gap until a better one came along?

Answer:
'3DES'.

Security Engineering Domain

Question:
What symmetric algorithm was broken in 1998 by a brute-force attack?

Answer:
'DES'.

Question:
What are the 4 modes of 3DES?

Answer:
'EEE3, EDE3, EE2 and EDE2'.

Question:
What symmetric algorithm is based on the Rijndael algorithm?

Answer:
'AES'.

Question:
What symmetric algorithm is GPG based on?

Answer:
'IDEA'.

Question:
What symmetric algorithm uses a block cipher with key sizes from 32 to 448 bits, and is in the public domain?

Answer:
'Blowfish'.

Question:
What symmetric stream algorithm was very poorly implemented in 802.11 WEP?

Answer:
'RC4'.

Question:
What is the primary difference between RC4 and RC5?

Answer:
'RC4 is a stream cipher while RC5 is a block cipher'.

Question:
What is the primary difference between RC5 and RC6?

Answer:
'RC6 is faster'.

Question:
What was the greatest weakness of the Diffie-Hellman algorithm?

Answer:
'It was susceptible to a man-in-the-middle-attack'.

Security Engineering Domain

Question:
What security attributes did Diffie-Hellman provide?

Answer:
'Confidentiality only'.

Question:
What are the 4 attributes of strong hashing?

Answer:
'the entire message is used, non-reversible, no collisions and birthday attack-resistant'.

Question:
What are the 10 minimal fields an X.509 certificate contains?

Answer:
'version, serial #, signature, issuer, issuer ID, subject, subject ID, validity, public key and extensions'.

Question:
What are the 11 best practices for key management?

Answer:
'encrypt, automated distribution, backup, multiparty key recovery, long keys, store securely, random keys, full keyspace, sensitivity drives lifetime, use drives lifetime and destroy'.

Question:
What are the two types of TMP memory?

Answer:
'persistent and versatile memory'.

Question:
What are the two types of TMP persistent memory?

Answer:
'Endorsement Key and Storage Root Key'.

Question:
What are the three types of TMP versatile memory?

Answer:
'Attestation Identity Key, Platform Configuration Registers and Storage Keys'.

Question:
What are the 3 types of attacks that can take place against cryptography systems?

Answer:
'Passive, active and adaptive'.

Question:
What are 4 types of physical threats?

Answer:
'natural environment, supply system, manmade and politically motivated'.

Security Engineering Domain

Question:
What are the 5 things the site planning process should address?

Answer:
'deterrence, delaying mechanisms, detection, incident assessment and response procedures'.

Question:
What are the two types of threats?

Answer:
'internal and external'.

Question:
What are the 3 strategies of CPTED?

Answer:
'natural access control, natural surveillance and natural territory reinforcement'.

Question:
What are 6 security zone guidelines?

Answer:
'limit entry points, sign in, reduce entry after hours, sidewalks and landscaping, back entrance, front parking'.

Question:
What are the 6 primary building entry points that must be secured?

Answer:
'Doors, windows, roof access, delivery access points, fire escapes and chimneys'.

Question:
What are the 7 types of doors?

Answer:
'personnel, industrial, vehicle access, bullet-resistant, Vault, hollow or solid core'.

Question:
What are the 7 types of windows?

Answer:
'standard, tempered, acrylic, wired, laminated, solar window film, security film'.

Question:
What are 6 physical threats to assets?

Answer:
'service interruption, theft, compromised systems, environment integrity, unauthorized access, physical damage'.

Question:
What are 5 types of safes?

Answer:
'wall, floor, chest, depositories, vaults'.

Security Engineering Domain

Question:
What are 4 ways in which power delivery can be protected?

Answer:
'online UPS, standby UPS, a redundant line feed and on onsite generator'.

Question:
What are the 3 components of fire?

Answer:
'fuel, oxygen and heat'.

Question:
How close to electrical equipment should fire extinguishers be located?

Answer:
'50 feet'.

Question:
What are the 5 types of fire suppression agents?

Answer:
'water, foam, carbon dioxide, gases, dry powders and wet chemicals'.

Question:
What are the 5 types of fires?

Answer:
'Classes A, B, C, D and K'.

Question:
What are the 4 types of water sprinklers?

Answer:
'wet pipe, dry pipe, precaution, deluge'.

Question:
What is the primary drawback to a wet pipe water sprinkler?

Answer:
'It is susceptible to burst pipes in freezing weather'.

Question:
Which type of water sprinkler should never be used in data centers?

Answer:
'Deluge'.

Question:
Which type of water sprinkler is the most common found in data centers, and provides people time to leave before activating?

Answer:
'Precaution'.

Communication and Network Security Domain

Definitions

Question:
What is the transmission of data through analog, digital or wireless mediums?

Answer:
'telecommunications'

Question:
What is a model that describe how network communication takes place?

Answer:
'Open Systems Interconnection Reference Model, or OSI'

Question:
What is a set of rules that systems use to communicate across a network?

Answer:
'network protocol'

Question:
What is the OSI layer that contains high-level networking protocols?

Answer:
'layer 7, or Application Layer'

Question:
What is the OSI layer that wraps more specific content into a generic wrapper?

Answer:
'layer 6, or Presentation Layer'

Question:
What is the OSI layer that establishes a session between the same application running on two different computers?

Answer:
'layer 5, or Session Layer'

Question:
What is a communication mode in which parties can communicate in one direction only?

Answer:
'simplex'

Question:
What is a communication mode in which parties can communicate in both directions, but one at a time?

Answer:
'half-duplex'

Communication and Network Security Domain

199

Question:
What is a communication mode in which parties can communicate in both directions simultaneously?

Answer:
'full-duplex'

Question:
What is how inter-process communication happens?

Answer:
'remote procedure call, or RPC'

Question:
What is RPC coupled with authentication?

Answer:
'secure RPC, or SRPC'

Question:
What is the OSI layer that ensures data arrives intact?

Answer:
'layer 4, or Transport Layer'

Question:
What is the OSI layer that ensures the packet gets to the correct location?

Answer:
'layer 3, or Network Layer'

Question:
What is the OSI layer that translates bits into voltage levels for the physical layer?

Answer:
'layer 2, or Data Link Layer'

Question:
What is the OSI layer 2 sublayer that provides multiplexing, flow control and error management?

Answer:
'Logical Link Control, or LLC'

Question:
What is the OSI layer 2 sublayer that decides the voltages to use?

Answer:
'Media Access Control, or MAC'

Question:
What is the OSI layer that generates electrical signals?

Answer:
'layer 1, or Physical Layer'

Communication and Network Security Domain

200

Question:
What is a simple 3-layer model for SCADA?

Answer:
'enhanced performance architecture, or EPA'

Question:
What is the protocol providing network connectivity for SCADA?

Answer:
'Distributed Network Protocol 3, or NDP3'

Question:
What is the network backbone found in vehicles?

Answer:
'CAN Bus'

Question:
What is an alternative network model that can map to OSI?

Answer:
'TCP/IP Model'

Question:
What is the TCP/IP model layer that maps to OSI layers 7 through 5?

Answer:
'layer 4, or Application Layer'

Question:
What is the TCP/IP model layer that maps to OSI Transport Layer 4?

Answer:
'layer 3, or Host-to-Host Layer'

Question:
What is the TCP/IP model layer that maps to OSI Network Layer 3?

Answer:
'layer 2, or Internet Layer'

Question:
What is the TCP/IP model layer that maps to OSI layers 2-1?

Answer:
'layer 1, or Network Access Layer'

Question:
What is a common connection-oriented protocol operating at OSI layer 4?

Answer:
'transport control protocol, or TCP'

Communication and Network Security Domain

201

Question:
What occurs when two computers negotiate how the remaining communication will take place?

Answer:
'handshaking'

Question:
What is a common connectionless protocol operating at OSI layer 4?

Answer:
'user datagram protocol, or UDP'

Question:
What occurs when each layer wraps the data from the layer above?

Answer:
'data encapsulation'

Question:
What is an attack where the attacker sends SYN but never responds with ACK?

Answer:
'SYN flood'

Question:
What is an attack where the attacker guesses the TCP sequence numbers and injects their own packets?

Answer:
'TCP session hijacking'

Question:
What is a common service found on port 7?

Answer:
'ECHO'

Question:
What is a common service found on ports 20 and 21?

Answer:
'FTP'

Question:
What is a common service found on port 22?

Answer:
'SSH'

Question:
What is a common service found on port 23?

Answer:
'Telnet'

Communication and Network Security Domain

Question:
What is a common service found on port 25?

Answer:
'SMTP'

Question:
What is a common service found on port 53?

Answer:
'DNS'

Question:
What is a common service found on port 80?

Answer:
'HTTP'

Question:
What is a common service found on port 110?

Answer:
'POP3'

Question:
What is a common service found on ports 161 and 162?

Answer:
'SNMP'

Question:
What are designated ports 1,024 through 49,151?

Answer:
'registered ports'

Question:
What are designated ports 49,152 through 65,535?

Answer:
'dynamic ports'

Question:
What defines IP addresses that can be reused within private networks?

Answer:
'classless interdomain routing, or CIDR, or Supernetting'

Question:
What are logical subdivisions within the network created by further segmenting host segments?

Answer:
'subnet'

Communication and Network Security Domain

Question:
What defines a subnet?

Answer:
'subnet mask'

Question:
What are the types of IP addresses used with normal subnet masks?

Answer:
'classful, or classical'

Question:
What is a flag that restricts how long a packet bounces around a network?

Answer:
'time to live, or TTL'

Question:
What occurs when large packets are broken into smaller packets in order to communicate with hosts that can't handle the larger packets?

Answer:
'packet fragmentation'

Question:
What is the newest version of the Internet Protocol?

Answer:
'iPV6, or IP next generation, or IPng'

Question:
What allows routers to automatically tunnel through IPv4?

Answer:
'automatic tunneling'

Question:
What is a type of automatic tunneling that wraps outgoing IPv6 packets in well-known IPv4 anycast addresses, and incoming IPv4 address data in IPv6 packets?

Answer:
'6to4'

Question:
What is a type of automatic tunneling that uses UDP encapsulation so that NAT is not affected?

Answer:
'Teredo'

Question:
What sees the IPv4 network as a virtual IPv6 local link?

Answer:
'intra-site automatic tunneling addressing protocol, or ISATAP'

Communication and Network Security Domain

Question:
What is a mechanism to connect two different networks?

Answer:
'intersite'

Question:
What is a term that represents communication within a network?

Answer:
'intrasite'

Question:
What is a protocol that protects MAC-layer traffic by providing CIA?

Answer:
'IEEE 8021AE, or MACSec'

Question:
What is a Layer 2 device configured with MACSec?

Answer:
'MACSec security entity, or SecY'

Question:
What is the standard that assigns and binds unique identifiers for SecY devices?

Answer:
'IEEE 802.1AR'

Question:
What is the standard that manages session keys used between SecY?

Answer:
'IEEE 802.1AF'

Question:
What is the combination of 802.1AE, 802.1AR, 802.1AF and RADIUS?

Answer:
'Extensible Authentication Protocol Transport Layer, or EAP-TLS'

Question:
What occurs when two separate protocols become one?

Answer:
'converged protocols'

Question:
What is a protocol that operates at layers 2 and 3, and is referred to as 2.5 protocol?

Answer:
'multiprotocol label switching, or MPLS'

Communication and Network Security Domain

Question:
What is a converged protocol between fiber and Ethernet?

Answer:
'fiber channel over Ethernet, or FCoE'

Question:
What is a converged protocol allowing SCSI to travel over a network?

Answer:
'internet small computer system interface, or iSCSI'

Question:
What is a protocol that transitions to ride on top of IP?

Answer:
'IP convergence'

Question:
What is any way to communicate information?

Answer:
'signal'

Question:
What is communication by varying amplitude and/or frequency of a signal?

Answer:
'signal wave'

Question:
What is a value that measures the height of a signal wave peak?

Answer:
'amplitude'

Question:
What is a value that measures the amount of space between peaks in a signal wave?

Answer:
'frequency'

Question:
What is the term for amplitude modulation?

Answer:
'AM'

Question:
What is the term for frequency modulation?

Answer:
'FM'

Communication and Network Security Domain

Question:
What is a type of signal where information is based on an infinite degrees of AM or FM?

Answer:
'analog signal'

Question:
What is a type of signal where information is based on two discrete ranges of AM or FM - '0' or '1'?

Answer:
'digital signal'

Question:
What measures the number of electrical pulses that can be sent over a signal within a given time period?

Answer:
'bandwidth'

Question:
What measures the number of bits that can be sent and received over a given period of time?

Answer:
'data throughput'

Question:
What occurs when two devices communicate based on exact timing?

Answer:
'synchronous communication'

Question:
What occurs when two devices communicate based on start and stop signals?

Answer:
'asynchronous communication'

Question:
What is the term used to describe an entire channel being in-use at once?

Answer:
'baseband'

Question:
What is the term used to describe a channel that has been split up into sub-channels?

Answer:
'broadband'

Question:
What is a type of cabling usually found in TV cable, and consists of a single copper wire?

Answer:
'coaxial cable'

Communication and Network Security Domain

Question:
What is the term describing a cable with pairs of thin copper wires twisted around each other wrapped in an outer jacket?

Answer:
'twisted-Pair cable'

Question:
What is comprised of wires, each wrapped in an outer foil shielding?

Answer:
'shielded twisted pair, or STP'

Question:
What is comprised of wires that do not have an outer foil shielding?

Answer:
'unshielded twisted pair, or UTP'

Question:
What is the type of Ethernet cabling supporting voice grade up to 1Mbs?

Answer:
'category 1 Ethernet cabling'

Question:
What is the type of Ethernet cabling supporting up to 4Mbs?

Answer:
'category 2 Ethernet cabling'

Question:
What is the type of Ethernet cabling supporting 10 Mbps?

Answer:
'category 3 Ethernet cabling'

Question:
What is the type of Ethernet cabling supporting 16 Mbps?

Answer:
'category 4 Ethernet cabling'

Question:
What is the type of Ethernet cabling supporting 100 Mbps?

Answer:
'category 5 Ethernet cabling'

Question:
What is the type of Ethernet cabling supporting 1 Gbps?

Answer:
'category 6 Ethernet cabling'

Communication and Network Security Domain

Question:
What is the type of Ethernet cabling supporting 10 Gbps?

Answer:
'category 7 Ethernet cabling'

Question:
What is a type of cabling using glass to carry light signals, and can travel long distances?

Answer:
'fiber-optic cable'

Question:
What is the component that converts electrical signal into a light signal in fiber-optic cables?

Answer:
'fiber-optic light source'

Question:
What is the component that carries the light signal in a fiber-optic cable?

Answer:
'fiber cable'

Question:
What is the fiber cable mode that has a small glass core, provides less bandwidth, but delivers data over a longer distance?

Answer:
'single mode'

Question:
What is the fiber cable mode that requires a larger glass core, provides higher bandwidth, but only over shorter distances?

Answer:
'multimode'

Question:
What is the component that converts the light signal back into an electrical signal in a fiber-optic cable?

Answer:
'light detector'

Question:
What is any undesired addition to a source signal that can interfere with the receiver turning it back into the original information?

Answer:
'noise'

Question:
What occurs when signal is lost due to the distance travelled?

Answer:
'attenuation'

Communication and Network Security Domain

Question:
What occurs when radiation from one cable interferes with the signal in another?

Answer:
'crosstalk'

Question:
What are spaces for cable runs above lowered ceilings or beneath raised floors?

Answer:
'plenum space'

Question:
What describes how computers are arranged relative to each other within a network?

Answer:
'network topology'

Question:
What describes how cables are laid out and connected to each computer?

Answer:
'physical topology'

Question:
What describes how computers communicate over physical cabling, including wireless?

Answer:
'logical topology'

Question:
What is a network topology in which all nodes are physically connected in a ring?

Answer:
'ring topology'

Question:
What is a network topology in which a single cable runs the entire length of the network?

Answer:
'bus topology'

Question:
What is a network topology in which all nodes attach directly to the bus?

Answer:
'linear bus topology'

Question:
What is a network topology in which branches connect directly to the bus, with nodes connected to branches?

Answer:
'tree bus topology'

Communication and Network Security Domain

Question:
What is a network topology in which all nodes are connected directly to a central device?

Answer:
'star topology'

Question:
What is a network topology in which all nodes are connected directly to each other?

Answer:
'full mesh topology'

Question:
What is a network topology in which any combination of other topologies, usually star, are used?

Answer:
'partial mesh topology'

Question:
What is a term describing anything that happens at Layer 2, specifically within the MAC sublayer?

Answer:
'media access technologies'

Question:
What is a media access technology in which only the computer possessing the 24-bit token can talk?

Answer:
'token passing'

Question:
What is a media access technology used by Ethernet networks?

Answer:
'carrier sense multiple access, or CSMA'

Question:
What occurs when two or more electronic signals collide, resulting in corruption of both?

Answer:
'collision'

Question:
What is the term for a frame transmitted across an Ethernet network?

Answer:
'carrier'

Question:
What is a flavor of CSMA in which two computers speak, recognize a collision, and then back off; used by Ethernet?

Answer:
'carrier sense multiple access with collision detection, or CSMA/CD'

Communication and Network Security Domain

Question:
What is a flavor of CSMA in which a computer announces it is about to speak, and all other computers back off; used by Wi-Fi?

Answer:
'carrier sense multiple access with collision avoidance, or CSMA/CA'

Question:
What is the term describing a network segmented with layer 2 switches?

Answer:
'collision domain'

Question:
What is the term describing a network segmented with layer 3 routers?

Answer:
'broadcast domain'

Question:
What is a technique used with mainframes, in which a server instructs a client when to communicate if it wishes to?

Answer:
'polling'

Question:
What is a technology in which all resources use the same shared medium?

Answer:
'contention-based technology'

Question:
What is the standard that is contention-based, uses collision and broadcast domains, employs CSMA/CD, and works with coaxial, UTP or fiber?

Answer:
'Ethernet, or IEEE 802.3'

Question:
What is a common name for 100Base-TX?

Answer:
'Fast Ethernet'

Question:
What is a common name for 1000Base-T?

Answer:
'Gigabit Ethernet'

Question:
What is the standard for Token Ring?

Answer:
'IEEE 802.5'

Communication and Network Security Domain

Question:
What is a process that removes frames that are continuously circulating?

Answer:
'active monitor'

Question:
What describes a frame being sent out when a computer encounters a problem?

Answer:
'beaconing'

Question:
What is a media access technology that uses token passing on fiber backbones with two rings for redundancy?

Answer:
'fiber distributed data interface, or FDDI'

Question:
What is the standard for FDDI?

Answer:
'IEEE 802.4'

Question:
What is an FDDI device that attaches to only one ring through a concentrator?

Answer:
'single-attachment station, or SAS'

Question:
What is an FDDI device that attaches to both rings through a concentrator?

Answer:
'dual-attachment station, or DAS'

Question:
What is an FDDI device that attaches an SAS device to the primary ring?

Answer:
'single-attachment concentrator, or SAC'

Question:
What is an FDDI device that attaches DAS, SAS and SAC to both rings?

Answer:
'dual-attachment concentrator, or DAC'

Question:
What is an enhancement to FDDI that added QoS?

Answer:
'FDDI-2'

Communication and Network Security Domain

Question:
What is a media access technology just like FDDI but over UTP and meant for LANs?

Answer:
'Copper Distributed Data Interface, or CDDI'

Question:
What is the normal method of communication with a single computer?

Answer:
'unicast'

Question:
What is communication with a group of computers?

Answer:
'multicast'

Question:
What is communication with all computers?

Answer:
'broadcast'

Question:
What is the name of the group which advances multicasting protocols?

Answer:
'Internet Group Management Protocol, or IGMP'

Question:
What is the version of IGMP that added the ability to be removed from a multicast group?

Answer:
'IGMP version 2'

Question:
What is the version of IGMP that allows recipients to specify the multicast source?

Answer:
'IGMP version 3'

Question:
What is a protocol that, given a MAC address, returns the IP address?

Answer:
'Address Resolution Protocol, or ARP'

Question:
What is a device that sends and receives signals directly from the physical medium?

Answer:
'Network Interface Card, or NIC'

Communication and Network Security Domain

Question:
What is a 48-bit globally unique identifier assigned by the manufacturer to NICs?

Answer:
'Media Access Control address, or MAC address'

Question:
What is an attack in which a device masquerades as the owner of a MAC address?

Answer:
'ARP table cache poisoning'

Question:
What is a service that assigns IP addresses from a pool in real-time?

Answer:
'Dynamic Host Configuration Protocol, or DHCP'

Question:
What is assigned to devices when they are manually configured with an IP address?

Answer:
'static IP address'

Question:
What is assigned to devices from a DHCP server?

Answer:
'dynamic IP address'

Question:
What is a device that receives a dynamic IP address?

Answer:
'DHCP client'

Question:
What is the value that dictates how long a client can keep a dynamic IP address?

Answer:
'DHCP lease'

Question:
What is a security precaution that allows DHCPDISCOVER requests only from trusted devices based on the device's MAC address?

Answer:
'DHCP snooping'

Question:
What is a protocol that, given an IP address, returns the MAC address?

Answer:
'Reverse Address Resolution Protocol, or RARP'

Communication and Network Security Domain

Question:
What is used by a client to retrieve the default gateway and DNS server IP addresses dynamically?

Answer:
'Bootstrap Protocol, or BOOTP'

Question:
What is a protocol used to test connectivity, provide status updates and report errors?

Answer:
'Internet Control Message Protocol, or ICMP'

Question:
What is an attack in which the attacker uses an ICMP packet to send data?

Answer:
'ICMP tunneling'

Question:
What is a protocol allowing a unified method to manage all of the devices on a network?

Answer:
'Simple Network Management Protocol, or SMNP'

Question:
What is SNMP software that runs on a central server?

Answer:
'SNMP manager'

Question:
What is SNMP software that runs on network devices?

Answer:
'SNMP agent'

Question:
What is an unrequested SNMP message an agent sends to a manager?

Answer:
'SNMP trap'

Question:
What is a small database of objects that an SNMP agent keeps track of?

Answer:
'Management Information Base, or MIB'

Question:
What includes the SNMP manager and its agents?

Answer:
'SNMP community'

Communication and Network Security Domain

Question:
What is the term for an SNMP community password?

Answer:
'SNMP community string'

Question:
What is the type of SNMP password that provides the ability to read an agent's MIB?

Answer:
'SNMP read password'

Question:
What is the type of SNMP password that provides the ability to both read and update an agent's MIB?

Answer:
'SNMP read-write password'

Question:
What is a service that translates domain names into an IP address?

Answer:
'Domain Name Service, or DNS'

Question:
What is the name of local process that carries out DNS services?

Answer:
'DNS resolver'

Question:
What is used if an address is not found locally, but is forwarded to the next-level DNS?

Answer:
'recursive query'

Question:
What is a type of query that is not forwarded if the information is not found locally?

Answer:
'non-recursive query'

Question:
What is a text file containing a list of domain names and matching IP addresses?

Answer:
'HOSTS file'

Question:
What is a standard that implements authentication and encryption around the DNS request and resolution exchange?

Answer:
'DNS Security, or DNSSEC'

Communication and Network Security Domain

Question:
What occurs when a hyperlink containing non-threatening text has an underlying link to a site where an attack is launched?

Answer:
'URL hiding'

Question:
What is implemented when using two DNS servers - one for external and another for internal entries?

Answer:
'split DNS'

Question:
What is the act of grabbing an attractive domain name and reselling it for a profit?

Answer:
'cyber squatting'

Question:
What is the act of purchasing a recently-expired domain name and charging a hefty price to get it back?

Answer:
'domain grabbing'

Question:
What is the protocol all mail servers use for sending email messages?

Answer:
'Simple Mail Transfer Protocol, or SMTP'

Question:
What is an extension to SMTP that added authentication?

Answer:
'SMTP authentication, or SMTP-AUTH'

Question:
What is used to download email messages from an email server, but deletes each message from the server?

Answer:
'Post Office Protocol, or POP'

Question:
What is the protocol version that added SASL support to POP?

Answer:
'POP version 3, or POP3'

Question:
What is a protocol-independent method for authentication?

Answer:
'Simple Authentication and Security Layer, or SASL'

Communication and Network Security Domain

Question:
What is a replacement for POP3 that allows messages to stay on the server and supports server-based searches?

Answer:
'Internet Message Access Protocol, or IMAP'

Question:
What is used by SMTP for server-to-server communication, and is often abused by spammers?

Answer:
'SMTP relay'

Question:
What is an attack in which emails appear to be coming from a legitimate source by manipulating the email header?

Answer:
'email spoofing'

Question:
What is a technique that detects bogus incoming messages from other servers?

Answer:
'Sender Policy Framework, or SPF'

Question:
What is an email-based social engineering attack with the goal of getting a victim to click a link?

Answer:
'phishing'

Question:
What is a phishing attack targeting a specific user?

Answer:
'spear phishing'

Question:
What is a spear fishing attack targeting a 'big fish' in an organization?

Answer:
'whaling attack'

Question:
What is a technology that increases the number of available IP addresses by creating a private range of addresses?

Answer:
'Network Address Translation, or NAT'

Question:
What is an IP address that is not routable on a public network?

Answer:
'private IP address'

Communication and Network Security Domain

Question:
What is the act of translating a network address from private to public, and back again?

Answer:
'NATing'

Question:
What is a technique in which a specific private IP address is mapped to a dedicated IP public address?

Answer:
'static IP mapping'

Question:
What is a technique in which a specific private IP address is mapped to a single public IP address pulled from a pre-defined pool of public addresses?

Answer:
'dynamic IP mapping'

Question:
What is used when a single public IP address is mapped to multiple private IP addresses by assigning a port to each private address?

Answer:
'Port Address Translation, or PAT'

Question:
What is a NATing technique in which the translation process must maintain a list of public and private mappings?

Answer:
'stateful NAT'

Question:
What is a small network communicating within a larger network?

Answer:
'autonomous system, or AS'

Question:
What is a routing protocol that is manually configured to route packets through a specific path?

Answer:
'static routing protocol'

Question:
What is a routing protocol that discovers the best path to send packets?

Answer:
'dynamic routing protocol'

Question:
What is a routing protocol that looks at distance and vector only?

Answer:
'distance-vector routing protocol'

Communication and Network Security Domain

Question:
What is a routing protocol that looks at distance, packet size, link speed, latency, traffic load and historical reliability?

Answer:
'link-state routing protocol'

Question:
What occurs when the availability of routers is constantly changing within an AS?

Answer:
'route flapping'

Question:
What is a term that represents the number of route hops?

Answer:
'route distance'

Question:
What is a term representing the direction of a link?

Answer:
'route vector'

Question:
What are routing protocols that operate inside of a network?

Answer:
'interior routing protocols'

Question:
What is a very slow distance vector protocol?

Answer:
'Routing Information Protocol, or RIP'

Question:
What is the name of a link-state protocol that supports a backbone link connecting subnets?

Answer:
'Open Shortest Path First, or OSPF'

Question:
What is a Cisco distance-vector protocol that uses 5 metrics (bandwidth, latency, load, reliability and MTU) instead of the usual distance and vector?

Answer:
'Interior Gateway Routing Protocol, or IGRP'

Question:
What is a successor to IGRP, and adds faster router table updates?

Answer:
'Enhanced Interior Gateway Routing Protocol, or EIGRP'

Communication and Network Security Domain

Question:
What is a router protocol that supports a primary and failover router to eliminate a single point of failure?

Answer:
'Virtual Router Redundancy Protocol, or VRRP'

Question:
What is a link-state protocol that is vendor-neutral and does not use IP addresses?

Answer:
'Intermediate System to Intermediate System, or IS-IS'

Question:
What is the name of routing protocols used between networks?

Answer:
'exterior routing protocols'

Question:
What is a protocol that employs a combination of both distance-vector and link-state algorithms?

Answer:
'Border Gateway Protocol, or BGP'

Question:
What allows administrators to apply weights to different metrics?

Answer:
'routing policy'

Question:
What is an attack in which one or more packets are captured and transported to another location in the network?

Answer:
'wormhole attack'

Question:
What is a packet header that limits the use of data?

Answer:
'leash'

Question:
What is a type of leash that ensures a packet can be used only within a certain distance, or hops, of the sender?

Answer:
'geographical leash'

Question:
What is a type of leash that ensures a packet must be used within a specific time window?

Answer:
'temporal leash'

Communication and Network Security Domain

Question:
What is a network device that amplifies a signal?

Answer:
'repeater'

Question:
What is a repeater with multiple ports?

Answer:
'hub'

Question:
What is a network device that connects multiple physical devices?

Answer:
'concentrator'

Question:
What is a network device that connects LAN segments and creates a collision domain?

Answer:
'bridge'

Question:
What is a bridge that connects LANs within a local area, usually a building?

Answer:
'local bridge'

Question:
What is a bridge that connects LANs over a MAN by using a telecommunication link?

Answer:
'remote bridge'

Question:
What is a bridge that connects LANs that use different protocols, for example Ethernet and Token Ring?

Answer:
'translation bridge'

Question:
What is a type of bridging where the bridge learns the mapping between frames and ports?

Answer:
'transparent bridging'

Question:
What is an algorithm that makes sure that rogue frames do not circulate forever, assigns priorities to certain paths and calculates costs for paths?

Answer:
'Spanning Tree Algorithm, or SPA'

Communication and Network Security Domain

Question:
What is the act of allowing a frame or packet to specify the exact network path it wants to travel through?

Answer:
'source routing'

Question:
What is a hub combined with a bridge, plus ACLs and VLANs, and creates collision domains?

Answer:
'switch'

Question:
What is a virtual network containing devices regardless of the physical location?

Answer:
'virtual LAN, or VLAN'

Question:
What performs routing functions but moves routing logic into hardware for speed?

Answer:
'layer 3 switch'

Question:
What operates based on IP addresses and creates broadcast domains?

Answer:
'router'

Question:
What is the term for the maximum size a packet can be?

Answer:
'Maximum Transmission Size, or MTU'

Question:
What describes the process of dividing a packet into smaller packets based on the MTU?

Answer:
'fragmenting'

Question:
What are devices that operate across more than one OSI layer?

Answer:
'multilayer devices'

Question:
What is a hardware device dedicated to carrying out a specific task that can be software-based?

Answer:
'Application-Specific Integrated Circuit, or ASIC'

Communication and Network Security Domain

Question:
What is a layer 3 and 4 capability to apply an attribute in real-time to a fragment or packet that other devices can look at?

Answer:
'Multiprotocol Label Switching, or MPLS'

Question:
What is an attack which uses MPLS to force a packet down a specific path?

Answer:
'double tagging attack'

Question:
What is an attack in which the attacker pretends to be a switch?

Answer:
'switch spoofing attack'

Question:
What is an attack in which the attacker gains access to traffic in a different VLAN?

Answer:
'VLAN hopping attack'

Question:
What is a piece of software that connects two dissimilar environments?

Answer:
'gateway'

Question:
What is a gateway that manages communication between different mail server platforms?

Answer:
'electronic mail gateway'

Question:
What is a private, company-owned telephone switch located on the company's premises?

Answer:
'Private Branch Exchange, or PBX'

Question:
What is an attached modem for service personnel to connect to while servicing a PBX?

Answer:
'hanging modem'

Question:
What is a term used for phone hackers?

Answer:
'phreakers'

Communication and Network Security Domain

Question:
What is a secure zone setup around public servers using a firewall?

Answer:
'Demilitarized Zone, or DMZ'

Question:
What describes traffic coming into a network?

Answer:
'ingress'

Question:
What describes traffic leaving a network?

Answer:
'egress'

Question:
What describes network devices that only look at individual packets, not the entire conversation?

Answer:
'stateless inspection'

Question:
What describes network devices that keep track of all packets until the socket is closed?

Answer:
'stateful inspection'

Question:
What is an attack that attempts to rob legitimate users of a resource, such as availability?

Answer:
'Denial of Service, or DoS'

Question:
What is a DoS attack carried out by many computers in different locations, often by Zombies?

Answer:
'Distributed Denial of Service, or DDoS'

Question:
What is a dedicated hardware/software platform?

Answer:
'appliance'

Question:
What is a stateless firewall that operates at layers 3 and 4?

Answer:
'Packet-Filtering Firewall'

Communication and Network Security Domain

Question:
What is the same as a packet-filtering firewall but stateful?

Answer:
'Stateful Firewall'

Question:
What is a firewall that breaks the communication path and communicates on behalf of two clients?

Answer:
'Proxy Firewall'

Question:
What is a firewall that operates at layer 5?

Answer:
'Circuit-Level Proxy'

Question:
What is a firewall that operates at layer 7, and is slower but more intelligent than a circuit-level proxy?

Answer:
'Application-Level Proxy'

Question:
What is a circuit-level protocol used to create a secure channel between two computers?

Answer:
'SOCKS'

Question:
What is a firewall that keeps high-numbered ports closed until a computer within its network needs to use one?

Answer:
'Dynamic Packet-Filtering Firewall'

Question:
What is a firewall that puts the packet inspection intelligence inside of the kernel itself, speeding up the inspection?

Answer:
'Kernel Proxy Firewall'

Question:
What is a firewall that add an IPS and allows configuration from a central server?

Answer:
'Next-Generation Firewall'

Question:
What is the name for devices connected directly to a packet-filtering firewall?

Answer:
'screened host'

Communication and Network Security Domain

Question:
What is the name for a network created by a packet-filtering firewall?

Answer:
'screened subnet'

Question:
What is the term used for a single firewall?

Answer:
'single-tiered configuration'

Question:
What is the term used when employing a screened host?

Answer:
'two-tiered configuration'

Question:
What is the term used when employing a screened subnet?

Answer:
'three-tiered configuration'

Question:
What is a device with 2 NICs - one internal and one external?

Answer:
'dual-homed device'

Question:
What is a device with 3 or more NICs?

Answer:
'multi-homed device'

Question:
What is a server hardened against attacks, usually residing in a DMZ?

Answer:
'bastion host'

Question:
What is a firewall that sits between virtual machines?

Answer:
'virtual firewall'

Question:
What is a policy that indicates that if there is no rule to explicitly accept a packet, then is should be discarded?

Answer:
'deny first policy'

Communication and Network Security Domain

Question:
What is a rule that drops 'noisy' traffic without logging it to avoid filling up the logs up too quickly?

Answer:
'silent rule'

Question:
What is a rule to not allow access to the firewall software except from authorized systems?

Answer:
'stealth rule'

Question:
What is a rule that any packet not meeting a rule should be discarded?

Answer:
'cleanup rule'

Question:
What is the name of a rule that is the same as 'deny first'?

Answer:
'negate rule'

Question:
What is an attack in which an attacker crafts packet fragments that cannot be reassembled, resulting in a software crash or an out of memory condition?

Answer:
'IP fragmentation attack'

Question:
What is an attack in which an attacker sneaks past firewalls that do not reassemble fragments before approving them?

Answer:
'overlapping fragment attack'

Question:
What is a proxy firewall that understands the software running on both the server and client?

Answer:
'proxy server'

Question:
What is a proxy server allowing the client to indicate which server it wishes to speak to?

Answer:
'forwarding proxy'

Question:
What is a forwarding proxy that is available for anyone to use?

Answer:
'open proxy'

Communication and Network Security Domain

Question:
What is a server that allows users to remain anonymous by concealing their real IP address?

Answer:
'anonymous open proxy'

Question:
What hides the servers behind it so the client never knows they exist, such as load balancers?

Answer:
'reverse proxy'

Question:
What is an attractive target for attackers that is designed to slow down and distract them?

Answer:
'honeypot'

Question:
What describes when more than one honeypot is put into place?

Answer:
'honeynet'

Question:
What is an attractive target for attackers purposefully designed to handicap them by being very slow to respond?

Answer:
'tarpit'

Question:
What is an appliance that implements a firewall, anti-malware, anti-spam, IDS and IPS, VPN support, information leak prevention and content filtering?

Answer:
'Unified Threat Management'

Question:
What describes caching content at various geographical places around the world to speed delivery and to mitigate DDoS attacks?

Answer:
'Content Distribution Networks, or CDN'

Question:
What describes implementing network management as distributed software?

Answer:
'Software Defined Networking, or SDN'

Question:
What is an SDN component where routing paths are tracked, discovered and discarded?

Answer:
'control plane'

Communication and Network Security Domain

Question:
What is an SDN network device, usually an ASIC, where actual forwarding decision are made based on control plane paths?

Answer:
'forwarding plane'

Question:
What is an SDN open source package providing communication between the control and forwarding planes?

Answer:
'OpenFlow'

Question:
What is an SDN approach in which open-source code and standards create the components of SDN?

Answer:
'open'

Question:
What is a CISCO SDN approach which extends OpenFlow to allow deeper packet inspection?

Answer:
'API'

Question:
What is an SDN approach which creates a virtual overlay on top of the physical network?

Answer:
'overlay'

Question:
What is an internal network of servers and clients that are inaccessible outside of the company's network?

Answer:
'intranet'

Question:
What is a network between two companies allowing real-time communication?

Answer:
'extranet'

Question:
What describes automated processes exchanging data?

Answer:
'Electronic Data Interchange, or EDI'

Question:
What is a network created and hosted by a third-party that allows two companies to connect in real-time?

Answer:
'Value-Added Network, or VAN'

Communication and Network Security Domain

231

Question:
What is a small geographical region covered by a single network?

Answer:
'Local Area Network, or LAN'

Question:
What describes two LANs connected by a router?

Answer:
'internetwork'

Question:
What is the term for two LANs connected by different layer 2 technology, such as frame relay or ATM?

Answer:
'Wide Area Network, or WAN'

Question:
What occurs when a single transmission path is broken up into multiple channels?

Answer:
'multiplexing'

Question:
What is a digital line with 24 calls over one UTP?

Answer:
'T1'

Question:
What is the label for 28 T1 lines?

Answer:
'T3'

Question:
What is the term describing T1 and T3 lines carrying both voice and data?

Answer:
't-carrier'

Question:
What is another name for shared T lines?

Answer:
'fractional T line'

Question:
What is the European version of a T-carrier, with E1 and E3 instead of T1 and T3?

Answer:
'e-carrier'

Communication and Network Security Domain

Question:
What is a version of multiplexing in which time slots are created within a single channel by modulating the amplitude?

Answer:
'Time-Division Multiplexing, or TDM'

Question:
What is a version of multiplexing like TDM but only includes data for each subchannel if it is being used?

Answer:
'Statistical Time-Division Multiplexing, or STDM'

Question:
What is a version of multiplexing which modulates the frequency to carry more data?

Answer:
'Frequency-Division Multiplexing, or FDM'

Question:
What is a fiber line carrying up to 52 Mbps?

Answer:
'OC-1'

Question:
What is a fiber line carrying up to 155 Mbps?

Answer:
'OC-3'

Question:
What is the fiber standard that the Internet backbone is based on, supporting up to 10 Gbps?

Answer:
'OC-192'

Question:
What is a standard that allows copper and fiber to work together?

Answer:
'Synchronous Optical Network, or SONET'

Question:
What is Europe's version of SONET?

Answer:
'Synchronous Digital Hierarchy, or SDH'

Question:
What is a protocol created specifically for SONET?

Answer:
'Asynchronous Transfer Mode, or ATM'

Communication and Network Security Domain

Question:
What are WAN devices that physically connect a LAN and a WAN?

Answer:
'Channel Service Unit/Data Service Unit, or CSU/DSU'

Question:
What is the WAN device within a company's network?

Answer:
'Data Terminal Equipment, or DTE'

Question:
What is a WAN device belonging to the carrier?

Answer:
'Data-Circuit Terminating Equipment, or DCE'

Question:
What is a method of transmitting packets such that they all follow the same path?

Answer:
'circuit-switching'

Question:
What is a method of transmitting packets such that they can follow different paths?

Answer:
'packet switching'

Question:
What is a number that is assigned to each packet when using packet switching?

Answer:
'Frame Check Sequence, or FCS'

Question:
What is a type of link that allows more than one party to share in a single dedicated line across a WAN?

Answer:
'frame relay'

Question:
What is a form of bandwidth guarantee to a company when using frame relay?

Answer:
'Committed Information Rate, or CIR'

Question:
What is a collection of DCEs which forward packets from Point A to Point B?

Answer:
'frame relay cloud'

Communication and Network Security Domain

Question:
What is used by frame relay or X.25 to send data across a WAN or MAN link?

Answer:
'virtual circuit'

Question:
What is a virtual circuit that is programmed into devices directly, resulting in a CIR?

Answer:
'Permanent Virtual Circuit, or PVC'

Question:
What is a virtual circuit that is built and destroyed as-needed?

Answer:
'Switched Virtual Circuit, or SVC'

Question:
What is a backbone, usually SONET, that connects LANS, WANs, the Internet and other telecommunications and cable networks?

Answer:
'Metropolitan Area Network, or MAN'

Question:
What occurs when a break in the primary ring of SONET results in traffic continuing on a back-up ring?

Answer:
'self-healing'

Question:
What is the term for Ethernet used with MANs?

Answer:
'Metro Ethernet'

Question:
What creates a distributed LAN over a MAN?

Answer:
'Virtual Private LAN service, or VPLS'

Question:
What is an older WAN protocol that defines how networks establish and maintain connections using packet switching?

Answer:
'X.25'

Question:
What is used on the Internet backbone, and is a connection-oriented technology that uses cells instead of packets providing QoS?

Answer:
'Asynchronous Transfer Mode, or ATM'

Communication and Network Security Domain

Question:
What is the act of distinguishing between different types of traffic and assigning delivery priority levels?

Answer:
'Quality of Service, or QoS'

Question:
What is a connectionless channel that pretty much promises nothing?

Answer:
'Unspecified Bit Rate Service, or UBR'

Question:
What is a connection-oriented channel that does not guarantee a minimum latency and provides a peak and sustained data rate?

Answer:
'Variable Bit Rate Service, or VBR'

Question:
What is a connection-oriented channel that allows the bit rate to be adjusted to match whatever bandwidth is available?

Answer:
'Available Bit Rate Service, or ABR'

Question:
What is a connection-oriented channel that is based on a bandwidth requirement that is specified when the connection is started?

Answer:
'Constant Bit Rate Service, or CBR'

Question:
What is a non-ATM QoS level that promises nothing – just the best effort after all other classes have been served?

Answer:
'best-effort service'

Question:
What is a non-ATM QoS level that promises nothing other than that this class gets priority over best-effort service?

Answer:
'differentiated service'

Question:
What is a non-ATM QoS level that promises a guaranteed speed?

Answer:
'guaranteed service'

Question:
What occurs when the QoS classification sets priorities for traffic?

Answer:
'traffic shaping'

Communication and Network Security Domain

Question:
What is an IBM mainframe network?

Answer:
'Systems Network Architecture, or SNA'

Question:
What is a polling protocol used on SNA networks?

Answer:
'Asynchronous Data Link Control, or SDLC'

Question:
What is used for communication between two devices on a WAN at layer 2?

Answer:
'High-level Data Link Control, or HDLC'

Question:
What is the protocol that encapsulates dissimilar protocols so that two different networks can communicate?

Answer:
'Point-to-Point Protocol, or PPP'

Question:
What is part of PPP and is the protocol that establishes, configures and maintains a connection?

Answer:
'Link Control Protocol, or LCP'

Question:
What is part of PPP and is the protocol that configures the network layer?

Answer:
'Network Control Protocol, or NCP'

Question:
What is an interface that works at layer 1, and allows ATM or frame relay to work on routers and multiplexers?

Answer:
'High-Speed Serial Interface, or HSSI'

Question:
What is the network used by regular phones with RJ-11 connections?

Answer:
'Public-Switched Telephone Network, or PSTN'

Question:
What is the protocol used by PSTN?

Answer:
'Signaling System 7, or SS7'

Communication and Network Security Domain

Question:
What occurs when a single transmission line is used to carry several types of communication categories?

Answer:
'multiservice access technologies'

Question:
What describes delays due to variable latency?

Answer:
'jitter'

Question:
What is a network that ensures a consistent bandwidth availability?

Answer:
'isochronous network'

Question:
What is a protocol that allows phone calls to be routed as IP packets?

Answer:
'Voice over IP, or VoIP'

Question:
What is the end-user software or hardware responsible for digitizing analog signals such as audio, and turning digital signals back into audio?

Answer:
'IP telephony device'

Question:
What is a VoIP component that routes packets and provides links to legacy and backup voice systems?

Answer:
'voice gateway'

Question:
What is a VoIP component that initiates and accepts calls?

Answer:
'call-processing manager'

Question:
What is a VoIP component that stores messages, forwards calls and provides direct lookup capabilities?

Answer:
'voicemail system'

Question:
What is a VoIP component that sets up and tears down conversation sessions?

Answer:
'Session Initiation Protocol , or SIP'

Communication and Network Security Domain

Question:
What is a VoIP component comprised of a user-facing software client?

Answer:
'User Agent Client, or UAC'

Question:
What is a VoIP server component that takes care of all routing and signaling?

Answer:
'User Agent Server, or UAS'

Question:
What is a layer 5 protocol that normally uses UDP to stream audio?

Answer:
'Real-time Transport Protocol, or RTP'

Question:
What provides the information RTP needs for QoS?

Answer:
'RTP Control Protocol, or RTCP'

Question:
What is the VoIP server that relays signals between the UAC and UAS?

Answer:
'proxy server'

Question:
What is the VoIP server that tracks the addresses of all participants?

Answer:
'registrar server'

Question:
What is the VoIP server that allows SIP devices to physically move without having to change identities?

Answer:
'redirect server'

Question:
What is an attack in which the attacker sends a voice message to a voicemail server?

Answer:
'SPam over Internet Telephony, or SPIT'

Question:
What is a device connected to a PSTN connection that allows a remote device to connect to the network?

Answer:
'modem, or modulator-demodulator'

Communication and Network Security Domain

Question:
What is the process of configuring a computer to automatically dial through a list of phone numbers in search of a modem?

Answer:
'war dialing'

Question:
What is the telephone company's neighborhood infrastructure?

Answer:
'Central Office, or CO'

Question:
What was the first truly digital connection over copper phone lines?

Answer:
'Integrated Services Digital Network, or ISDN'

Question:
What is an ISDN implementation of 2 x 64 Kbps B channels, and 1 x 16 Kbps D channel for 144 Kbps total?

Answer:
'Basic Rate Interface ISDN, or BRI'

Question:
What is an ISDN implementation of 23 x 64 Kbps B channels and 1 x 16 Kbps D channel for 1544 Mbps total?

Answer:
'Primary Rate Interface ISDN, or PRI'

Question:
What is an ISDN implementation used within a backbone, such as with ATM and SONET?

Answer:
'Broadband ISDN, or BISDN'

Question:
What is the successor to ISDN and operates at rates up to 52 Mbps?

Answer:
'Digital Subscriber Line, or DSL'

Question:
What is a DSL implementation delivering 768 Kbps down and 128 to 384 Kbps up?

Answer:
'Asymmetric DSL, or ADSL'

Question:
What is a DSL implementation delivering 192 to 1100 Kbps down and up?

Answer:
'Symmetric DSL, or SDSL'

Communication and Network Security Domain

Question:
What is a DSL implementation delivering T1 speeds?

Answer:
'High-bit-rate DSL, or HDSL'

Question:
What is a DSL implementation delivering 13 Mbps down and 2 Mbps up?

Answer:
'Very high-bit-rate DSL, or VDSL'

Question:
What is a DSL implementation in which the rates adjust to match the signal quality?

Answer:
'Rate-Adaptive DSL, or RADSL'

Question:
What is a specification that addresses how to provide high-speed data over existing cable TV networks?

Answer:
'Data-Over-Cable Service Interface Specification, or DOCSIS'

Question:
What is created when two trusted networks securely communicate over untrusted infrastructure?

Answer:
'Virtual Private Network, or VPN'

Question:
What is a protocol that tunnels PPP connections through an IP network, but only system-to-system?

Answer:
'Point-to-Point Tunneling Protocol, or PPTP'

Question:
What is the method through which PPTP encrypts data?

Answer:
'Generic Routing Encapsulation, or GRE'

Question:
What is a very insecure implementation of encryption over PPTP?

Answer:
'Microsoft Point-to-Point Encryption, or MPPE'

Question:
What is Cisco's PPP protocol?

Answer:
'Layer 2 Forwarding, or L2F'

Communication and Network Security Domain

Question:
What is a tunneling wrapper for L2F that can communicate over non-IP networks?

Answer:
'Layer 2 Tunneling Protocol, or L2TP'

Question:
What is a standard invented to provide security for the IP protocol?

Answer:
'Internet Protocol Security, or IPSec'

Question:
What is an IPSec protocol in which a hash provides integrity and system authentication, and protects from replay attacks?

Answer:
'Authentication Header, or AH'

Question:
What is an IPSec protocol which provides confidentiality, integrity and authentication through encryption?

Answer:
'Encapsulating Security Payload, or ESP'

Question:
What is an IPSec protocol which controls the management and storage of all possible connection variables?

Answer:
'Internet Security Association and Key Management Protocol, or ISAKMP'

Question:
What is an IPSec protocol that allows for key creation and secure exchange for ISAKMP?

Answer:
'Internet Key Exchange, or IKE'

Question:
What describes the parameters that a remote router has specified?

Answer:
'Security Association, or SA'

Question:
What is a protocol encryptor that NSA created based on IPSec?

Answer:
'High Assurance Internet Protocol Encryptor, or HAIPE'

Question:
What occurs when more than one security protocol is being used together in IPSec?

Answer:
'transport adjacency'

Communication and Network Security Domain

Question:
What occurs when wrapping a tunneled packet inside of another tunnel?

Answer:
'iterated tunneling'

Question:
What is the successor to SSL working at layer 5?

Answer:
'Transport Level Security, or TLS'

Question:
What is an implementation of TLS in which a single user connects to a web site acting as a gateway into more services?

Answer:
'TLS portal VPN'

Question:
What is an implementation of TLS in which a single browser connects to multiple non-web-based network services?

Answer:
'TLS tunnel VPN'

Question:
What is an authentication protocol that sends passwords in clear text?

Answer:
'Password Authentication Protocol, or PAP'

Question:
What is an authentication protocol in which the password is never sent, and randomly forces re-authentication?

Answer:
'Challenge Handshake Authentication Protocol, or CHAP'

Question:
What is Microsoft's version of CHAP?

Answer:
'MS-CHAP'

Question:
What is a framework that supports multiple authentication protocols?

Answer:
'Extensible Authentication Protocol, or EAP'

Question:
What is Cisco's wireless version of EAP?

Answer:
'Lightweight EAP, or LEAP'

Communication and Network Security Domain

Question:
What is an EAP protocol that is based on digital certificates?

Answer:
'EAP-TLS'

Question:
What is an EAP protocol that uses hashing and is weak?

Answer:
'EAP-MD5'

Question:
What is an EAP protocol that uses symmetric key mutual authentication?

Answer:
'EAP-PSK'

Question:
What is an EAP protocol that extends EAP-TLS?

Answer:
'EAP-TTLS'

Question:
What is an EAP protocol that uses asymmetric or symmetric mutual authentication?

Answer:
'EAP-IKE2'

Question:
What is an EAP protocol that is similar to EAP-TTLS but requires a server certificate?

Answer:
'PEAP-v0/EAP-MSCHAPv2'

Question:
What is an EAP protocol that is based on Cisco's Generic Token Card?

Answer:
'PEAPv1/EAP-GTC'

Question:
What is an EAP protocol that is Cisco's replacement for LEAP?

Answer:
'EAP-FAST'

Question:
What is an EAP protocol that is used for GSM cell SIM cards?

Answer:
'EAP-SIM'

Communication and Network Security Domain

Question:
What is an EAP protocol that is used for UMTS cell SIM cards?

Answer:
'EAP-AKA'

Question:
What is an EAP protocol that uses Kerberos with the Generic Security Service?

Answer:
'EAP-GSS'

Question:
What consists of electromagnetic signals varying both frequency and amplitude as they travel through air and space?

Answer:
'wireless network'

Question:
What is a spread spectrum technology in which only a single channel is used at any given time?

Answer:
'Frequency Hopping Spread Spectrum, or FHSS'

Question:
What is a spread spectrum technology in which extra information is encoded so that it can be rebuilt if a collision occurs?

Answer:
'Direct Sequence Spread Spectrum, or DSSS'

Question:
What is an extra bit added to each packet in DSSS to create redundancy?

Answer:
'DSSS chip'

Question:
What is the pattern of applying chips to data in DSSS?

Answer:
'DSSS chipping code'

Question:
What is a spread spectrum technology in which each channel is perpendicular to the next channel?

Answer:
'Orthogonal Frequency-Division Multiplexing, or OFDM'

Question:
What is created when a LAN is connected not with cables but wirelessly?

Answer:
'Wireless LAN, or WLAN'

Communication and Network Security Domain

Question:
What describes two computers talking to each other directly?

Answer:
'ad hoc WLAN'

Question:
What describes a network using a wireless access point?

Answer:
'stand-alone WLAN'

Question:
What is created when the access point is connected to another network?

Answer:
'infrastructure WLAN'

Question:
What is a specific frequency range on a WLAN?

Answer:
'WLAN channel'

Question:
What is a group of wireless devices communicating in infrastructure mode?

Answer:
'Basic Service Set, or BSS'

Question:
What is the name of a wireless BSS?

Answer:
'Service Set ID, or SSID'

Question:
What was the initial security provided for wireless networks, and was very poorly implemented?

Answer:
'Wired Equivalent Protocol, or WEP'

Question:
What is a WEP authentication mode requiring only the SSID, and supports no encryption?

Answer:
'Open System Authentication, or OSA'

Question:
What is a WEP authentication mode in which the access point and client possess a shared key, and use the CHAP method for authentication?

Answer:
'Shared Key Authentication, or SKA'

Communication and Network Security Domain

Question:
What is the successor to WEP that kept RC4, but added TKIP, EAP and 902.1X port authentication?

Answer:
'Wi-Fi Protected Access, or WPA'

Question:
What is the successor to WPA and added AES and CBC-MAC?

Answer:
'WPA2'

Question:
What is a term describing WPA2 relative to WPA?

Answer:
'robust security network'

Question:
What is the standard that replaced 802.11 when WPA came out?

Answer:
'802.11i'

Question:
What implements port-based network access and mutual authentication?

Answer:
'802.1X'

Question:
What ensures that a user cannot make a full network connection until authentication has properly happened?

Answer:
'port-based network access'

Question:
What is the wireless client for 802.1x authentication?

Answer:
'802.1x supplicant'

Question:
What is the access point for 802.1x authentication?

Answer:
'802.1x authenticator'

Question:
What is usually implemented using RADIUS for 802.1x authentication?

Answer:
'802.1x authentication server'

Communication and Network Security Domain

Question:
What occurs when both devices authenticate to each other in 802.1x authentication?

Answer:
'802.1x mutual authentication'

Question:
What is the standard that defines support for MANs?

Answer:
'802.16'

Question:
What is a laser system that transmits light across open air requiring a clear line of sight?

Answer:
'Free-Space Optics, or FSO'

Question:
What uses FSO to provide a point-to-point connection?

Answer:
'optical wireless'

Question:
What is a wireless personal network used for short-distance communication?

Answer:
'WPAN'

Question:
What implements a WPAN over 2.4 Ghz for 100 meters?

Answer:
'802.15.4'

Question:
What is the most popular 802.15.4 protocol, providing 250 Kbps and 128-bit symmetric encryption?

Answer:
'Zigbee'

Question:
What is the standard that uses the 2.5 Ghz spectrum and provides 1 to 3 Mbps speed up to 100 meters away?

Answer:
'Bluetooth'

Question:
What is an attack in which an unsolicited message is sent to a Bluetooth device?

Answer:
'bluejacking'

Communication and Network Security Domain

Question:
What is an attack in which data is retrieved from the victim's device via Bluetooth?

Answer:
'bluesnarking'

Question:
What is a communications relay that is placed into a low-earth orbit?

Answer:
'satellite'

Question:
What is the term for the area visible to a satellite?

Answer:
'satellite footprint'

Question:
What links a remote satellite site to a service provider?

Answer:
'Very Small Aperture Terminal or VSAT'

Question:
What is a wireless network divided into cells usually less than 1 mile in diameter?

Answer:
'cellular network'

Question:
What is a multiple access technology that divides the frequency range into sub-bands, with each assigned to a single phone call?

Answer:
'Frequency Division Multiple Access or FDMA'

Question:
What is a multiple access technology that divides FDMA sub-bands into time slots, so that multiple calls can share them?

Answer:
'Time Division Multiple Access or TDMA'

Question:
What is a technology that supported both voice and data?

Answer:
'Personal Communications Service or PCS'

Question:
What is a multiple access technology that added 3G speeds and packet switching by assigning a unique code to each call or data stream?

Answer:
'Code Division Multiple Access or CDMA'

Communication and Network Security Domain

Question:
What is a technology added to SMS to allow media messaging?

Answer:
'Multimedia Messaging Service or MMS'

Question:
What is a multiple access technology that combines FDMA and TDMA?

Answer:
'Orthogonal Frequency Division Multiple Access or OFDMA'

Question:
What is a layer 2 encryption process?

Answer:
'link encryption or online encryption'

Question:
What is encryption that happens at the application level?

Answer:
'end-to-end encryption'

Question:
What is a specification on how systems should handle binary email attachments?

Answer:
'Multipurpose Internet Mail Extension or MIME'

Question:
What is designed to encrypt mail, and was the first widely-adopted public key encryption program?

Answer:
'Pretty Good Privacy or PGP'

Question:
What is a file in PGP containing a list of public keys that have been received?

Answer:
'key ring'

Question:
What is a connectionless protocol used by browsers, in which everything is sent in clear text?

Answer:
'Hypertext Transfer Protocol or HTTP'

Question:
What is HTTP encrypted by SSL or TLS?

Answer:
'HTTP Secure or HTTPS'

Communication and Network Security Domain

Question:
What are 2 PKI-based encryption technologies?

Answer:
'SSL and TLS'

Question:
What is an attack that proved that SSL v3.0 was flawed?

Answer:
'Padding Oracle On Downgraded Legacy Encryption, or POODLE'

Question:
What is essentially SSL v3.0 but POODLE-proof, and is no longer considered secure?

Answer:
'TLS v1.0'

Question:
What is the current version of TLS and is considered to be secure?

Answer:
'TLS v1.2'

Question:
What is a file that a browser stores on the local computer's hard drive?

Answer:
'cookie'

Question:
What is a tunneling mechanism that allows remote users to execute commands, securely transfer files and redirect ports?

Answer:
'Secure Shell or SSH'

Question:
What is an attack that prevents a system or service from being available for use?

Answer:
'Denial of Service or DoS'

Question:
What is an attack that crashes an OS by sending a single ICMP Echo Request greater than the maximum size of 65,536 bytes?

Answer:
'Ping of Death'

Question:
What is an attack in which computer is sent so much traffic that it is unable to respond to new requests?

Answer:
'flooding'

Communication and Network Security Domain

Question:
What is an attack where SYN packets are sent, but the corresponding ACK never follows?

Answer:
'SYN flood'

Question:
What is a network of compromised computers participating in a single DoS attack?

Answer:
'Distributed Denial of Service or DDoS'

Question:
What is the centralized authority controlling a botnet?

Answer:
'Command and Control or C&C'

Question:
What is a computer that has malware installed that carries out C&C instructions?

Answer:
'zombie'

Question:
What is another name for a zombie?

Answer:
'bot'

Question:
What is the collection of bots reporting to the same C&C?

Answer:
'botnet'

Question:
What is malware that locks some resource and blackmails victims into paying a fee to unlock it?

Answer:
'ransomware'

Question:
What is the ability to eavesdrop on passing network packets?

Answer:
'sniffing'

Question:
What is the mode a NIC must be put into in order to enable sniffing?

Answer:
'promiscuous mode'

Communication and Network Security Domain

Question:
What occurs when user is forced to unknowingly use a malicious DNS server?

Answer:
'DNS Hijacking'

Question:
What is an attack that modifies the DNS settings a computer uses to point to the attacker's own server?

Answer:
'host based attack'

Question:
What is an attack in which the attacker redirects DNS traffic to his own server using tactics such as ARP table poisoning?

Answer:
'network based attack'

Question:
What is an attack in which the attacker convinces a legitimate DNS server that his own DNS server is authoritative for the victim domain?

Answer:
'server based attack'

Question:
What is an attack in which visiting a single page results in malware being downloaded and installed?

Answer:
'drive-by download attack'

Communication and Network Security Domain

Terms

Question:
What is 'telecommunications'?

Answer:
'telecommunications' is the transmission of data through analog, digital or wireless mediums.

Question:
What is the 'Open Systems Interconnection Reference Model, or OSI'?

Answer:
The 'Open Systems Interconnection Reference Model, or OSI' is a model that describe how network communication takes place.

Question:
What is a 'network protocol'?

Answer:
A 'network protocol' is a set of rules that systems use to communicate across a network.

Question:
What is 'layer 7, or Application Layer'?

Answer:
'layer 7, or Application Layer' is the OSI layer that contains high-level networking protocols.

Question:
What is 'layer 6, or Presentation Layer'?

Answer:
'layer 6, or Presentation Layer' is the OSI layer that wraps more specific content into a generic wrapper.

Question:
What is 'layer 5, or Session Layer'?

Answer:
'layer 5, or Session Layer' is the OSI layer that establishes a session between the same application running on two different computers.

Question:
What is 'simplex'?

Answer:
'simplex' is a communication mode in which parties can communicate in one direction only.

Question:
What is 'half-duplex'?

Answer:
'half-duplex' is a communication mode in which parties can communicate in both directions, but one at a time.

Communication and Network Security Domain

Question:
What is 'full-duplex'?

Answer:
'full-duplex' is a communication mode in which parties can communicate in both directions simultaneously.

Question:
What is 'remote procedure call, or RPC'?

Answer:
'remote procedure call, or RPC' is how inter-process communication happens.

Question:
What is a 'secure RPC, or SRPC'?

Answer:
A 'secure RPC, or SRPC' is RPC coupled with authentication.

Question:
What is 'layer 4, or Transport Layer'?

Answer:
'layer 4, or Transport Layer' is the OSI layer that ensures data arrives intact.

Question:
What is 'layer 3, or Network Layer'?

Answer:
'layer 3, or Network Layer' is the OSI layer that ensures the packet gets to the correct location.

Question:
What is 'layer 2, or Data Link Layer'?

Answer:
'layer 2, or Data Link Layer' is the OSI layer that translates bits into voltage levels for the physical layer.

Question:
What is 'Logical Link Control, or LLC'?

Answer:
'Logical Link Control, or LLC' is the OSI layer 2 sublayer that provides multiplexing, flow control and error management.

Question:
What is 'Media Access Control, or MAC'?

Answer:
'Media Access Control, or MAC' is the OSI layer 2 sublayer that decides the voltages to use.

Question:
What is 'layer 1, or Physical Layer'?

Answer:
'layer 1, or Physical Layer' is the OSI layer that generates electrical signals.

Communication and Network Security Domain

Question:
What is 'enhanced performance architecture, or EPA'?

Answer:
'enhanced performance architecture, or EPA' is a simple 3-layer model for SCADA.

Question:
What is 'Distributed Network Protocol 3, or NDP3'?

Answer:
'Distributed Network Protocol 3, or NDP3' is the protocol providing network connectivity for SCADA.

Question:
What is the 'CAN Bus'?

Answer:
The 'CAN Bus' is the network backbone found in vehicles.

Question:
What is the 'TCP/IP Model'?

Answer:
The 'TCP/IP Model' is an alternative network model that can map to OSI.

Question:
What is 'layer 4, or Application Layer'?

Answer:
'layer 4, or Application Layer' is the TCP/IP model layer that maps to OSI layers 7 through 5.

Question:
What is 'layer 3, or Host-to-Host Layer'?

Answer:
'layer 3, or Host-to-Host Layer' is the TCP/IP model layer that maps to OSI Transport Layer 4.

Question:
What is 'layer 2, or Internet Layer'?

Answer:
'layer 2, or Internet Layer' is the TCP/IP model layer that maps to OSI Network Layer 3.

Question:
What is 'layer 1, or Network Access Layer'?

Answer:
'layer 1, or Network Access Layer' is the TCP/IP model layer that maps to OSI layers 2-1.

Question:
What is the 'transport control protocol, or TCP'?

Answer:
The 'transport control protocol, or TCP' is a common connection-oriented protocol operating at OSI layer 4.

Communication and Network Security Domain

Question:
What is 'handshaking'?

Answer:
'handshaking' occurs when two computers negotiate how the remaining communication will take place.

Question:
What is the 'user datagram protocol, or UDP'?

Answer:
The 'user datagram protocol, or UDP' is a common connectionless protocol operating at OSI layer 4.

Question:
What is 'data encapsulation'?

Answer:
'data encapsulation' occurs when each layer wraps the data from the layer above.

Question:
What is 'SYN flood'?

Answer:
'SYN flood' is an attack where the attacker sends SYN but never responds with ACK.

Question:
What is 'TCP session hijacking'?

Answer:
'TCP session hijacking' is an attack where the attacker guesses the TCP sequence numbers and injects their own packets.

Question:
What is 'ECHO'?

Answer:
'ECHO' is a common service found on port 7.

Question:
What is 'FTP'?

Answer:
'FTP' is a common service found on ports 20 and 21.

Question:
What is 'SSH'?

Answer:
'SSH' is a common service found on port 22.

Question:
What is 'Telnet'?

Answer:
'Telnet' is a common service found on port 23.

Communication and Network Security Domain

Question:
What is 'SMTP'?

Answer:
'SMTP' is a common service found on port 25.

Question:
What is 'DNS'?

Answer:
'DNS' is a common service found on port 53.

Question:
What is 'HTTP'?

Answer:
'HTTP' is a common service found on port 80.

Question:
What is 'POP3'?

Answer:
'POP3' is a common service found on port 110.

Question:
What is 'SNMP'?

Answer:
'SNMP' is a common service found on ports 161 and 162.

Question:
What is 'registered ports'?

Answer:
'registered ports' are designated ports 1,024 through 49,151.

Question:
What is 'dynamic ports'?

Answer:
'dynamic ports' are designated ports 49,152 through 65,535.

Question:
What is 'classless interdomain routing, or CIDR, or Supernetting'?

Answer:
'classless interdomain routing, or CIDR, or Supernetting' defines IP addresses that can be reused within private networks.

Question:
What is a 'subnet'?

Answer:
A 'subnet' are logical subdivisions within the network created by further segmenting host segments.

Communication and Network Security Domain

Question:
What is a 'subnet mask'?

Answer:
A 'subnet mask' defines a subnet.

Question:
What is 'classful, or classical'?

Answer:
'classful, or classical' are the types of IP addresses used with normal subnet masks.

Question:
What is the 'time to live, or TTL'?

Answer:
The 'time to live, or TTL' is a flag that restricts how long a packet bounces around a network.

Question:
What is 'packet fragmentation'?

Answer:
'packet fragmentation' occurs when large packets are broken into smaller packets in order to communicate with hosts that can't handle the larger packets.

Question:
What is 'iPV6, or IP next generation, or IPng'?

Answer:
'iPV6, or IP next generation, or IPng' is the newest version of the Internet Protocol.

Question:
What is 'automatic tunneling'?

Answer:
'automatic tunneling' allows routers to automatically tunnel through IPv4.

Question:
What is '6to4'?

Answer:
'6to4' is a type of automatic tunneling that wraps outgoing IPv6 packets in well-known IPv4 anycast addresses, and incoming IPv4 address data in IPv6 packets.

Question:
What is 'Teredo'?

Answer:
'Teredo' is a type of automatic tunneling that uses UDP encapsulation so that NAT is not affected.

Question:
What is 'intra-site automatic tunneling addressing protocol, or ISATAP'?

Answer:
'intra-site automatic tunneling addressing protocol, or ISATAP' sees the IPv4 network as a virtual IPv6 local link.

Communication and Network Security Domain

Question:
What is 'intersite'?

Answer:
'intersite' is a mechanism to connect two different networks.

Question:
What is 'intrasite'?

Answer:
'intrasite' is a term that represents communication within a network.

Question:
What is 'IEEE 8021AE, or MACSec'?

Answer:
'IEEE 8021AE, or MACSec' is a protocol that protects MAC-layer traffic by providing CIA.

Question:
What is 'MACSec security entity, or SecY'?

Answer:
'MACSec security entity, or SecY' is a Layer 2 device configured with MACSec.

Question:
What is 'IEEE 802.1AR'?

Answer:
'IEEE 802.1AR' is the standard that assigns and binds unique identifiers for SecY devices.

Question:
What is 'IEEE 802.1AF'?

Answer:
'IEEE 802.1AF' is the standard that manages session keys used between SecY.

Question:
What is the 'Extensible Authentication Protocol Transport Layer, or EAP-TLS'?

Answer:
The 'Extensible Authentication Protocol Transport Layer, or EAP-TLS' is the combination of 802.1AE, 802.1AR, 802.1AF and RADIUS.

Question:
What is 'converged protocols'?

Answer:
'converged protocols' occurs when two separate protocols become one.

Question:
What is 'multiprotocol label switching, or MPLS'?

Answer:
'multiprotocol label switching, or MPLS' is a protocol that operates at layers 2 and 3, and is referred to as 2.5 protocol.

Communication and Network Security Domain

Question:
What is 'fiber channel over Ethernet, or FCoE'?

Answer:
'fiber channel over Ethernet, or FCoE' is a converged protocol between fiber and Ethernet.

Question:
What is 'internet small computer system interface, or iSCSI'?

Answer:
'internet small computer system interface, or iSCSI' is a converged protocol allowing SCSI to travel over a network.

Question:
What is 'IP convergence'?

Answer:
'IP convergence' is a protocol that transitions to ride on top of IP.

Question:
What is a 'signal'?

Answer:
A 'signal' is any way to communicate information.

Question:
What is a 'signal wave'?

Answer:
A 'signal wave' is communication by varying amplitude and/or frequency of a signal.

Question:
What is 'amplitude'?

Answer:
'amplitude' is a value that measures the height of a signal wave peak.

Question:
What is 'frequency'?

Answer:
'frequency' is a value that measures the amount of space between peaks in a signal wave.

Question:
What is 'AM'?

Answer:
'AM' is the term for amplitude modulation.

Question:
What is 'FM'?

Answer:
'FM' is the term for frequency modulation.

Communication and Network Security Domain

Question:
What is an 'analog signal'?

Answer:
An 'analog signal' is a type of signal where information is based on an infinite degrees of AM or FM.

Question:
What is a 'digital signal'?

Answer:
A 'digital signal' is a type of signal where information is based on two discrete ranges of AM or FM - '0' or '1'.

Question:
What is 'bandwidth'?

Answer:
'bandwidth' measures the number of electrical pulses that can be sent over a signal within a given time period.

Question:
What is 'data throughput'?

Answer:
'data throughput' measures the number of bits that can be sent and received over a given period of time.

Question:
What is 'synchronous communication'?

Answer:
'synchronous communication' occurs when two devices communicate based on exact timing.

Question:
What is 'asynchronous communication'?

Answer:
'asynchronous communication' occurs when two devices communicate based on start and stop signals.

Question:
What is 'baseband'?

Answer:
'baseband' is the term used to describe an entire channel being in-use at once.

Question:
What is 'broadband'?

Answer:
'broadband' is the term used to describe a channel that has been split up into sub-channels.

Question:
What is 'coaxial cable'?

Answer:
'coaxial cable' is a type of cabling usually found in TV cable, and consists of a single copper wire.

Communication and Network Security Domain

Question:
What is 'twisted-Pair cable'?

Answer:
'twisted-Pair cable' is the term describing a cable with pairs of thin copper wires twisted around each other wrapped in an outer jacket.

Question:
What is 'shielded twisted pair, or STP'?

Answer:
'shielded twisted pair, or STP' is comprised of wires, each wrapped in an outer foil shielding.

Question:
What is 'unshielded twisted pair, or UTP'?

Answer:
'unshielded twisted pair, or UTP' is comprised of wires that do not have an outer foil shielding.

Question:
What is 'category 1 Ethernet cabling'?

Answer:
'category 1 Ethernet cabling' is the type of Ethernet cabling supporting voice grade up to 1Mbs.

Question:
What is 'category 2 Ethernet cabling'?

Answer:
'category 2 Ethernet cabling' is the type of Ethernet cabling supporting up to 4Mbs.

Question:
What is 'category 3 Ethernet cabling'?

Answer:
'category 3 Ethernet cabling' is the type of Ethernet cabling supporting 10 Mbps.

Question:
What is 'category 4 Ethernet cabling'?

Answer:
'category 4 Ethernet cabling' is the type of Ethernet cabling supporting 16 Mbps.

Question:
What is 'category 5 Ethernet cabling'?

Answer:
'category 5 Ethernet cabling' is the type of Ethernet cabling supporting 100 Mbps.

Question:
What is 'category 6 Ethernet cabling'?

Answer:
'category 6 Ethernet cabling' is the type of Ethernet cabling supporting 1 Gbps.

Communication and Network Security Domain

Question:
What is 'category 7 Ethernet cabling'?

Answer:
'category 7 Ethernet cabling' is the type of Ethernet cabling supporting 10 Gbps.

Question:
What is a 'fiber-optic cable'?

Answer:
A 'fiber-optic cable' is a type of cabling using glass to carry light signals, and can travel long distances.

Question:
What is a 'fiber-optic light source'?

Answer:
A 'fiber-optic light source' is the component that converts electrical signal into a light signal in fiber-optic cables.

Question:
What is a 'fiber cable'?

Answer:
A 'fiber cable' is the component that carries the light signal in a fiber-optic cable.

Question:
What is 'single mode'?

Answer:
'single mode' is the fiber cable mode that has a small glass core, provides less bandwidth, but delivers data over a longer distance.

Question:
What is 'multimode'?

Answer:
'multimode' is the fiber cable mode that requires a larger glass core, provides higher bandwidth, but only over shorter distances.

Question:
What is a 'light detector'?

Answer:
A 'light detector' is the component that converts the light signal back into an electrical signal in a fiber-optic cable.

Question:
What is 'noise'?

Answer:
'noise' is any undesired addition to a source signal that can interfere with the receiver turning it back into the original information.

Question:
What is 'attenuation'?

Answer:
'attenuation' occurs when signal is lost due to the distance travelled.

Communication and Network Security Domain

Question:
What is 'crosstalk'?

Answer:
'crosstalk' occurs when radiation from one cable interferes with the signal in another.

Question:
What is 'plenum space'?

Answer:
'plenum space' are spaces for cable runs above lowered ceilings or beneath raised floors.

Question:
What is 'network topology'?

Answer:
'network topology' describes how computers are arranged relative to each other within a network.

Question:
What is 'physical topology'?

Answer:
'physical topology' describes how cables are laid out and connected to each computer.

Question:
What is 'logical topology'?

Answer:
'logical topology' describes how computers communicate over physical cabling, including wireless.

Question:
What is 'ring topology'?

Answer:
'ring topology' is a network topology in which all nodes are physically connected in a ring.

Question:
What is 'bus topology'?

Answer:
'bus topology' is a network topology in which a single cable runs the entire length of the network.

Question:
What is 'linear bus topology'?

Answer:
'linear bus topology' is a network topology in which all nodes attach directly to the bus.

Question:
What is 'tree bus topology'?

Answer:
'tree bus topology' is a network topology in which branches connect directly to the bus, with nodes connected to branches.

Communication and Network Security Domain

Question:
What is 'star topology'?

Answer:
'star topology' is a network topology in which all nodes are connected directly to a central device.

Question:
What is 'full mesh topology'?

Answer:
'full mesh topology' is a network topology in which all nodes are connected directly to each other.

Question:
What is 'partial mesh topology'?

Answer:
'partial mesh topology' is a network topology in which any combination of other topologies, usually star, are used.

Question:
What is 'media access technologies'?

Answer:
'media access technologies' is a term describing anything that happens at Layer 2, specifically within the MAC sublayer.

Question:
What is 'token passing'?

Answer:
'token passing' is a media access technology in which only the computer possessing the 24-bit token can talk.

Question:
What is 'carrier sense multiple access, or CSMA'?

Answer:
'carrier sense multiple access, or CSMA' is a media access technology used by Ethernet networks.

Question:
What is a 'collision'?

Answer:
A 'collision' occurs when two or more electronic signals collide, resulting in corruption of both.

Question:
What is a 'carrier'?

Answer:
A 'carrier' is the term for a frame transmitted across an Ethernet network.

Question:
What is 'carrier sense multiple access with collision detection, or CSMA/CD'?

Answer:
'carrier sense multiple access with collision detection, or CSMA/CD' is a flavor of CSMA in which two computers speak, recognize a collision, and then back off; used by Ethernet.

Communication and Network Security Domain

Question:
What is 'carrier sense multiple access with collision avoidance, or CSMA/CA'?

Answer:
'carrier sense multiple access with collision avoidance, or CSMA/CA' is a flavor of CSMA in which a computer announces it is about to speak, and all other computers back off; used by Wi-Fi.

Question:
What is a 'collision domain'?

Answer:
A 'collision domain' is the term describing a network segmented with layer 2 switches.

Question:
What is a 'broadcast domain'?

Answer:
A 'broadcast domain' is the term describing a network segmented with layer 3 routers.

Question:
What is 'polling'?

Answer:
'polling' is a technique used with mainframes, in which a server instructs a client when to communicate if it wishes to.

Question:
What is 'contention-based technology'?

Answer:
'contention-based technology' is a technology in which all resources use the same shared medium.

Question:
What is 'Ethernet, or IEEE 802.3'?

Answer:
'Ethernet, or IEEE 802.3' is the standard that is contention-based, uses collision and broadcast domains, employs CSMA/CD, and works with coaxial, UTP or fiber.

Question:
What is 'Fast Ethernet'?

Answer:
'Fast Ethernet' is a common name for 100Base-TX.

Question:
What is 'Gigabit Ethernet'?

Answer:
'Gigabit Ethernet' is a common name for 1000Base-T.

Question:
What is 'IEEE 802.5'?

Answer:
'IEEE 802.5' is the standard for Token Ring.

Communication and Network Security Domain

Question:
What is an 'active monitor'?

Answer:
An 'active monitor' is a process that removes frames that are continuously circulating.

Question:
What is 'beaconing'?

Answer:
'beaconing' describes a frame being sent out when a computer encounters a problem.

Question:
What is 'fiber distributed data interface, or FDDI'?

Answer:
'fiber distributed data interface, or FDDI' is a media access technology that uses token passing on fiber backbones with two rings for redundancy.

Question:
What is 'IEEE 802.4'?

Answer:
'IEEE 802.4' is the standard for FDDI.

Question:
What is a 'single-attachment station, or SAS'?

Answer:
A 'single-attachment station, or SAS' is an FDDI device that attaches to only one ring through a concentrator.

Question:
What is a 'dual-attachment station, or DAS'?

Answer:
A 'dual-attachment station, or DAS' is an FDDI device that attaches to both rings through a concentrator.

Question:
What is a 'single-attachment concentrator, or SAC'?

Answer:
A 'single-attachment concentrator, or SAC' is an FDDI device that attaches an SAS device to the primary ring.

Question:
What is a 'dual-attachment concentrator, or DAC'?

Answer:
A 'dual-attachment concentrator, or DAC' is an FDDI device that attaches DAS, SAS and SAC to both rings.

Question:
What is 'FDDI-2'?

Answer:
'FDDI-2' is an enhancement to FDDI that added QoS.

Communication and Network Security Domain

Question:
What is the 'Copper Distributed Data Interface, or CDDI'?

Answer:
The 'Copper Distributed Data Interface, or CDDI' is a media access technology just like FDDI but over UTP and meant for LANs.

Question:
What is 'unicast'?

Answer:
'unicast' is the normal method of communication with a single computer.

Question:
What is 'multicast'?

Answer:
'multicast' is communication with a group of computers.

Question:
What is 'broadcast'?

Answer:
'broadcast' is communication with all computers.

Question:
What is the 'Internet Group Management Protocol, or IGMP'?

Answer:
The 'Internet Group Management Protocol, or IGMP' is the name of the group which advances multicasting protocols.

Question:
What is 'IGMP version 2'?

Answer:
'IGMP version 2' is the version of IGMP that added the ability to be removed from a multicast group.

Question:
What is 'IGMP version 3'?

Answer:
'IGMP version 3' is the version of IGMP that allows recipients to specify the multicast source.

Question:
What is the 'Address Resolution Protocol, or ARP'?

Answer:
The 'Address Resolution Protocol, or ARP' is a protocol that, given a MAC address, returns the IP address.

Question:
What is a 'Network Interface Card, or NIC'?

Answer:
A 'Network Interface Card, or NIC' is a device that sends and receives signals directly from the physical medium.

Communication and Network Security Domain

Question:
What is a 'Media Access Control address, or MAC address'?

Answer:
A 'Media Access Control address, or MAC address' is a 48-bit globally unique identifier assigned by the manufacturer to NICs.

Question:
What is 'ARP table cache poisoning'?

Answer:
'ARP table cache poisoning' is an attack in which a device masquerades as the owner of a MAC address.

Question:
What is the 'Dynamic Host Configuration Protocol, or DHCP'?

Answer:
The 'Dynamic Host Configuration Protocol, or DHCP' is a service that assigns IP addresses from a pool in real-time.

Question:
What is a 'static IP address'?

Answer:
A 'static IP address' is assigned to devices when they are manually configured with an IP address.

Question:
What is a 'dynamic IP address'?

Answer:
A 'dynamic IP address' is assigned to devices from a DHCP server.

Question:
What is a 'DHCP client'?

Answer:
A 'DHCP client' is a device that receives a dynamic IP address.

Question:
What is a 'DHCP lease'?

Answer:
A 'DHCP lease' is the value that dictates how long a client can keep a dynamic IP address.

Question:
What is 'DHCP snooping'?

Answer:
'DHCP snooping' is a security precaution that allows DHCPDISCOVER requests only from trusted devices based on the device's MAC address.

Question:
What is the 'Reverse Address Resolution Protocol, or RARP'?

Answer:
The 'Reverse Address Resolution Protocol, or RARP' is a protocol that, given an IP address, returns the MAC address.

Communication and Network Security Domain

Question:
What is the 'Bootstrap Protocol, or BOOTP'?

Answer:
The 'Bootstrap Protocol, or BOOTP' is used by a client to retrieve the default gateway and DNS server IP addresses dynamically.

Question:
What is the 'Internet Control Message Protocol, or ICMP'?

Answer:
The 'Internet Control Message Protocol, or ICMP' is a protocol used to test connectivity, provide status updates and report errors.

Question:
What is 'ICMP tunneling'?

Answer:
'ICMP tunneling' is an attack in which the attacker uses an ICMP packet to send data.

Question:
What is the 'Simple Network Management Protocol, or SMNP'?

Answer:
The 'Simple Network Management Protocol, or SMNP' is a protocol allowing a unified method to manage all of the devices on a network.

Question:
What is an 'SNMP manager'?

Answer:
An 'SNMP manager' is SNMP software that runs on a central server.

Question:
What is an 'SNMP agent'?

Answer:
An 'SNMP agent' is SNMP software that runs on network devices.

Question:
What is an 'SNMP trap'?

Answer:
An 'SNMP trap' is an unrequested SNMP message an agent sends to a manager.

Question:
What is the 'Management Information Base, or MIB'?

Answer:
The 'Management Information Base, or MIB' is a small database of objects that an SNMP agent keeps track of.

Question:
What is an 'SNMP community'?

Answer:
An 'SNMP community' includes the SNMP manager and its agents.

Communication and Network Security Domain

Question:
What is an 'SNMP community string'?

Answer:
An 'SNMP community string' is the term for an SNMP community password.

Question:
What is an 'SNMP read password'?

Answer:
An 'SNMP read password' is the type of SNMP password that provides the ability to read an agent's MIB.

Question:
What is an 'SNMP read-write password'?

Answer:
An 'SNMP read-write password' is the type of SNMP password that provides the ability to both read and update an agent's MIB.

Question:
What is the 'Domain Name Service, or DNS'?

Answer:
The 'Domain Name Service, or DNS' is a service that translates domain names into an IP address.

Question:
What is a 'DNS resolver'?

Answer:
A 'DNS resolver' is the name of local process that carries out DNS services.

Question:
What is a 'recursive query'?

Answer:
A 'recursive query' is used if an address is not found locally, but is forwarded to the next-level DNS.

Question:
What is a 'non-recursive query'?

Answer:
A 'non-recursive query' is a type of query that is not forwarded if the information is not found locally.

Question:
What is the 'HOSTS file'?

Answer:
The 'HOSTS file' is a text file containing a list of domain names and matching IP addresses.

Question:
What is 'DNS Security, or DNSSEC'?

Answer:
'DNS Security, or DNSSEC' is a standard that implements authentication and encryption around the DNS request and resolution exchange.

Communication and Network Security Domain

Question:
What is 'URL hiding'?

Answer:
'URL hiding' occurs when a hyperlink containing non-threatening text has an underlying link to a site where an attack is launched.

Question:
What is 'split DNS'?

Answer:
'split DNS' is implemented when using two DNS servers - one for external and another for internal entries.

Question:
What is 'cyber squatting'?

Answer:
'cyber squatting' is the act of grabbing an attractive domain name and reselling it for a profit.

Question:
What is 'domain grabbing'?

Answer:
'domain grabbing' is the act of purchasing a recently-expired domain name and charging a hefty price to get it back.

Question:
What is the 'Simple Mail Transfer Protocol, or SMTP'?

Answer:
The 'Simple Mail Transfer Protocol, or SMTP' is the protocol all mail servers use for sending email messages.

Question:
What is 'SMTP authentication, or SMTP-AUTH'?

Answer:
'SMTP authentication, or SMTP-AUTH' is an extension to SMTP that added authentication.

Question:
What is the 'Post Office Protocol, or POP'?

Answer:
The 'Post Office Protocol, or POP' is used to download email messages from an email server, but deletes each message from the server.

Question:
What is 'POP version 3, or POP3'?

Answer:
'POP version 3, or POP3' is the protocol version that added SASL support to POP.

Question:
What is 'Simple Authentication and Security Layer, or SASL'?

Answer:
'Simple Authentication and Security Layer, or SASL' is a protocol-independent method for authentication.

Communication and Network Security Domain

Question:
What is 'Internet Message Access Protocol, or IMAP'?

Answer:
'Internet Message Access Protocol, or IMAP' is a replacement for POP3 that allows messages to stay on the server and supports server-based searches.

Question:
What is 'SMTP relay'?

Answer:
'SMTP relay' is used by SMTP for server-to-server communication, and is often abused by spammers.

Question:
What is 'email spoofing'?

Answer:
'email spoofing' is an attack in which emails appear to be coming from a legitimate source by manipulating the email header.

Question:
What is the 'Sender Policy Framework, or SPF'?

Answer:
The 'Sender Policy Framework, or SPF' is a technique that detects bogus incoming messages from other servers.

Question:
What is 'phishing'?

Answer:
'phishing' is an email-based social engineering attack with the goal of getting a victim to click a link.

Question:
What is 'spear phishing'?

Answer:
'spear phishing' is a phishing attack targeting a specific user.

Question:
What is 'whaling attack'?

Answer:
'whaling attack' is a spear fishing attack targeting a 'big fish' in an organization.

Question:
What is 'Network Address Translation, or NAT'?

Answer:
'Network Address Translation, or NAT' is a technology that increases the number of available IP addresses by creating a private range of addresses.

Question:
What is a 'private IP address'?

Answer:
A 'private IP address' is an IP address that is not routable on a public network.

Communication and Network Security Domain

Question:
What is 'NATing'?

Answer:
'NATing' is the act of translating a network address from private to public, and back again.

Question:
What is 'static IP mapping'?

Answer:
'static IP mapping' is a technique in which a specific private IP address is mapped to a dedicated IP public address.

Question:
What is 'dynamic IP mapping'?

Answer:
'dynamic IP mapping' is a technique in which a specific private IP address is mapped to a single public IP address pulled from a pre-defined pool of public addresses.

Question:
What is 'Port Address Translation, or PAT'?

Answer:
'Port Address Translation, or PAT' is used when a single public IP address is mapped to multiple private IP addresses by assigning a port to each private address.

Question:
What is 'stateful NAT'?

Answer:
'stateful NAT' is a NATing technique in which the translation process must maintain a list of public and private mappings.

Question:
What is an 'autonomous system, or AS'?

Answer:
An 'autonomous system, or AS' is a small network communicating within a larger network.

Question:
What is the 'static routing protocol'?

Answer:
The 'static routing protocol' is a routing protocol that is manually configured to route packets through a specific path.

Question:
What is the 'dynamic routing protocol'?

Answer:
The 'dynamic routing protocol' is a routing protocol that discovers the best path to send packets.

Question:
What is the 'distance-vector routing protocol'?

Answer:
The 'distance-vector routing protocol' is a routing protocol that looks at distance and vector only.

Communication and Network Security Domain

Question:
What is the 'link-state routing protocol'?

Answer:
The 'link-state routing protocol' is a routing protocol that looks at distance, packet size, link speed, latency, traffic load and historical reliability.

Question:
What is 'route flapping'?

Answer:
'route flapping' occurs when the availability of routers is constantly changing within an AS.

Question:
What is the 'route distance'?

Answer:
The 'route distance' is a term that represents the number of route hops.

Question:
What is the 'route vector'?

Answer:
The 'route vector' is a term representing the direction of a link.

Question:
What is 'interior routing protocols'?

Answer:
'interior routing protocols' are routing protocols that operate inside of a network.

Question:
What is the 'Routing Information Protocol, or RIP'?

Answer:
The 'Routing Information Protocol, or RIP' is a very slow distance vector protocol.

Question:
What is 'Open Shortest Path First, or OSPF'?

Answer:
'Open Shortest Path First, or OSPF' is the name of a link-state protocol that supports a backbone link connecting subnets.

Question:
What is the 'Interior Gateway Routing Protocol, or IGRP'?

Answer:
The 'Interior Gateway Routing Protocol, or IGRP' is a Cisco distance-vector protocol that uses 5 metrics (bandwidth, latency, load, reliability and MTU) instead of the usual distance and vector.

Question:
What is the 'Enhanced Interior Gateway Routing Protocol, or EIGRP'?

Answer:
The 'Enhanced Interior Gateway Routing Protocol, or EIGRP' is a successor to IGRP, and adds faster router table updates.

Communication and Network Security Domain

Question:
What is the 'Virtual Router Redundancy Protocol, or VRRP'?

Answer:
The 'Virtual Router Redundancy Protocol, or VRRP' is a router protocol that supports a primary and failover router to eliminate a single point of failure.

Question:
What is 'Intermediate System to Intermediate System, or IS-IS'?

Answer:
'Intermediate System to Intermediate System, or IS-IS' is a link-state protocol that is vendor-neutral and does not use IP addresses.

Question:
What is 'exterior routing protocols'?

Answer:
'exterior routing protocols' is the name of routing protocols used between networks.

Question:
What is the 'Border Gateway Protocol, or BGP'?

Answer:
The 'Border Gateway Protocol, or BGP' is a protocol that employs a combination of both distance-vector and link-state algorithms.

Question:
What is a 'routing policy'?

Answer:
A 'routing policy' allows administrators to apply weights to different metrics.

Question:
What is a 'wormhole attack'?

Answer:
A 'wormhole attack' is an attack in which one or more packets are captured and transported to another location in the network.

Question:
What is a 'leash'?

Answer:
A 'leash' is a packet header that limits the use of data.

Question:
What is a 'geographical leash'?

Answer:
A 'geographical leash' is a type of leash that ensures a packet can be used only within a certain distance, or hops, of the sender.

Question:
What is a 'temporal leash'?

Answer:
A 'temporal leash' is a type of leash that ensures a packet must be used within a specific time window.

Communication and Network Security Domain

Question:
What is a 'repeater'?

Answer:
A 'repeater' is a network device that amplifies a signal.

Question:
What is a 'hub'?

Answer:
A 'hub' is a repeater with multiple ports.

Question:
What is a 'concentrator'?

Answer:
A 'concentrator' is a network device that connects multiple physical devices.

Question:
What is a 'bridge'?

Answer:
A 'bridge' is a network device that connects LAN segments and creates a collision domain.

Question:
What is a 'local bridge'?

Answer:
A 'local bridge' is a bridge that connects LANs within a local area, usually a building.

Question:
What is a 'remote bridge'?

Answer:
A 'remote bridge' is a bridge that connects LANs over a MAN by using a telecommunication link.

Question:
What is a 'translation bridge'?

Answer:
A 'translation bridge' is a bridge that connects LANs that use different protocols, for example Ethernet and Token Ring.

Question:
What is 'transparent bridging'?

Answer:
'transparent bridging' is a type of bridging where the bridge learns the mapping between frames and ports.

Question:
What is the 'Spanning Tree Algorithm, or SPA'?

Answer:
The 'Spanning Tree Algorithm, or SPA' is an algorithm that makes sure that rogue frames do not circulate forever, assigns priorities to certain paths and calculates costs for paths.

Communication and Network Security Domain

Question:
What is 'source routing'?

Answer:
'source routing' is the act of allowing a frame or packet to specify the exact network path it wants to travel through.

Question:
What is a 'switch'?

Answer:
A 'switch' is a hub combined with a bridge, plus ACLs and VLANs, and creates collision domains.

Question:
What is a 'virtual LAN, or VLAN'?

Answer:
A 'virtual LAN, or VLAN' is a virtual network containing devices regardless of the physical location.

Question:
What is a 'layer 3 switch'?

Answer:
A 'layer 3 switch' performs routing functions but moves routing logic into hardware for speed.

Question:
What is a 'router'?

Answer:
A 'router' operates based on IP addresses and creates broadcast domains.

Question:
What is the 'Maximum Transmission Size, or MTU'?

Answer:
The 'Maximum Transmission Size, or MTU' is the term for the maximum size a packet can be.

Question:
What is 'fragmenting'?

Answer:
'fragmenting' describes the process of dividing a packet into smaller packets based on the MTU.

Question:
What is 'multilayer devices'?

Answer:
'multilayer devices' are devices that operate across more than one OSI layer.

Question:
What is an 'Application-Specific Integrated Circuit, or ASIC'?

Answer:
An 'Application-Specific Integrated Circuit, or ASIC' is a hardware device dedicated to carrying out a specific task that can be software-based.

Communication and Network Security Domain

Question:
What is 'Multiprotocol Label Switching, or MPLS'?

Answer:
'Multiprotocol Label Switching, or MPLS' is a layer 3 and 4 capability to apply an attribute in real-time to a fragment or packet that other devices can look at.

Question:
What is a 'double tagging attack'?

Answer:
A 'double tagging attack' is an attack which uses MPLS to force a packet down a specific path.

Question:
What is a 'switch spoofing attack'?

Answer:
A 'switch spoofing attack' is an attack in which the attacker pretends to be a switch.

Question:
What is a 'VLAN hopping attack'?

Answer:
A 'VLAN hopping attack' is an attack in which the attacker gains access to traffic in a different VLAN.

Question:
What is a 'gateway'?

Answer:
A 'gateway' is a piece of software that connects two dissimilar environments.

Question:
What is an 'electronic mail gateway'?

Answer:
An 'electronic mail gateway' is a gateway that manages communication between different mail server platforms.

Question:
What is a 'Private Branch Exchange, or PBX'?

Answer:
A 'Private Branch Exchange, or PBX' is a private, company-owned telephone switch located on the company's premises.

Question:
What is a 'hanging modem'?

Answer:
A 'hanging modem' is an attached modem for service personnel to connect to while servicing a PBX.

Question:
What is 'phreakers'?

Answer:
'phreakers' is a term used for phone hackers.

Communication and Network Security Domain

Question:
What is a 'Demilitarized Zone, or DMZ'?

Answer:
A 'Demilitarized Zone, or DMZ' is a secure zone setup around public servers using a firewall.

Question:
What is 'ingress'?

Answer:
'ingress' describes traffic coming into a network.

Question:
What is 'egress'?

Answer:
'egress' describes traffic leaving a network.

Question:
What is 'stateless inspection'?

Answer:
'stateless inspection' describes network devices that only look at individual packets, not the entire conversation.

Question:
What is 'stateful inspection'?

Answer:
'stateful inspection' describes network devices that keep track of all packets until the socket is closed.

Question:
What is 'Denial of Service, or DoS'?

Answer:
'Denial of Service, or DoS' is an attack that attempts to rob legitimate users of a resource, such as availability.

Question:
What is 'Distributed Denial of Service, or DDoS'?

Answer:
'Distributed Denial of Service, or DDoS' is a DoS attack carried out by many computers in different locations, often by Zombies.

Question:
What is an 'appliance'?

Answer:
An 'appliance' is a dedicated hardware/software platform.

Question:
What is a 'Packet-Filtering Firewall'?

Answer:
A 'Packet-Filtering Firewall' is a stateless firewall that operates at layers 3 and 4.

Communication and Network Security Domain

Question:
What is a 'Stateful Firewall'?

Answer:
A 'Stateful Firewall' is the same as a packet-filtering firewall but stateful.

Question:
What is a 'Proxy Firewall'?

Answer:
A 'Proxy Firewall' is a firewall that breaks the communication path and communicates on behalf of two clients.

Question:
What is a 'Circuit-Level Proxy'?

Answer:
A 'Circuit-Level Proxy' is a firewall that operates at layer 5.

Question:
What is an 'Application-Level Proxy'?

Answer:
An 'Application-Level Proxy' is a firewall that operates at layer 7, and is slower but more intelligent than a circuit-level proxy.

Question:
What is 'SOCKS'?

Answer:
'SOCKS' is a circuit-level protocol used to create a secure channel between two computers.

Question:
What is a 'Dynamic Packet-Filtering Firewall'?

Answer:
A 'Dynamic Packet-Filtering Firewall' is a firewall that keeps high-numbered ports closed until a computer within its network needs to use one.

Question:
What is a 'Kernel Proxy Firewall'?

Answer:
A 'Kernel Proxy Firewall' is a firewall that puts the packet inspection intelligence inside of the kernel itself, speeding up the inspection.

Question:
What is a 'Next-Generation Firewall'?

Answer:
A 'Next-Generation Firewall' is a firewall that add an IPS and allows configuration from a central server.

Question:
What is a 'screened host'?

Answer:
A 'screened host' is the name for devices connected directly to a packet-filtering firewall.

Communication and Network Security Domain

Question:
What is a 'screened subnet'?

Answer:
A 'screened subnet' is the name for a network created by a packet-filtering firewall.

Question:
What is a 'single-tiered configuration'?

Answer:
A 'single-tiered configuration' is the term used for a single firewall.

Question:
What is a 'two-tiered configuration'?

Answer:
A 'two-tiered configuration' is the term used when employing a screened host.

Question:
What is a 'three-tiered configuration'?

Answer:
A 'three-tiered configuration' is the term used when employing a screened subnet.

Question:
What is a 'dual-homed device'?

Answer:
A 'dual-homed device' is a device with 2 NICs - one internal and one external.

Question:
What is a 'multi-homed device'?

Answer:
A 'multi-homed device' is a device with 3 or more NICs.

Question:
What is a 'bastion host'?

Answer:
A 'bastion host' is a server hardened against attacks, usually residing in a DMZ.

Question:
What is a 'virtual firewall'?

Answer:
A 'virtual firewall' is a firewall that sits between virtual machines.

Question:
What is a 'deny first policy'?

Answer:
A 'deny first policy' is a policy that indicates that if there is no rule to explicitly accept a packet, then is should be discarded.

Communication and Network Security Domain

Question:
What is the 'silent rule'?

Answer:
The 'silent rule' is a rule that drops 'noisy' traffic without logging it to avoid filling up the logs up too quickly.

Question:
What is the 'stealth rule'?

Answer:
The 'stealth rule' is a rule to not allow access to the firewall software except from authorized systems.

Question:
What is the 'cleanup rule'?

Answer:
The 'cleanup rule' is a rule that any packet not meeting a rule should be discarded.

Question:
What is the 'negate rule'?

Answer:
The 'negate rule' is the name of a rule that is the same as 'deny first'.

Question:
What is an 'IP fragmentation attack'?

Answer:
An 'IP fragmentation attack' is an attack in which an attacker crafts packet fragments that cannot be reassembled, resulting in a software crash or an out of memory condition.

Question:
What is an 'overlapping fragment attack'?

Answer:
An 'overlapping fragment attack' is an attack in which an attacker sneaks past firewalls that do not reassemble fragments before approving them.

Question:
What is a 'proxy server'?

Answer:
A 'proxy server' is a proxy firewall that understands the software running on both the server and client.

Question:
What is a 'forwarding proxy'?

Answer:
A 'forwarding proxy' is a proxy server allowing the client to indicate which server it wishes to speak to.

Question:
What is a 'open proxy'?

Answer:
A 'open proxy' is a forwarding proxy that is available for anyone to use.

Communication and Network Security Domain

Question:
What is a 'anonymous open proxy'?

Answer:
A 'anonymous open proxy' is a server that allows users to remain anonymous by concealing their real IP address.

Question:
What is a 'reverse proxy'?

Answer:
A 'reverse proxy' hides the servers behind it so the client never knows they exist, such as load balancers.

Question:
What is a 'honeypot'?

Answer:
A 'honeypot' is an attractive target for attackers that is designed to slow down and distract them.

Question:
What is a 'honeynet'?

Answer:
A 'honeynet' describes when more than one honeypot is put into place.

Question:
What is a 'tarpit'?

Answer:
A 'tarpit' is an attractive target for attackers purposefully designed to handicap them by being very slow to respond.

Question:
What is 'Unified Threat Management'?

Answer:
'Unified Threat Management' is an appliance that implements a firewall, anti-malware, anti-spam, IDS and IPS, VPN support, information leak prevention and content filtering.

Question:
What is 'Content Distribution Networks, or CDN'?

Answer:
'Content Distribution Networks, or CDN' describes caching content at various geographical places around the world to speed delivery and to mitigate DDoS attacks.

Question:
What is 'Software Defined Networking, or SDN'?

Answer:
'Software Defined Networking, or SDN' describes implementing network management as distributed software.

Question:
What is a 'control plane'?

Answer:
A 'control plane' is an SDN component where routing paths are tracked, discovered and discarded.

Communication and Network Security Domain

Question:
What is a 'forwarding plane'?

Answer:
A 'forwarding plane' is an SDN network device, usually an ASIC, where actual forwarding decision are made based on control plane paths.

Question:
What is 'OpenFlow'?

Answer:
'OpenFlow' is an SDN open source package providing communication between the control and forwarding planes.

Question:
What is 'open'?

Answer:
'open' is an SDN approach in which open-source code and standards create the components of SDN.

Question:
What is 'API'?

Answer:
'API' is a CISCO SDN approach which extends OpenFlow to allow deeper packet inspection.

Question:
What is an 'overlay'?

Answer:
An 'overlay' is an SDN approach which creates a virtual overlay on top of the physical network.

Question:
What is an 'intranet'?

Answer:
An 'intranet' is an internal network of servers and clients that are inaccessible outside of the company's network.

Question:
What is an 'extranet'?

Answer:
An 'extranet' is a network between two companies allowing real-time communication.

Question:
What is 'Electronic Data Interchange, or EDI'?

Answer:
'Electronic Data Interchange, or EDI' describes automated processes exchanging data.

Question:
What is a 'Value-Added Network, or VAN'?

Answer:
A 'Value-Added Network, or VAN' is a network created and hosted by a third-party that allows two companies to connect in real-time.

Communication and Network Security Domain

Question:
What is a 'Local Area Network, or LAN'?

Answer:
A 'Local Area Network, or LAN' is a small geographical region covered by a single network.

Question:
What is an 'internetwork'?

Answer:
An 'internetwork' describes two LANs connected by a router.

Question:
What is a 'Wide Area Network, or WAN'?

Answer:
A 'Wide Area Network, or WAN' is the term for two LANs connected by different layer 2 technology, such as frame relay or ATM.

Question:
What is 'multiplexing'?

Answer:
'multiplexing' occurs when a single transmission path is broken up into multiple channels.

Question:
What is a 'T1'?

Answer:
A 'T1' is a digital line with 24 calls over one UTP.

Question:
What is a 'T3'?

Answer:
A 'T3' is the label for 28 T1 lines.

Question:
What is a 't-carrier'?

Answer:
A 't-carrier' is the term describing T1 and T3 lines carrying both voice and data.

Question:
What is a 'fractional T line'?

Answer:
A 'fractional T line' is another name for shared T lines.

Question:
What is an 'e-carrier'?

Answer:
An 'e-carrier' is the European version of a T-carrier, with E1 and E3 instead of T1 and T3.

Communication and Network Security Domain

Question:
What is 'Time-Division Multiplexing, or TDM'?

Answer:
'Time-Division Multiplexing, or TDM' is a version of multiplexing in which time slots are created within a single channel by modulating the amplitude.

Question:
What is 'Statistical Time-Division Multiplexing, or STDM'?

Answer:
'Statistical Time-Division Multiplexing, or STDM' is a version of multiplexing like TDM but only includes data for each subchannel if it is being used.

Question:
What is 'Frequency-Division Multiplexing, or FDM'?

Answer:
'Frequency-Division Multiplexing, or FDM' is a version of multiplexing which modulates the frequency to carry more data.

Question:
What is an 'OC-1'?

Answer:
An 'OC-1' is a fiber line carrying up to 52 Mbps.

Question:
What is an 'OC-3'?

Answer:
An 'OC-3' is a fiber line carrying up to 155 Mbps.

Question:
What is an 'OC-192'?

Answer:
An 'OC-192' is the fiber standard that the Internet backbone is based on, supporting up to 10 Gbps.

Question:
What is 'Synchronous Optical Network, or SONET'?

Answer:
'Synchronous Optical Network, or SONET' is a standard that allows copper and fiber to work together.

Question:
What is 'Synchronous Digital Hierarchy, or SDH'?

Answer:
'Synchronous Digital Hierarchy, or SDH' is Europe's version of SONET.

Question:
What is 'Asynchronous Transfer Mode, or ATM'?

Answer:
'Asynchronous Transfer Mode, or ATM' is a protocol created specifically for SONET.

Communication and Network Security Domain

Question:
What is 'Channel Service Unit/Data Service Unit, or CSU/DSU'?

Answer:
'Channel Service Unit/Data Service Unit, or CSU/DSU' are WAN devices that physically connect a LAN and a WAN.

Question:
What is 'Data Terminal Equipment, or DTE'?

Answer:
'Data Terminal Equipment, or DTE' is the WAN device within a company's network.

Question:
What is 'Data-Circuit Terminating Equipment, or DCE'?

Answer:
'Data-Circuit Terminating Equipment, or DCE' is a WAN device belonging to the carrier.

Question:
What is 'circuit-switching'?

Answer:
'circuit-switching' is a method of transmitting packets such that they all follow the same path.

Question:
What is 'packet switching'?

Answer:
'packet switching' is a method of transmitting packets such that they can follow different paths.

Question:
What is 'Frame Check Sequence, or FCS'?

Answer:
'Frame Check Sequence, or FCS' is a number that is assigned to each packet when using packet switching.

Question:
What is a 'frame relay'?

Answer:
A 'frame relay' is a type of link that allows more than one party to share in a single dedicated line across a WAN.

Question:
What is 'Committed Information Rate, or CIR'?

Answer:
'Committed Information Rate, or CIR' is a form of bandwidth guarantee to a company when using frame relay.

Question:
What is a 'frame relay cloud'?

Answer:
A 'frame relay cloud' is a collection of DCEs which forward packets from Point A to Point B.

Communication and Network Security Domain

Question:
What is a 'virtual circuit'?

Answer:
A 'virtual circuit' is used by frame relay or X.25 to send data across a WAN or MAN link.

Question:
What is a 'Permanent Virtual Circuit, or PVC'?

Answer:
A 'Permanent Virtual Circuit, or PVC' is a virtual circuit that is programmed into devices directly, resulting in a CIR.

Question:
What is a 'Switched Virtual Circuit, or SVC'?

Answer:
A 'Switched Virtual Circuit, or SVC' is a virtual circuit that is built and destroyed as-needed.

Question:
What is a 'Metropolitan Area Network, or MAN'?

Answer:
A 'Metropolitan Area Network, or MAN' is a backbone, usually SONET, that connects LANS, WANs, the Internet and other telecommunications and cable networks.

Question:
What is 'self-healing'?

Answer:
'self-healing' occurs when a break in the primary ring of SONET results in traffic continuing on a back-up ring.

Question:
What is 'Metro Ethernet'?

Answer:
'Metro Ethernet' is the term for Ethernet used with MANs.

Question:
What is a 'Virtual Private LAN service, or VPLS'?

Answer:
A 'Virtual Private LAN service, or VPLS' creates a distributed LAN over a MAN.

Question:
What is 'X.25'?

Answer:
'X.25' is an older WAN protocol that defines how networks establish and maintain connections using packet switching.

Question:
What is 'Asynchronous Transfer Mode, or ATM'?

Answer:
'Asynchronous Transfer Mode, or ATM' is used on the Internet backbone, and is a connection-oriented technology that uses cells instead of packets providing QoS.

Communication and Network Security Domain

Question:
What is 'Quality of Service, or QoS'?

Answer:
'Quality of Service, or QoS' is the act of distinguishing between different types of traffic and assigning delivery priority levels.

Question:
What is 'Unspecified Bit Rate Service, or UBR'?

Answer:
'Unspecified Bit Rate Service, or UBR' is a connectionless channel that pretty much promises nothing.

Question:
What is 'Variable Bit Rate Service, or VBR'?

Answer:
'Variable Bit Rate Service, or VBR' is a connection-oriented channel that does not guarantee a minimum latency and provides a peak and sustained data rate.

Question:
What is 'Available Bit Rate Service, or ABR'?

Answer:
'Available Bit Rate Service, or ABR' is a connection-oriented channel that allows the bit rate to be adjusted to match whatever bandwidth is available.

Question:
What is 'Constant Bit Rate Service, or CBR'?

Answer:
'Constant Bit Rate Service, or CBR' is a connection-oriented channel that is based on a bandwidth requirement that is specified when the connection is started.

Question:
What is a 'best-effort service'?

Answer:
A 'best-effort service' is a non-ATM QoS level that promises nothing – just the best effort after all other classes have been served.

Question:
What is a 'differentiated service'?

Answer:
A 'differentiated service' is a non-ATM QoS level that promises nothing other than that this class gets priority over best-effort service.

Question:
What is a 'guaranteed service'?

Answer:
A 'guaranteed service' is a non-ATM QoS level that promises a guaranteed speed.

Communication and Network Security Domain

Question:
What is 'traffic shaping'?

Answer:
'traffic shaping' occurs when the QoS classification sets priorities for traffic.

Question:
What is 'Systems Network Architecture, or SNA'?

Answer:
'Systems Network Architecture, or SNA' is an IBM mainframe network.

Question:
What is 'Asynchronous Data Link Control, or SDLC'?

Answer:
'Asynchronous Data Link Control, or SDLC' is a polling protocol used on SNA networks.

Question:
What is 'High-level Data Link Control, or HDLC'?

Answer:
'High-level Data Link Control, or HDLC' is used for communication between two devices on a WAN at layer 2.

Question:
What is the 'Point-to-Point Protocol, or PPP'?

Answer:
The 'Point-to-Point Protocol, or PPP' is the protocol that encapsulates dissimilar protocols so that two different networks can communicate.

Question:
What is the 'Link Control Protocol, or LCP'?

Answer:
The 'Link Control Protocol, or LCP' is part of PPP and is the protocol that establishes, configures and maintains a connection.

Question:
What is the 'Network Control Protocol, or NCP'?

Answer:
The 'Network Control Protocol, or NCP' is part of PPP and is the protocol that configures the network layer.

Question:
What is 'High-Speed Serial Interface, or HSSI'?

Answer:
'High-Speed Serial Interface, or HSSI' is an interface that works at layer 1, and allows ATM or frame relay to work on routers and multiplexers.

Question:
What is 'Public-Switched Telephone Network, or PSTN'?

Answer:
'Public-Switched Telephone Network, or PSTN' is the network used by regular phones with RJ-11 connections.

Communication and Network Security Domain

Question:
What is 'Signaling System 7, or SS7'?

Answer:
'Signaling System 7, or SS7' is the protocol used by PSTN.

Question:
What is 'multiservice access technologies'?

Answer:
'multiservice access technologies' occurs when a single transmission line is used to carry several types of communication categories.

Question:
What is 'jitter'?

Answer:
'jitter' describes delays due to variable latency.

Question:
What is an 'isochronous network'?

Answer:
An 'isochronous network' is a network that ensures a consistent bandwidth availability.

Question:
What is 'Voice over IP, or VoIP'?

Answer:
'Voice over IP, or VoIP' is a protocol that allows phone calls to be routed as IP packets.

Question:
What is an 'IP telephony device'?

Answer:
An 'IP telephony device' is the end-user software or hardware responsible for digitizing analog signals such as audio, and turning digital signals back into audio.

Question:
What is a 'voice gateway'?

Answer:
A 'voice gateway' is a VoIP component that routes packets and provides links to legacy and backup voice systems.

Question:
What is a 'call-processing manager'?

Answer:
A 'call-processing manager' is a VoIP component that initiates and accepts calls.

Question:
What is a 'voicemail system'?

Answer:
A 'voicemail system' is a VoIP component that stores messages, forwards calls and provides direct lookup capabilities.

Communication and Network Security Domain

Question:
What is the 'Session Initiation Protocol, or SIP'?

Answer:
The 'Session Initiation Protocol, or SIP' is a VoIP component that sets up and tears down conversation sessions.

Question:
What is 'User Agent Client, or UAC'?

Answer:
'User Agent Client, or UAC' is a VoIP component comprised of a user-facing software client.

Question:
What is 'User Agent Server, or UAS'?

Answer:
'User Agent Server, or UAS' is a VoIP server component that takes care of all routing and signaling.

Question:
What is the 'Real-time Transport Protocol, or RTP'?

Answer:
The 'Real-time Transport Protocol, or RTP' is a layer 5 protocol that normally uses UDP to stream audio.

Question:
What is the 'RTP Control Protocol, or RTCP'?

Answer:
The 'RTP Control Protocol, or RTCP' provides the information RTP needs for QoS.

Question:
What is a 'proxy server'?

Answer:
A 'proxy server' is the VoIP server that relays signals between the UAC and UAS.

Question:
What is a 'registrar server'?

Answer:
A 'registrar server' is the VoIP server that tracks the addresses of all participants.

Question:
What is a 'redirect server'?

Answer:
A 'redirect server' is the VoIP server that allows SIP devices to physically move without having to change identities.

Question:
What is 'SPam over Internet Telephony, or SPIT'?

Answer:
'SPam over Internet Telephony, or SPIT' is an attack in which the attacker sends a voice message to a voicemail server.

Communication and Network Security Domain

Question:
What is a 'modem, or modulator-demodulator'?

Answer:
A 'modem, or modulator-demodulator' is a device connected to a PSTN connection that allows a remote device to connect to the network.

Question:
What is 'war dialing'?

Answer:
'war dialing' is the process of configuring a computer to automatically dial through a list of phone numbers in search of a modem.

Question:
What is a 'Central Office, or CO'?

Answer:
A 'Central Office, or CO' is the telephone company's neighborhood infrastructure.

Question:
What is 'Integrated Services Digital Network, or ISDN'?

Answer:
'Integrated Services Digital Network, or ISDN' was the first truly digital connection over copper phone lines.

Question:
What is 'Basic Rate Interface ISDN, or BRI'?

Answer:
'Basic Rate Interface ISDN, or BRI' is an ISDN implementation of 2 x 64 Kbps B channels, and 1 x 16 Kbps D channel for 144 Kbps total.

Question:
What is 'Primary Rate Interface ISDN, or PRI'?

Answer:
'Primary Rate Interface ISDN, or PRI' is an ISDN implementation of 23 x 64 Kbps B channels and 1 x 16 Kbps D channel for 1544 Mbps total.

Question:
What is 'Broadband ISDN, or BISDN'?

Answer:
'Broadband ISDN, or BISDN' is an ISDN implementation used within a backbone, such as with ATM and SONET.

Question:
What is 'Digital Subscriber Line, or DSL'?

Answer:
'Digital Subscriber Line, or DSL' is the successor to ISDN and operates at rates up to 52 Mbps.

Question:
What is 'Asymmetric DSL, or ADSL'?

Answer:
'Asymmetric DSL, or ADSL' is a DSL implementation delivering 768 Kbps down and 128 to 384 Kbps up.

Communication and Network Security Domain

Question:
What is 'Symmetric DSL, or SDSL'?

Answer:
'Symmetric DSL, or SDSL' is a DSL implementation delivering 192 to 1100 Kbps down and up.

Question:
What is 'High-bit-rate DSL, or HDSL'?

Answer:
'High-bit-rate DSL, or HDSL' is a DSL implementation delivering T1 speeds.

Question:
What is 'Very high-bit-rate DSL, or VDSL'?

Answer:
'Very high-bit-rate DSL, or VDSL' is a DSL implementation delivering 13 Mbps down and 2 Mbps up.

Question:
What is 'Rate-Adaptive DSL, or RADSL'?

Answer:
'Rate-Adaptive DSL, or RADSL' is a DSL implementation in which the rates adjust to match the signal quality.

Question:
What is 'Data-Over-Cable Service Interface Specification, or DOCSIS'?

Answer:
'Data-Over-Cable Service Interface Specification, or DOCSIS' is a specification that addresses how to provide high-speed data over existing cable TV networks.

Question:
What is 'Virtual Private Network, or VPN'?

Answer:
'Virtual Private Network, or VPN' is created when two trusted networks securely communicate over untrusted infrastructure.

Question:
What is the 'Point-to-Point Tunneling Protocol, or PPTP'?

Answer:
The 'Point-to-Point Tunneling Protocol, or PPTP' is a protocol that tunnels PPP connections through an IP network, but only system-to-system.

Question:
What is 'Generic Routing Encapsulation, or GRE'?

Answer:
'Generic Routing Encapsulation, or GRE' is the method through which PPTP encrypts data.

Question:
What is 'Microsoft Point-to-Point Encryption, or MPPE'?

Answer:
'Microsoft Point-to-Point Encryption, or MPPE' is a very insecure implementation of encryption over PPTP.

Communication and Network Security Domain

Question:
What is 'Layer 2 Forwarding, or L2F'?

Answer:
'Layer 2 Forwarding, or L2F' is Cisco's PPP protocol.

Question:
What is the 'Layer 2 Tunneling Protocol, or L2TP'?

Answer:
The 'Layer 2 Tunneling Protocol, or L2TP' is a tunneling wrapper for L2F that can communicate over non-IP networks.

Question:
What is 'Internet Protocol Security, or IPSec'?

Answer:
'Internet Protocol Security, or IPSec' is a standard invented to provide security for the IP protocol.

Question:
What is 'Authentication Header, or AH'?

Answer:
'Authentication Header, or AH' is an IPSec protocol in which a hash provides integrity and system authentication, and protects from replay attacks.

Question:
What is 'Encapsulating Security Payload, or ESP'?

Answer:
'Encapsulating Security Payload, or ESP' is an IPSec protocol which provides confidentiality, integrity and authentication through encryption.

Question:
What is 'Internet Security Association and Key Management Protocol, or ISAKMP'?

Answer:
'Internet Security Association and Key Management Protocol, or ISAKMP' is an IPSec protocol which controls the management and storage of all possible connection variables.

Question:
What is 'Internet Key Exchange, or IKE'?

Answer:
'Internet Key Exchange, or IKE' is an IPSec protocol that allows for key creation and secure exchange for ISAKMP.

Question:
What is 'Security Association, or SA'?

Answer:
'Security Association, or SA' describes the parameters that a remote router has specified.

Communication and Network Security Domain

Question:
What is 'High Assurance Internet Protocol Encryptor, or HAIPE'?

Answer:
'High Assurance Internet Protocol Encryptor, or HAIPE' is a protocol encryptor that NSA created based on IPSec.

Question:
What is 'transport adjacency'?

Answer:
'transport adjacency' occurs when more than one security protocol is being used together in IPSec.

Question:
What is 'iterated tunneling'?

Answer:
'iterated tunneling' occurs when wrapping a tunneled packet inside of another tunnel.

Question:
What is 'Transport Level Security, or TLS'?

Answer:
'Transport Level Security, or TLS' is the successor to SSL working at layer 5.

Question:
What is 'TLS portal VPN'?

Answer:
'TLS portal VPN' is an implementation of TLS in which a single user connects to a web site acting as a gateway into more services.

Question:
What is 'TLS tunnel VPN'?

Answer:
'TLS tunnel VPN' is an implementation of TLS in which a single browser connects to multiple non-web-based network services.

Question:
What is the 'Password Authentication Protocol, or PAP'?

Answer:
The 'Password Authentication Protocol, or PAP' is an authentication protocol that sends passwords in clear text.

Question:
What is the 'Challenge Handshake Authentication Protocol, or CHAP'?

Answer:
The 'Challenge Handshake Authentication Protocol, or CHAP' is an authentication protocol in which the password is never sent, and randomly forces re-authentication.

Question:
What is 'MS-CHAP'?

Answer:
'MS-CHAP' is Microsoft's version of CHAP.

Communication and Network Security Domain

Question:
What is the 'Extensible Authentication Protocol, or EAP'?

Answer:
The 'Extensible Authentication Protocol, or EAP' is a framework that supports multiple authentication protocols.

Question:
What is 'Lightweight EAP, or LEAP'?

Answer:
'Lightweight EAP, or LEAP' is Cisco's wireless version of EAP.

Question:
What is 'EAP-TLS'?

Answer:
'EAP-TLS' is an EAP protocol that is based on digital certificates.

Question:
What is 'EAP-MD5'?

Answer:
'EAP-MD5' is an EAP protocol that uses hashing and is weak.

Question:
What is 'EAP-PSK'?

Answer:
'EAP-PSK' is an EAP protocol that uses symmetric key mutual authentication.

Question:
What is 'EAP-TTLS'?

Answer:
'EAP-TTLS' is an EAP protocol that extends EAP-TLS.

Question:
What is 'EAP-IKE2'?

Answer:
'EAP-IKE2' is an EAP protocol that uses asymmetric or symmetric mutual authentication.

Question:
What is 'PEAP-v0/EAP-MSCHAPv2'?

Answer:
'PEAP-v0/EAP-MSCHAPv2' is an EAP protocol that is similar to EAP-TTLS but requires a server certificate.

Question:
What is 'PEAPv1/EAP-GTC'?

Answer:
'PEAPv1/EAP-GTC' is an EAP protocol that is based on Cisco's Generic Token Card.

Communication and Network Security Domain

Question:
What is 'EAP-FAST'?

Answer:
'EAP-FAST' is an EAP protocol that is Cisco's replacement for LEAP.

Question:
What is 'EAP-SIM'?

Answer:
'EAP-SIM' is an EAP protocol that is used for GSM cell SIM cards.

Question:
What is 'EAP-AKA'?

Answer:
'EAP-AKA' is an EAP protocol that is used for UMTS cell SIM cards.

Question:
What is 'EAP-GSS'?

Answer:
'EAP-GSS' is an EAP protocol that uses Kerberos with the Generic Security Service.

Question:
What is a 'wireless network'?

Answer:
A 'wireless network' consists of electromagnetic signals varying both frequency and amplitude as they travel through air and space.

Question:
What is 'Frequency Hopping Spread Spectrum, or FHSS'?

Answer:
'Frequency Hopping Spread Spectrum, or FHSS' is a spread spectrum technology in which only a single channel is used at any given time.

Question:
What is 'Direct Sequence Spread Spectrum, or DSSS'?

Answer:
'Direct Sequence Spread Spectrum, or DSSS' is a spread spectrum technology in which extra information is encoded so that it can be rebuilt if a collision occurs.

Question:
What is a 'DSSS chip'?

Answer:
A 'DSSS chip' is an extra bit added to each packet in DSSS to create redundancy.

Question:
What is a 'DSSS chipping code'?

Answer:
A 'DSSS chipping code' is the pattern of applying chips to data in DSSS.

Communication and Network Security Domain

Question:
What is 'Orthogonal Frequency-Division Multiplexing, or OFDM'?

Answer:
'Orthogonal Frequency-Division Multiplexing, or OFDM' is a spread spectrum technology in which each channel is perpendicular to the next channel.

Question:
What is a 'Wireless LAN, or WLAN'?

Answer:
A 'Wireless LAN, or WLAN' is created when a LAN is connected not with cables but wirelessly.

Question:
What is an 'ad hoc WLAN'?

Answer:
An 'ad hoc WLAN' describes two computers talking to each other directly.

Question:
What is a 'stand-alone WLAN'?

Answer:
A 'stand-alone WLAN' describes a network using a wireless access point.

Question:
What is an 'infrastructure WLAN'?

Answer:
An 'infrastructure WLAN' is created when the access point is connected to another network.

Question:
What is a 'WLAN channel'?

Answer:
A 'WLAN channel' is a specific frequency range on a WLAN.

Question:
What is the 'Basic Service Set, or BSS'?

Answer:
The 'Basic Service Set, or BSS' is a group of wireless devices communicating in infrastructure mode.

Question:
What is a 'Service Set ID, or SSID'?

Answer:
A 'Service Set ID, or SSID' is the name of a wireless BSS.

Question:
What is 'Wired Equivalent Protocol, or WEP'?

Answer:
'Wired Equivalent Protocol, or WEP' was the initial security provided for wireless networks, and was very poorly implemented.

Communication and Network Security Domain

301

Question:
What is 'Open System Authentication, or OSA'?

Answer:
'Open System Authentication, or OSA' is a WEP authentication mode requiring only the SSID, and supports no encryption.

Question:
What is 'Shared Key Authentication, or SKA'?

Answer:
'Shared Key Authentication, or SKA' is a WEP authentication mode in which the access point and client possess a shared key, and use the CHAP method for authentication.

Question:
What is 'Wi-Fi Protected Access, or WPA'?

Answer:
'Wi-Fi Protected Access, or WPA' is the successor to WEP that kept RC4, but added TKIP, EAP and 902.1X port authentication.

Question:
What is 'WPA2'?

Answer:
'WPA2' is the successor to WPA and added AES and CBC-MAC.

Question:
What is a 'robust security network'?

Answer:
A 'robust security network' is a term describing WPA2 relative to WPA.

Question:
What is '802.11i'?

Answer:
'802.11i' is the standard that replaced 802.11 when WPA came out.

Question:
What is '802.1X'?

Answer:
'802.1X' implements port-based network access and mutual authentication.

Question:
What is 'port-based network access'?

Answer:
'port-based network access' ensures that a user cannot make a full network connection until authentication has properly happened.

Question:
What is an '802.1x supplicant'?

Answer:
An '802.1x supplicant' is the wireless client for 802.1x authentication.

Communication and Network Security Domain

Question:
What is an '802.1x authenticator'?

Answer:
An '802.1x authenticator' is the access point for 802.1x authentication.

Question:
What is an '802.1x authentication server'?

Answer:
An '802.1x authentication server' is usually implemented using RADIUS for 802.1x authentication.

Question:
What is an '802.1x mutual authentication'?

Answer:
An '802.1x mutual authentication' occurs when both devices authenticate to each other in 802.1x authentication.

Question:
What is '802.16'?

Answer:
'802.16' is the standard that defines support for MANs.

Question:
What is 'Free-Space Optics, or FSO'?

Answer:
'Free-Space Optics, or FSO' is a laser system that transmits light across open air requiring a clear line of sight.

Question:
What is 'optical wireless'?

Answer:
'optical wireless' uses FSO to provide a point-to-point connection.

Question:
What is 'WPAN'?

Answer:
'WPAN' is a wireless personal network used for short-distance communication.

Question:
What is '802.15.4'?

Answer:
'802.15.4' implements a WPAN over 2.4 Ghz for 100 meters.

Question:
What is 'Zigbee'?

Answer:
'Zigbee' is the most popular 802.15.4 protocol, providing 250 Kbps and 128-bit symmetric encryption.

Communication and Network Security Domain

Question:
What is 'Bluetooth'?

Answer:
'Bluetooth' is the standard that uses the 2.5 Ghz spectrum and provides 1 to 3 Mbps speed up to 100 meters away.

Question:
What is 'bluejacking'?

Answer:
'bluejacking' is an attack in which an unsolicited message is sent to a Bluetooth device.

Question:
What is 'bluesnarking'?

Answer:
'bluesnarking' is an attack in which data is retrieved from the victim's device via Bluetooth.

Question:
What is a 'satellite'?

Answer:
A 'satellite' is a communications relay that is placed into a low-earth orbit.

Question:
What is a 'satellite footprint'?

Answer:
A 'satellite footprint' is the term for the area visible to a satellite.

Question:
What is 'Very Small Aperture Terminal or VSAT'?

Answer:
'Very Small Aperture Terminal or VSAT' links a remote satellite site to a service provider.

Question:
What is a 'cellular network'?

Answer:
A 'cellular network' is a wireless network divided into cells usually less than 1 mile in diameter.

Question:
What is 'Frequency Division Multiple Access or FDMA'?

Answer:
'Frequency Division Multiple Access or FDMA' is a multiple access technology that divides the frequency range into sub-bands, with each assigned to a single phone call.

Question:
What is 'Time Division Multiple Access or TDMA'?

Answer:
'Time Division Multiple Access or TDMA' is a multiple access technology that divides FDMA sub-bands into time slots, so that multiple calls can share them.

Communication and Network Security Domain

Question:
What is 'Personal Communications Service or PCS'?

Answer:
'Personal Communications Service or PCS' is a technology that supported both voice and data.

Question:
What is 'Code Division Multiple Access or CDMA'?

Answer:
'Code Division Multiple Access or CDMA' is a multiple access technology that added 3G speeds and packet switching by assigning a unique code to each call or data stream.

Question:
What is 'Multimedia Messaging Service or MMS'?

Answer:
'Multimedia Messaging Service or MMS' is a technology added to SMS to allow media messaging.

Question:
What is 'Orthogonal Frequency Division Multiple Access or OFDMA'?

Answer:
'Orthogonal Frequency Division Multiple Access or OFDMA' is a multiple access technology that combines FDMA and TDMA.

Question:
What is 'link encryption or online encryption'?

Answer:
'link encryption or online encryption' is a layer 2 encryption process.

Question:
What is 'end-to-end encryption'?

Answer:
'end-to-end encryption' is encryption that happens at the application level.

Question:
What is 'Multipurpose Internet Mail Extension or MIME'?

Answer:
'Multipurpose Internet Mail Extension or MIME' is a specification on how systems should handle binary email attachments.

Question:
What is 'Pretty Good Privacy or PGP'?

Answer:
'Pretty Good Privacy or PGP' is designed to encrypt mail, and was the first widely-adopted public key encryption program.

Question:
What is a 'key ring'?

Answer:
A 'key ring' is a file in PGP containing a list of public keys that have been received.

Communication and Network Security Domain

Question:
What is 'Hypertext Transfer Protocol or HTTP'?

Answer:
'Hypertext Transfer Protocol or HTTP' is a connectionless protocol used by browsers, in which everything is sent in clear text.

Question:
What is 'HTTP Secure or HTTPS'?

Answer:
'HTTP Secure or HTTPS' is HTTP encrypted by SSL or TLS.

Question:
What is 'SSL and TLS'?

Answer:
'SSL and TLS' are 2 PKI-based encryption technologies.

Question:
What is 'Padding Oracle On Downgraded Legacy Encryption, or POODLE'?

Answer:
'Padding Oracle On Downgraded Legacy Encryption, or POODLE' is an attack that proved that SSL v3.0 was flawed.

Question:
What is 'TLS v1.0'?

Answer:
'TLS v1.0' is essentially SSL v3.0 but POODLE-proof, and is no longer considered secure.

Question:
What is 'TLS v1.2'?

Answer:
'TLS v1.2' is the current version of TLS and is considered to be secure.

Question:
What is a 'cookie'?

Answer:
A 'cookie' is a file that a browser stores on the local computer's hard drive.

Question:
What is 'Secure Shell or SSH'?

Answer:
'Secure Shell or SSH' is a tunneling mechanism that allows remote users to execute commands, securely transfer files and redirect ports.

Question:
What is 'Denial of Service or DoS'?

Answer:
'Denial of Service or DoS' is an attack that prevents a system or service from being available for use.

Communication and Network Security Domain

Question:
What is 'Ping of Death'?

Answer:
'Ping of Death' is an attack that crashes an OS by sending a single ICMP Echo Request greater than the maximum size of 65,536 bytes.

Question:
What is 'flooding'?

Answer:
'flooding' is an attack in which computer is sent so much traffic that it is unable to respond to new requests.

Question:
What is 'SYN flood'?

Answer:
'SYN flood' is an attack where SYN packets are sent, but the corresponding ACK never follows.

Question:
What is 'Distributed Denial of Service or DDoS'?

Answer:
'Distributed Denial of Service or DDoS' is a network of compromised computers participating in a single DoS attack.

Question:
What is 'Command and Control or C&C'?

Answer:
'Command and Control or C&C' is the centralized authority controlling a botnet.

Question:
What is a 'zombie'?

Answer:
A 'zombie' is a computer that has malware installed that carries out C&C instructions.

Question:
What is a 'bot'?

Answer:
A 'bot' is another name for a zombie.

Question:
What is a 'botnet'?

Answer:
A 'botnet' is the collection of bots reporting to the same C&C.

Question:
What is 'ransomware'?

Answer:
'ransomware' is malware that locks some resource and blackmails victims into paying a fee to unlock it.

Communication and Network Security Domain

Question:
What is 'sniffing'?

Answer:
'sniffing' is the ability to eavesdrop on passing network packets.

Question:
What is 'promiscuous mode'?

Answer:
'promiscuous mode' is the mode a NIC must be put into in order to enable sniffing.

Question:
What is 'DNS Hijacking'?

Answer:
'DNS Hijacking' occurs when user is forced to unknowingly use a malicious DNS server.

Question:
What is a 'host based attack'?

Answer:
A 'host based attack' is an attack that modifies the DNS settings a computer uses to point to the attacker's own server.

Question:
What is a 'network based attack'?

Answer:
A 'network based attack' is an attack in which the attacker redirects DNS traffic to his own server using tactics such as ARP table poisoning.

Question:
What is a 'server based attack'?

Answer:
A 'server based attack' is an attack in which the attacker convinces a legitimate DNS server that his own DNS server is authoritative for the victim domain.

Question:
What is a 'drive-by download attack'?

Answer:
A 'drive-by download attack' is an attack in which visiting a single page results in malware being downloaded and installed.

Quiz

Question:
What are the 9 primary protocols in OSI layer 7?

Answer:
'FTP, TFTP, SNMP, Telnet, LDP, DNS, HTTP, IRC, SMTP'.

Question:
What are the 8 primary protocols in OSI layer 6?

Answer:
'ACII, EBCDIC, MIDI, MIME, TIFF, GIF, JPG, MPEG'.

Question:
What are the 5 primary protocols in OSI layer 5?

Answer:
'NetBIOS, PAP, PPTP, RPC, SRPC'.

Question:
What are the 3 primary protocols in OSI layer 4?

Answer:
'TCP, UDP, SPX'.

Question:
At what OSI layer are TCP and UDP ports specified?

Answer:
'Layer 4, the transport layer'.

Question:
What is the name of a TCP envelope at OSI layer 4?

Answer:
'segment'.

Question:
What is the name of a UDP envelope at OSI layer 4?

Answer:
'datagram'.

Question:
What 3 things must computers agree on before they can communicate?

Answer:
'how much data to send at a time, how to verify integrity, and how to know if something got lost'.

Communication and Network Security Domain

Question:
What are the 7 primary protocols in OSI layer 3?

Answer:
'IP, IPX, ICM, RIP, OSPF, BGP, IGMP'.

Question:
What is the name of an envelope at OSI layer 3?

Answer:
'packet'.

Question:
What are the 10 primary protocols in OSI layer 2?

Answer:
'ARP, RARP, SLIP, PPP, ATM, L2PP, FDDI, Ethernet, Token Ring, 802.11'.

Question:
What is the name of an envelope at OSI layer 2?

Answer:
'frame'.

Question:
What are the 2 sublayers of OSI layer 2?

Answer:
'logical link control and media access control'.

Question:
What are the 6 primary protocols in OSI layer 1?

Answer:
'10XBaseY, ISDN, DSL, SONET, FDDI, CDDI'.

Question:
What are the headers that TCP and UDP have in common?

Answer:
'source port, destination port, checksum, data'.

Question:
What is a header that only UDP contains?

Answer:
'length'.

Question:
What are the headers that only TCP contains?

Answer:
'seq #, ack #, offset, reserved, flags, window, urgent pointer, options, padding'.

Communication and Network Security Domain

Question:
Between TCP or UDP, which protocol ensures packets reach their destination?

Answer:
'TCP'.

Question:
Between TCP or UDP, which protocol is connectionless?

Answer:
'UDP'.

Question:
Between TCP or UDP, which protocol uses sequence numbers?

Answer:
'TCP'.

Question:
Between TCP or UDP, which protocol can slow the transmission rate?

Answer:
'TCP'.

Question:
Between TCP or UDP, which protocol ensures reliable delivery of packets?

Answer:
'TCP'.

Question:
Between TCP or UDP, which protocol has the highest resource usage?

Answer:
'UDP'.

Question:
What are the steps of the TCP Handshake?

Answer:
'SYN, SYN/ACK, ACK'.

Question:
What is the range for well-known ports?

Answer:
'0-1,023'.

Question:
What is the range of addresses in IPV4 class A?

Answer:
'0.0.0.0 to 127.255.255.255'.

Communication and Network Security Domain

Question:
What is the range of addresses in IPV4 class B?

Answer:
'128.0.0.0 to 191.255.255.255'.

Question:
What is the range of addresses in IPV4 class C?

Answer:
'192.0.0.0 to 223.255.255.255'.

Question:
What is the range of addresses in IPV4 class D?

Answer:
'224.0.0.0 to 239.255.255.255'.

Question:
What is the range of addresses in IPV4 class E?

Answer:
'240.0.0.0 to 255.255.255.255'.

Question:
What class of IPV4 addresses are used for multicast?

Answer:
'Class D'.

Question:
What class of IPV4 addresses are used for research?

Answer:
'Class E'.

Question:
Does the host or network portion of an IPV4 address come first?

Answer:
'Network'.

Question:
What are the 7 best features of IPV6 over IPV4?

Answer:
'supports IPSec, QoS, anycast, optional headers, CIA, jumbograms and no NATing is required'.

Question:
At what OSI layer are frames secured?

Answer:
'layer 2'.

Communication and Network Security Domain

Question:
Between bandwidth and data throughput, which value can increase due to compression?

Answer:
'data throughput'.

Question:
Between synchronous and asynchronous, which method requires timing agreement?

Answer:
'synchronous'.

Question:
Between synchronous and asynchronous, which method uses a parity bit for error control?

Answer:
'asynchronous'.

Question:
Between synchronous and asynchronous, which method supports robust integrity via CRC?

Answer:
'synchronous'.

Question:
Between synchronous and asynchronous, which method can use all bits for data?

Answer:
'synchronous'.

Question:
Between synchronous and asynchronous, which method uses 3 bits for start, stop and parity?

Answer:
'asynchronous'.

Question:
Between synchronous and asynchronous, which method is very forgiving when using an unstable path?

Answer:
'asynchronous'.

Question:
Between synchronous and asynchronous, which method has the least overhead?

Answer:
'synchronous'.

Question:
Between synchronous and asynchronous, which method does not need a timing agreement?

Answer:
'asynchronous'.

Communication and Network Security Domain

Question:
Which is cheaper - coaxial or twisted-pair?

Answer:
'twisted-Pair'.

Question:
Which is more secure - coaxial or twisted-pair?

Answer:
'coaxial'.

Question:
How many categories of Ethernet cabling are there?

Answer:
'7'.

Question:
What is the Ethernet cable category that is normally used in new installations requiring high-speed transmissions?

Answer:
'category 7'.

Question:
What is the Ethernet cable category that is used in most new installations?

Answer:
'category 6'.

Question:
What is the Ethernet cable category that is required for Gigabyte Ethernet?

Answer:
'category 6'.

Question:
What is the Ethernet cable category that is the most widely used?

Answer:
'category 5'.

Question:
What is the Ethernet cable category that is used for Token Ring networks?

Answer:
'category 4'.

Question:
What is the Ethernet cable category that can be used for both Ethernet and Token Ring networks?

Answer:
'category 3'.

Communication and Network Security Domain

314

Question:
What 4 things does copper cable transmission speed depend on?

Answer:
'copper quality, insulation quality, tightly twisting and type of shielding'.

Question:
What are the 3 components of fiber-optic cabling?

Answer:
'a light-source, the fiber cable and a light detector'.

Question:
What are the two types of fiber-optic light sources?

Answer:
'light-emitting diodes, and diode lasers'.

Question:
What are the 2 modes in fiber cable?

Answer:
'single mode and multimode'.

Question:
What are the 3 major sources of cabling problems?

Answer:
'noise, attenuation and crosstalk'.

Question:
What network topology does the Internet represent?

Answer:
'partial mesh topology'.

Question:
Which media access technology is used by Token Ring and FDDI networks?

Answer:
'token passing'.

Question:
What are the 2 types of CSMA?

Answer:
'CSMA/CD and CASMA/CA'.

Question:
What kind of CSMA is used by Ethernet?

Answer:
'CSMA/CD'.

Communication and Network Security Domain

Question:
What kind of CSMA is used by Wi-Fi?

Answer:
'CASMA/CA'.

Question:
What is the most common cabling for Ethernet?

Answer:
'4 pairs of UTP'.

Question:
What is the Ethernet category used for 10Base-T?

Answer:
'category 3'.

Question:
What is the Ethernet category used for 100Base-TX?

Answer:
'category 5'.

Question:
What is the Ethernet category used for 1000Base-T?

Answer:
'category 5'.

Question:
What is the Ethernet category used for 10GBase-T?

Answer:
'category 6'.

Question:
What are the 3 types of recipients within a network?

Answer:
'unicast, multicast and broadcast'.

Question:
Which bits in a MAC address represent the manufacturer?

Answer:
'the first 24'.

Question:
What are the 4 DHCP messages?

Answer:
'DHCPDISCOVER, DHCPOFFER, DHCPREQUEST, DHCPACK'.

Communication and Network Security Domain

Question:
What are the 2 most common ICMP messages?

Answer:
'Echo Request (type 8), and Echo Reply (type 0)'.

Question:
What are the 5 most important data elements that SNMP provides?

Answer:
'shares, usernames, services, domain information and resource utilization'.

Question:
What version of SNMP sent passwords in clear text?

Answer:
'versions 1 and 2'.

Question:
What version of SNMP added CIA?

Answer:
'version 3'.

Question:
What are the 6 top-level domains?

Answer:
'com, edu, mil, gov, org, net'.

Question:
Where is the HOSTS file found on Windows systems?

Answer:
"%systemroot%\system32\drivers\etc".

Question:
Where is the HOSTS file found on Linux systems?

Answer:
"/etc/hosts".

Question:
What version of the RIP routing protocol has no authentication?

Answer:
'Version 1'.

Question:
What version of the RIP routing protocol sends passwords in clear text or as MD5 hashes?

Answer:
'Version 2'.

Communication and Network Security Domain

317

Question:
What version of the RIP routing protocol adds support for IPv6?

Answer:
'RIPng'.

Question:
What routing protocol has mostly replaced RIP and supports authentication?

Answer:
'OSPF'.

Question:
What did version 3 of OSPF add?

Answer:
'support for IPv6 and IPSec'.

Question:
What version of EIGRP supports IPv6?

Answer:
'Version 4'.

Question:
What are the 5 most common types of networking devices?

Answer:
'Repeaters, Hubs, Bridges, Switches and Routers'.

Question:
What are the 3 types of bridges?

Answer:
'Local, remote and translation'.

Question:
What network devices amplify a signal?

Answer:
'Repeater, hub or concentrator'.

Question:
What network devices create collision domains?

Answer:
'Bridge, switch or router'.

Question:
What network device creates a broadcast domain?

Answer:
'router'.

Communication and Network Security Domain

Question:
What network device can create a VLAN?

Answer:
'switch'.

Question:
What network device operates using a MAC access control list?

Answer:
'switch'.

Question:
What network device operates using an IP Address access control list?

Answer:
'router'.

Question:
What 6 items do packet-filtering firewalls examine?

Answer:
'source IP and port, destination IP and port, protocol and direction'.

Question:
What are the 3 approaches to SDN?

Answer:
'Open, API and overlays'.

Question:
What are the 4 levels of QoS provided with ATM?

Answer:
'UBR, VBR, ABR and CBR'.

Question:
Which level of ATM QoS is good for delay-insensitive applications?

Answer:
'VBR'.

Question:
Which level of ATM QoS is good for voice and video applications?

Answer:
'CBR'.

Question:
What are the levels of QoS provided by non-ATM implementations?

Answer:
'best-effort service, differentiated service and guaranteed service'.

Communication and Network Security Domain

Question:
What non-ATM QoS level does most traffic on the Internet fall under?

Answer:
'best-effort service'.

Question:
What are the 3 types of user authentication that PPP supports?

Answer:
'PAP, CHAP and EAP'.

Question:
What are the 6 most common SIP messages in order of appearance?

Answer:
'INVITE, TRYING, RINGING, OK, ACK, BYE'.

Question:
Why is a VoIP SPIT attack impactful?

Answer:
'because the entire message must be played before it will end'.

Question:
What are the 3 ISDN implementations?

Answer:
'BRI, PRI and BISDN'.

Question:
What ISDN implementation is best used for home and small offices?

Answer:
'BRI'.

Question:
What ISDN implementation is best for companies with higher bandwidth requirements?

Answer:
'PRI'.

Question:
What are the 5 implementations of DSL?

Answer:
'ADSL, SDSL, HDSL, VDSL and RADSL'.

Question:
What DSL implementation is best used for residences?

Answer:
'ADSL'.

Communication and Network Security Domain

Question:
What DSL implementation is best used for businesses?

Answer:
'SDSL'.

Question:
What DSL implementation requires 2 UTP?

Answer:
'HDSL'.

Question:
What are the 4 methods in which PPTP can perform authentication?

Answer:
'PAP, CHAP, MS-CHAP and EAP-TLS'.

Question:
What are the 4 main IPSec protocols?

Answer:
'AH, ESP, ISAKMP and IKE'.

Question:
What is the TLS implementation this a browser normally uses?

Answer:
'TLS portal VPN'.

Question:
What are the 2 WEP modes?

Answer:
'OSA or SKA'.

Question:
What are the 3 weaknesses of WEP, even when using SKA?

Answer:
'a shared key that is hard to update, a lack of random IVs, and poorly implement ICVs'.

Question:
What are the weaknesses of WPA?

Answer:
'uses RC4 and TKIP'.

Question:
What are the 3 components in 802.11i?

Answer:
'TKIP, CCMP and 802.1x'.

Communication and Network Security Domain

Question:
What standard should you use in the lower layer of 802.11i?

Answer:
'Either TKIP or CCMP, but only one'.

Question:
What are the top 10 best practices for securing WLANs?

Answer:
'change the SSID, use port access, separate guest, use VLANs, deploy a WIDS, place in the physical center, create a DMZ, implement a VPN, use MAC filtering and pen test'.

Question:
Describe the 802.11 wireless standard.

Answer:
'Operated in the 2.4 Ghz range, provided speeds up to 2 Mbps'.

Question:
Describe the 802.11b wireless standard.

Answer:
'Used DSSS, operated in the 2.4 Ghz range, provided speeds up to 11 Mbps'.

Question:
Describe the 802.11i wireless standard.

Answer:
'Added WPA'.

Question:
Describe the 802.11a wireless standard.

Answer:
'Used ODFM, operated in the 5 Ghz range, 5provided speeds up to 4 Mbps'.

Question:
Describe the 802.11e wireless standard.

Answer:
'Added QoS multimedia traffic'.

Question:
Describe the 802.11f wireless standard.

Answer:
'Added roaming'.

Question:
Describe the 802.11g wireless standard.

Answer:
'Operated in the 2.4 Ghz range, provided speeds up to 54 Mbps'.

Communication and Network Security Domain

Question:
Describe the 802.11h wireless standard.

Answer:
'Increased usability of 802.11a outside of the US'.

Question:
Describe the 802.11j wireless standard.

Answer:
'Aligned standards across countries'.

Question:
Describe the 802.11n wireless standard.

Answer:
'Used MIMO, operated in the 5 Ghz range, provided speeds up to 100 Mbps'.

Question:
Describe the 802.11ac wireless standard.

Answer:
'Used beamforming, operated in the 2.4 and 5 Ghz ranges, provided speeds up to 1.3 Gbps'.

Question:
What are 3 1G implementations of FDMA?

Answer:
'AMPS, TACS and NMT'.

Question:
What 3 technologies comprise 2G networks?

Answer:
'TDMA, GSM and PCS'.

Question:
What 4 technologies comprise 3.5G networks, sometimes called 3GPP?

Answer:
'EDGE, HSPDA, CDMA2000 and WiMAX'.

Question:
What 3 technologies comprise 4G networks?

Answer:
'OFDMA, WiMAX and LTE'.

Question:
What capabilities did 1G deliver?

Answer:
'supported voice calls only, was analog, and used circuit-switching'.

Communication and Network Security Domain

Question:
What capabilities did 2G deliver?

Answer:
'added paging support, caller ID and low-speed data, such as email'.

Question:
What capabilities did 2.5G deliver?

Answer:
'added always on for email and pages, and increased the bandwidth'.

Question:
What capabilities did 3G deliver?

Answer:
'provided true Internet connectivity, and changed to packet-switching'.

Question:
What capabilities did 3.5G deliver?

Answer:
'used OFDMA, and increased bandwidth'.

Question:
What capabilities does 4G deliver?

Answer:
'was finally 100% all IP, and increased bandwidth up to 1 Gbps'.

Question:
What are the two types of network encryption?

Answer:
'link encryption, and End-to-End Encryption'.

Question:
Which network encryption is the best for performance?

Answer:
'end-to-end encryption'.

Question:
What security attributes does PGP provide?

Answer:
'confidentiality, integrity, nonrepudiation and authentication'.

Identity and Access Management Domain

Definitions

Question:
What is the flow of information between a subject and an object?

Answer:
'access'

Question:
What is an active entity that requests access to an object?

Answer:
'subject'

Question:
What is a passive entity that contains the desired information or functionality?

Answer:
'object'

Question:
What is assurance that information is not disclosed to an unauthorized subject?

Answer:
'confidentiality'

Question:
What is assurance that information has not been altered by an unauthorized subject?

Answer:
'integrity'

Question:
What is assurance that an object is available when a subject needs it?

Answer:
'availability'

Question:
What are software components used to carry out identification, authentication, authorization and accountability?

Answer:
'logical access controls'

Question:
What is a subject within a given environment?

Answer:
'identity'

Identity and Access Management Domain

Question:
What specifies that the identity should represent something unique about the subject?

Answer:
'identity uniqueness'

Question:
What specifies that the identity name should not describe the role or purpose of the account?

Answer:
'identity non-descriptive'

Question:
What specifies how an identity is issued to a subject, such as an email or ID card?

Answer:
'identity issuance'

Question:
What is the process of creating, managing and retiring identities?

Answer:
'Identity Management, or IdM'

Question:
What is a central location where all subjects and objects are tracked?

Answer:
'directory'

Question:
What is a standard which defines a hierarchical format?

Answer:
'X.500'

Question:
What allows other applications to interact with the directory?

Answer:
'Lightweight Directory Access Protocol, or LDAP'

Question:
What manages objects in a directory?

Answer:
'directory service'

Question:
What is a hierarchical naming convention that uniquely identifies a location or object?

Answer:
'namespace'

Identity and Access Management Domain

Question:
What is a friendly name in LDAP?

Answer:
'common name, or CN'

Question:
What identifies the object uniquely in the directory in LDAP?

Answer:
'distinguished name, or DN'

Question:
What makes up a DN, and together are unique in LDAP?

Answer:
'domain components, or DC'

Question:
What is the name of the directory service in a Windows LDAP network?

Answer:
'domain controller, or DC'

Question:
What is a directory that aggregates information from multiple sources and presents a unified view?

Answer:
'meta-directory'

Question:
What is a directory that points to an external database only?

Answer:
'virtual directory'

Question:
What is a software layer that controls authentication and authorization within a web-based environment?

Answer:
'Web Access Management, or WAM'

Question:
What is the process in which a subject proves it is who it claims to be?

Answer:
'authentication'

Question:
What is something a person stores in their memory, such as a password, pin, entry code for a vehicle or combination for a lock?

Answer:
'something a person knows'

Identity and Access Management Domain

Question:
What is a physical possession, such as a swipe card, a smart token, keys or an access badge?

Answer:
'something a person has'

Question:
What is a unique physical attribute, such as fingerprint, retina pattern, a gait or voice print?

Answer:
'something a person is'

Question:
What is authentication requiring at least 2 factors?

Answer:
'strong authentication'

Question:
What is another name for strong authentication?

Answer:
'multifactor authentication'

Question:
What occurs when multiple systems update their own respective passwords for the same user account at the same time?

Answer:
'password synchronization'

Question:
What occurs when multiple systems use a common authentication mechanism?

Answer:
'single sign on'

Question:
What occurs when password is reset through automated means, such as via an email with a link?

Answer:
'self-service password reset'

Question:
What occurs when a helpdesk person types in the answers to password reset questions?

Answer:
'assisted password reset'

Question:
What is the process of creating, modifying and decommissioning user accounts on all appropriate systems?

Answer:
'account management'

Identity and Access Management Domain

Question:
What is the act of creating user objects and attributes?

Answer:
'user provisioning'

Question:
What accompanies a user account, and contains such things as addresses, phone numbers and email addresses?

Answer:
'profile'

Question:
What verifies an individual's identity based on physiological or behavioral attributes?

Answer:
'biometrics'

Question:
What are physical attributes that are unique to the individual, and are reflected by 'what you are'?

Answer:
'physiological traits'

Question:
What is a characteristic of an individual that is not guaranteed to be unique, such as signature, height or a walking gait, and is reflected by 'what you do'?

Answer:
'behavioral trait'

Question:
What is a biometric error that rejects an authorized individual?

Answer:
'type 1 biometric error'

Question:
What is a biometric error that accepts an unauthorized individual?

Answer:
'type 2 biometric error'

Question:
What increases when a type 1 error occurs?

Answer:
'False Rejection Rate, or FRR'

Question:
What increases when a type 2 error occurs?

Answer:
'False Acceptance Rate, or FAR'

Identity and Access Management Domain

Question:
What is the point at which FRR = FAR?

Answer:
'Crossover Error Rate, or CER'

Question:
What is a complete record of ridges and valley on a finger?

Answer:
'fingerprints'

Question:
What contains certain features of a fingerprint?

Answer:
'finger scan'

Question:
What includes fingerprint and the creases, ridges and grooves of the palm?

Answer:
'palm scan'

Question:
What includes the shape, length and width of hand and fingers?

Answer:
'hand geometry'

Question:
What records the blood-vessel patterns on the back of an eyeball, and is most invasive?

Answer:
'retina scan'

Question:
What records the colored portion surrounding the pupil, and is the most accurate?

Answer:
'iris scan'

Question:
What are the speed and movements produced when signing a name?

Answer:
'signature dynamics'

Question:
What are the speed and pauses between each keypress as a password is typed?

Answer:
'keystroke dynamics'

Identity and Access Management Domain

Question:
What is created by recording a number of words during enrollment?

Answer:
'voice print'

Question:
What records the bone structure, nose ridge, eye widths, forehead size and chin shape?

Answer:
'facial scan'

Question:
What is captured by a side camera looking at the contour of the palm and fingers?

Answer:
'hand topography'

Question:
What occurs when an attacker sniffs network traffic or records keystrokes?

Answer:
'electronic monitoring'

Question:
What is a file stored on the authentication server?

Answer:
'password file'

Question:
What is a password attack using an automated tool to try and login by cycling through many possible combinations of characters, numbers and symbols until a match is found?

Answer:
'brute-force attack'

Question:
What is a password attack in which words in the native language are used to guess the password?

Answer:
'dictionary attack'

Question:
What is used in an attack where all likely passwords exist in a table in a pre-hashed state?

Answer:
'rainbow table'

Question:
What is an attack where the attacker convinces the owner to reveal their password?

Answer:
'social engineering'

Identity and Access Management Domain

331

Question:
What is the number of failed authentication attempts before the system locks the account?

Answer:
'clipping level'

Question:
What forces a user to change the password at recurring intervals?

Answer:
'password aging'

Question:
What is a software tool that attempts to guess passwords?

Answer:
'password checker'

Question:
What is the same as a password checker but is used by an attacker?

Answer:
'password cracker'

Question:
What is the location where Linux systems store passwords?

Answer:
'shadow file'

Question:
What is created when a user answers opinion-based questions during enrollment?

Answer:
'cognitive password'

Question:
What occurs when any password or phrase is used to authenticate?

Answer:
'authentication by knowledge'

Question:
What is a technique in which a person is forced to enter information about a graphical image that is very difficult for computers to process?

Answer:
'CAPTCHA'

Question:
What is a password that can be used once?

Answer:
'One-Time Password, or OTP'

Identity and Access Management Domain

Question:
What is a device that will generate the same password simultaneously with the server?

Answer:
'synchronized device'

Question:
What is a token device that requires the user to push a button, resulting in both server and device advancing to the next token?

Answer:
'counter-synchronized, or event-based device'

Question:
What is a device which retrieves a nonce from the server, and when the user enters the same nonce, the device generates a shared key?

Answer:
'asynchronous token device'

Question:
What is a software-only token generator, as opposed to a hardware device?

Answer:
'soft token'

Question:
What is secret key made up of multiple words?

Answer:
'passphrase'

Question:
What is a card that stores data only?

Answer:
'memory card'

Question:
What is a memory card with one or more chips?

Answer:
'smart card'

Question:
What is a card which must be inserted into a reader and makes physical contact?

Answer:
'contact card'

Question:
What is a card with an antenna around the perimeter and communicates via an electromagnetic field?

Answer:
'contactless card'

Identity and Access Management Domain

333

Question:
What is a contactless card that is normally not encrypted due to power requirements?

Answer:
'Radio Frequency Identification, or RFID'

Question:
What is a card with one chip supporting both connection methods?

Answer:
'combi card'

Question:
What is a card with two chips, one for each connection method?

Answer:
'hybrid card'

Question:
What is a non-invasive attack which leaves the environment alone and simply watches for behavioral differences?

Answer:
'side-channel attack'

Question:
What is a side-channel attack in which the attacker monitors the power emissions during processing?

Answer:
'differential power analysis'

Question:
What is a side-channel attack in which the attacker monitors the frequencies emitted?

Answer:
'electromagnetic analysis'

Question:
What is a side-channel attack in which the attacker monitors how long a process takes?

Answer:
'timing analysis'

Question:
What is a non-invasive attack that provides instructions to exploit a vulnerability?

Answer:
'software attack'

Question:
What is an invasive card attack that changes the environment of the card, such as voltage, temperature or clock rate, and watches for differences?

Answer:
'fault generation'

Identity and Access Management Domain

Question:
What is an invasive card attack that accesses the internal circuitry directly?

Answer:
'microprobing'

Question:
What is the ISO standard detailing card physical attributes?

Answer:
'ISO 14443-1'

Question:
What is the ISO standard detailing card initialization and anti-collision?

Answer:
'ISO 14443-2'

Question:
What is the ISO standard detailing card transmission protocols?

Answer:
'ISO 14443-3'

Question:
What is the act of ensuring the subject is allowed to access an object?

Answer:
'authorization'

Question:
What are the rules used to determine if a subject has access to an object?

Answer:
'access criteria'

Question:
What represents access rights based on a subject's task?

Answer:
'role'

Question:
What contains multiple roles?

Answer:
'group'

Question:
What is the act of restricting physical access to a device?

Answer:
'physical location restriction'

Identity and Access Management Domain

335

Question:
What is the act of restricting access based on IP address?

Answer:
'logical location restriction'

Question:
What is the act of restricting access so that an object is available only during business hours or week days?

Answer:
'time-of-day restriction'

Question:
What is the act of restricting access based on the time of day?

Answer:
'temporal restriction'

Question:
What is the act of restricting access depending on the activity the subject is engaged in?

Answer:
'transaction-type restriction'

Question:
What is the approach that no features are allowed unless explicitly indicated?

Answer:
'Default to No Access'

Question:
What is the approach that data is accessible only if the subject needs it?

Answer:
'need-to-know'

Question:
What is the approach that subjects should be given just enough access to get a job done, and no more?

Answer:
'least-privilege'

Question:
What is the tendency for an employee to gain more and more access over time as positions are changed?

Answer:
'authorization creep'

Question:
What is the most common SSO implementation?

Answer:
'Kerberos'

Identity and Access Management Domain

Question:
What is a KDC component that authenticates a principal?

Answer:
'Authentication Service, or AS'

Question:
What is a KDC component that creates a ticket for a principal?

Answer:
'Ticket Granting Service, or TGS'

Question:
What is a user, application or network service?

Answer:
'Kerberos principal'

Question:
What passes proof of identity from principal to principal?

Answer:
'Kerberos ticket'

Question:
What is a packet of data containing a principal's information?

Answer:
'Kerberos authenticator'

Question:
What is a set of principals?

Answer:
'Kerberos realm'

Question:
What is a logical groupings of resources that are managed by the same security policy?

Answer:
'security domain'

Question:
What is a portable identity that can be used across organizational boundaries?

Answer:
'federated identity'

Question:
What is a browser-based plug-in?

Answer:
'portlet'

Identity and Access Management Domain

337

Question:
What is a text-based format used for data representation?

Answer:
'eXtensible Markup Language, or XML'

Question:
What is used to create browser-based user interfaces?

Answer:
'Hypertext Markup Language, or HTML'

Question:
What is used for automated configuration of users and entitlements?

Answer:
'Service Provisioning Markup Language, or SMPL'

Question:
What is the software sending a change request to a PSP?

Answer:
'Requesting Authority, or RA'

Question:
What is the software that will validate and distribute the change request to one or more PSTs?

Answer:
'Provisioning Service Provider, or PSP'

Question:
What is the system acting on the change request?

Answer:
'Provisioning Service Target, or PST'

Question:
What is used for real-time authentication in a federation?

Answer:
'Security Assertion Markup Language, or SAML'

Question:
What is a standardized way of communicating access rights and security policies?

Answer:
'eXtensible Access Control Markup Language, or XACML'

Question:
What are services that are accessible using HTTP across the web?

Answer:
'web services'

Identity and Access Management Domain

Question:
What is a very simple web-based communication format that has low overhead but provides no security?

Answer:
'Representative State Transfer, or REST'

Question:
What is a very heavy web-based communication format that has considerable security built in?

Answer:
'Simple Object Access Protocol, or SOAP'

Question:
What is a pattern for creating independent web-based services across business domains that can work together?

Answer:
'Service Oriented Approach, or SOA'

Question:
What is a method for 2 sites to leverage the same set of credentials without having to trust each other?

Answer:
'OpenID'

Question:
What is a user wanting to access a resource party using an OpenID provider?

Answer:
'OpenID end user'

Question:
What is a site the end user wants to access, and is OpenID-enabled?

Answer:
'OpenID resource party'

Question:
What is a third-party that stores end user's OpenID credentials?

Answer:
'OpenID provider'

Question:
What is a standard that adds authorization capabilities to OpenID?

Answer:
'OAuth'

Question:
What is an update to OAuth that implements both authentication and authorization, and is replacing OpenID?

Answer:
'OAuth2'

Identity and Access Management Domain

339

Question:
What is outsourced identity management that includes SSO, federated IdM and password-management services?

Answer:
'Identity as a Service, or IaaS'

Question:
What defines access rules and how they are applied to subjects and objects?

Answer:
'Access Control Models'

Question:
What is a discretionary model that allows each user to dictate access to anything that user owns?

Answer:
'Discretionary Access Control, or DAC'

Question:
What represents 'read' in the Discretionary Access Control model?

Answer:
'with DAC, the letter 'r''

Question:
What represents 'write' in the Discretionary Access Control model?

Answer:
'with DAC, the letter 'w''

Question:
What represents 'execute' in the Discretionary Access Control model?

Answer:
'with DAC, the letter 'x''

Question:
What represents 'delete' in the Discretionary Access Control model?

Answer:
'with DAC, the letter 'd''

Question:
What represents 'change' in the Discretionary Access Control model?

Answer:
'with DAC, the letter 'c''

Question:
What is an access control model used primarily for high-security systems such as SE Linux and Trusted Solaris?

Answer:
'Mandatory Access Control, or MAC'

Identity and Access Management Domain

340

Question:
What is an attribute dictating that the user cannot make decisions on access?

Answer:
'nondiscretionary'

Question:
What is a label that is assigned to every subject and object to provide security?

Answer:
'security label, or sensitivity label'

Question:
What is assigned to each subject or object to provide security, but only one per?

Answer:
'classification, or clearance level'

Question:
What is assigned to each subject or object for security, and more than one is allowed?

Answer:
'category'

Question:
What is a MAC system that allows a subject to access an object at a different classification?

Answer:
'Multilevel Security System, or MLS'

Question:
What occurs when an object's classification is at or below the subject's clearance, and can therefore be accessed?

Answer:
'domination'

Question:
What is a process that monitors the exchange of information and transfer of data between two systems?

Answer:
'guard'

Question:
What is an access control model that provides roles?

Answer:
'Role-Based Access Control, or RBAC'

Question:
What represents a user logging into an RBAC?

Answer:
'session'

Identity and Access Management Domain

Question:
What is an RBAC component that gathers all roles and permissions for a session?

Answer:
'core RBAC'

Question:
What is an RBAC component that allows the roles to be modeled on the actual organizational structure?

Answer:
'hierarchical RBAC'

Question:
What is a flavor of RBAC in which role inheritance is allowed only once; for example, Role 1 inherits from Role 2 but not from any other role?

Answer:
'limited hierarchies'

Question:
What is a flavor of RBAC in which role inheritance is allowed for multiple levels simultaneously; for example, Role 1 inherits from Role 2 AND from Role 3?

Answer:
'general hierarchies'

Question:
What occurs in hierarchical RBAC when we constrain the combination of privileges; for example, a user cannot be a member of both 'dock worker' and 'manifest clerk'?

Answer:
'static separation of duty, or SSD'

Question:
What occurs in hierarchical RBAC when we constrain the combination of privileges that can be active within the same session; for example, a user can belong to both 'dock worker' and 'manifest clerk', but not at the same time?

Answer:
'dynamic separation of duty, or DSD'

Question:
What is an RBAC management mode in which there are no roles; users are mapped directly to applications and no roles are used?

Answer:
'non-RBAC'

Question:
What is an RBAC management mode in which roles are optional; users are mapped to multiple roles as well as being mapped to applications that do not have role-based support?

Answer:
'limited RBAC'

Identity and Access Management Domain

Question:
What is an RBAC management mode in which we have pseudo roles; users are mapped to roles for multiple applications with only selected rights assigned?

Answer:
'hybrid RBAC'

Question:
What is an RBAC management mode in which we have enterprise roles; users are mapped to enterprise roles?

Answer:
'full RBAC'

Question:
What is a special version of RBAC geared to PHI and PII?

Answer:
'privacy-aware RBAC'

Question:
What is built on top of RBAC and extends its capabilities to include if...then rules?

Answer:
'Rule-Based Access Control, or RB-RBAC'

Question:
What is a user interface that limits a user's ability to access data or functionality?

Answer:
'constrained user interface'

Question:
What is a user interface constraint method that limits the options the user can chose from?

Answer:
'menus'

Question:
What is a user interface constraint method that limits the commands available when a shell, or virtual environment, opens?

Answer:
'shells'

Question:
What is a user interface constraint method that limits the data that can be viewed by creating a virtual view of the data?

Answer:
'database views'

Question:
What is a user interface constraint method that limits the physical controls the user can access such as keys or touch-screen buttons?

Answer:
'physical constraints'

Identity and Access Management Domain

Question:
What is a table of subjects and objects that dictates the level of access?

Answer:
'access control matrix'

Question:
What specifies the rights a subject has to a specific object?

Answer:
'capability table'

Question:
What is a term used to describe a token, ticket or key?

Answer:
'capability'

Question:
What is something that represents an object that a subject wishes to access?

Answer:
'capability component'

Question:
What is a list of subjects who may access an object, and the permissions available for that subject?

Answer:
'access control list, or ACL'

Question:
What occurs when we control access based only on the content of an object?

Answer:
'content-based access control'

Question:
What occurs when we add context decisions to content-based access control?

Answer:
'context-based access control'

Question:
What occurs when a single individual or department controls all access to resources?

Answer:
'centralized access control administration'

Question:
What is a network protocol that provides authentication and authorization services to remote clients?

Answer:
'Remote Authentication Dial-In User Service, or RADIUS'

Identity and Access Management Domain

344

Question:
What is a flexible list of permissions implemented by access control systems?

Answer:
'Attribute Value Pairs, or AVPS'

Question:
What is competitor to RADIUS?

Answer:
'Terminal Access Controller Access Control System, or TACACS'

Question:
What is a successor to TACACS and separates authentication from authorization?

Answer:
'eXtended TACACS, or XTACACS'

Question:
What is a protocol that added many features to TACACS, including TCP, encryption, and allowed more AVPs?

Answer:
'TACACS+'

Question:
What is a protocol similar to TACACS+ but is peer-to-peer, and is the latest standard?

Answer:
'Diameter'

Question:
What is a Diameter protocol that covers just about everything but AAA?

Answer:
'Diameter base protocol'

Question:
What is a Diameter protocol that allows other protocols to implement AAA?

Answer:
'Diameter extensions'

Question:
What is a capability allowing a mobile device to move from network to network without changing its IP address?

Answer:
'mobile IP'

Question:
What is a quasi-permanent IP that traffic can be sent to?

Answer:
'home IP address'

Identity and Access Management Domain

Question:
What is the current IP address of the mobile device?

Answer:
'care-of address'

Question:
What occurs when we trust the data owners to take care of managing access to their own data?

Answer:
'decentralized access control administration'

Question:
What are security controls that deal with personnel policies, employee training and periodic testing to make sure all controls are in-place and effective?

Answer:
'administrative controls'

Question:
What are security controls that deal with physically securing assets?

Answer:
'physical controls'

Question:
What are security controls that always have a software component and are used to restrict access?

Answer:
'technical controls'

Question:
What is the result of implementing audit tracking?

Answer:
'accountability'

Question:
What captures user actions, application events and system activities?

Answer:
'auditing'

Question:
What is the act of erasing log files entries after an attack?

Answer:
'scrubbing'

Question:
What is achieved by physically severing the "receive" pairs in an Ethernet cable?

Answer:
'simplex communication'

Identity and Access Management Domain

Question:
What allows us to detect the addition or removal of log entries by including the hash of the previous entry?

Answer:
'cryptographic hash chaining'

Question:
What occurs when we apply the proper level of filtering such that only important details are logged?

Answer:
'clipping'

Question:
What is a log review resulting from a disruption or security breach?

Answer:
'event-oriented log review'

Question:
What is a periodic log review to detect unusual behaviors from users, applications or systems?

Answer:
'audit trail log review'

Question:
What is a log review in which an automated system correlates logs from various systems, such as SEM or SIEM?

Answer:
'real-time analysis log review'

Question:
What discards irrelevant data to make reviews easier?

Answer:
'audit-reduction tool'

Question:
What automates the sifting and correlation of all logs?

Answer:
'Security Event Management, or SEM'

Question:
What is another name for SEM?

Answer:
'Security Information and Event Management, or SIEM'

Question:
What is the ability to make sense of the current state in spite of a large number of data points and complex relationships?

Answer:
'situational awareness'

Identity and Access Management Domain

Question:
What captures each keystroke and records the resulting characters in a file?

Answer:
'keystroke monitoring'

Question:
What is a device inserted between a wired keyboard connection and the computer?

Answer:
'dongle'

Question:
What is a metal shield that prevents electronic signals from leaking out?

Answer:
'faraday cage'

Question:
What is the use of random electrical signals across the entire communication band to hide valid signals?

Answer:
'white noise'

Question:
What is a room or building wrapped in a faraday cage?

Answer:
'control zone'

Question:
What is a standard that requires equipment to include a Faraday cage?

Answer:
'TEMPEST'

Question:
What is a system that detects intrusion attempts against network or network devices?

Answer:
'Intrusion Detection System, or IDS'

Question:
What within an IDS collects information and sends the resulting data to an analyzer?

Answer:
'sensor'

Question:
What within an IDS looks for suspicious activity and send alerts to the administration interface?

Answer:
'analyzer'

Identity and Access Management Domain

348

Question:
What within an IDS processes alerts, which can result in an email, text message, phone call, a visual alert on a screen or sending a message to some other system?

Answer:
'administration interface'

Question:
What is a NIC mode that captures all traffic whether it was intended for that device or not?

Answer:
'promiscuous mode'

Question:
What is the act of examining traffic as it passes by?

Answer:
'sniffing'

Question:
What understands and detects specific traffic protocols?

Answer:
'protocol analyzer'

Question:
What occurs when security vendors allow malicious software to execute on a host and then gather the changes that were made to the system?

Answer:
'behavior blocking'

Question:
What is an attack in which a rogue client pretends to own an IP it does not?

Answer:
'ARP poisoning'

Question:
What is an attack in which ICMP packets are used to hide data?

Answer:
'Loki attack'

Question:
What is an attack in which an attacker uses sequence numbers to jump in and take over a socket connection?

Answer:
'session hijacking'

Question:
What is an attack in which the source and destination IP addresses are the same?

Answer:
'Land attack'

Identity and Access Management Domain

Question:
What is an attack in which all TCP header flags are set to '1'?

Answer:
'Xmas attack'

Question:
What is a device that watches network traffic?

Answer:
'Network-based IDS, or NIDS'

Question:
What is a NIDS that compares traffic patterns in real-time to a list of patterns known to represent an attack?

Answer:
'signature-based, or knowledge-based or pattern-matching'

Question:
What is a NIDS that detects new patterns relative to a known 'normal' baseline?

Answer:
'anomaly-based IDS or behavioral-based'

Question:
What is a NIDS that understands certain protocols, allowing it to add context to patterns?

Answer:
'protocol anomaly-based IDS'

Question:
What is a NIDS that watches for known patterns that are suspicious due to the time or frequency?

Answer:
'traffic anomaly-based IDS'

Question:
What is a NIDS that is considered to be an expert system?

Answer:
'rule-based IDS, or a heuristic-based IDS'

Question:
What describes any NIDS data that comes in from a sensor or system that is being monitored?

Answer:
'rule-based facts'

Question:
What is a collection of NIDS 'if...then' rules that analyze facts and takes action?

Answer:
'rule-based knowledge base'

Identity and Access Management Domain

350

Question:
What uses 5th generation programming languages, such as artificial intelligence, and can infer relationships?

Answer:
'rule-based inference engine'

Question:
What is an IDS that watches everything on the local computer?

Answer:
'Host-based IDS, or HIDS'

Question:
What is a snapshot of the contents of volatile and non-volatile memory within a host?

Answer:
'HIDS state'

Question:
What is a host-based IDS which compares memory states to known attacks?

Answer:
'stateful matching IDS'

Question:
What is an IDS that watches certain software applications running on a host?

Answer:
'Application-based IDS, or AIDS'

Question:
What is an AIDS that takes action according to some predefined rules?

Answer:
'Intrusion Prevention System, or IPS'

Question:
What is the act of redirecting an attacker's efforts that he or she has already determined to carry out?

Answer:
'enticement'

Question:
What is the act of convincing an attacker to take action by encouraging or tricking them?

Answer:
'entrapment'

Question:
What is an attack that iterates through all commonly used words or combinations of characters trying to guess a password?

Answer:
'dictionary attack'

Identity and Access Management Domain

Question:
What is an attack that iterates through every possible character in increasing lengths until a password match is found?

Answer:
'brute-force attack, or exhaustive attack'

Question:
What is an attack that automatically dials through a list of phone numbers until a modem answers?

Answer:
'war-dialing'

Question:
What is an attack using a combination of dictionary and brute-force attacks?

Answer:
'hybrid attack'

Question:
What is an attack for which hashes for all relevant values are pre-computed into a 'rainbow table'?

Answer:
'rainbow attack'

Question:
What is an attack in which a software program mimics an OS interface to collect credentials?

Answer:
'spoofing at logon'

Identity and Access Management Domain

Terms

Question:
What is 'access'?

Answer:
'access' is the flow of information between a subject and an object.

Question:
What is a 'subject'?

Answer:
A 'subject' is an active entity that requests access to an object.

Question:
What is an 'object'?

Answer:
An 'object' is a passive entity that contains the desired information or functionality.

Question:
What is 'confidentiality'?

Answer:
'confidentiality' is assurance that information is not disclosed to an unauthorized subject.

Question:
What is 'integrity'?

Answer:
'integrity' is assurance that information has not been altered by an unauthorized subject.

Question:
What is 'availability'?

Answer:
'availability' is assurance that an object is available when a subject needs it.

Question:
What is 'logical access controls'?

Answer:
'logical access controls' are software components used to carry out identification, authentication, authorization and accountability.

Question:
What is an 'identity'?

Answer:
An 'identity' is a subject within a given environment.

Identity and Access Management Domain

Question:
What is 'identity uniqueness'?

Answer:
'identity uniqueness' specifies that the identity should represent something unique about the subject.

Question:
What is 'identity non-descriptive'?

Answer:
'identity non-descriptive' specifies that the identity name should not describe the role or purpose of the account.

Question:
What is 'identity issuance'?

Answer:
'identity issuance' specifies how an identity is issued to a subject, such as an email or ID card.

Question:
What is 'Identity Management, or IdM'?

Answer:
'Identity Management, or IdM' is the process of creating, managing and retiring identities.

Question:
What is a 'directory'?

Answer:
A 'directory' is a central location where all subjects and objects are tracked.

Question:
What is 'X.500'?

Answer:
'X.500' is a standard which defines a hierarchical format.

Question:
What is the 'Lightweight Directory Access Protocol, or LDAP'?

Answer:
The 'Lightweight Directory Access Protocol, or LDAP' allows other applications to interact with the directory.

Question:
What is a 'directory service'?

Answer:
A 'directory service' manages objects in a directory.

Question:
What is a 'namespace'?

Answer:
A 'namespace' is a hierarchical naming convention that uniquely identifies a location or object.

Identity and Access Management Domain

Question:
What is a 'common name, or CN'?

Answer:
A 'common name, or CN' is a friendly name in LDAP.

Question:
What is a 'distinguished name, or DN'?

Answer:
A 'distinguished name, or DN' identifies the object uniquely in the directory in LDAP.

Question:
What is 'domain components, or DC'?

Answer:
'domain components, or DC' makes up a DN, and together are unique in LDAP.

Question:
What is a 'domain controller, or DC'?

Answer:
A 'domain controller, or DC' is the name of the directory service in a Windows LDAP network.

Question:
What is a 'meta-directory'?

Answer:
A 'meta-directory' is a directory that aggregates information from multiple sources and presents a unified view.

Question:
What is a 'virtual directory'?

Answer:
A 'virtual directory' is a directory that points to an external database only.

Question:
What is 'Web Access Management, or WAM'?

Answer:
'Web Access Management, or WAM' is a software layer that controls authentication and authorization within a web-based environment.

Question:
What is 'authentication'?

Answer:
'authentication' is the process in which a subject proves it is who it claims to be.

Question:
What is 'something a person knows'?

Answer:
'something a person knows' is something a person stores in their memory, such as a password, pin, entry code for a vehicle or combination for a lock.

Identity and Access Management Domain

Question:
What is 'something a person has'?

Answer:
'something a person has' is a physical possession, such as a swipe card, a smart token, keys or an access badge.

Question:
What is 'something a person is'?

Answer:
'something a person is' is a unique physical attribute, such as fingerprint, retina pattern, a gait or voice print.

Question:
What is 'strong authentication'?

Answer:
'strong authentication' is authentication requiring at least 2 factors.

Question:
What is 'multifactor authentication'?

Answer:
'multifactor authentication' is another name for strong authentication.

Question:
What is 'password synchronization'?

Answer:
'password synchronization' occurs when multiple systems update their own respective passwords for the same user account at the same time.

Question:
What is 'single sign on'?

Answer:
'single sign on' occurs when multiple systems use a common authentication mechanism.

Question:
What is 'self-service password reset'?

Answer:
'self-service password reset' occurs when password is reset through automated means, such as via an email with a link.

Question:
What is 'assisted password reset'?

Answer:
'assisted password reset' occurs when a helpdesk person types in the answers to password reset questions.

Question:
What is 'account management'?

Answer:
'account management' is the process of creating, modifying and decommissioning user accounts on all appropriate systems.

Identity and Access Management Domain

Question:
What is 'user provisioning'?

Answer:
'user provisioning' is the act of creating user objects and attributes.

Question:
What is a 'profile'?

Answer:
A 'profile' accompanies a user account, and contains such things as addresses, phone numbers and email addresses.

Question:
What is 'biometrics'?

Answer:
'biometrics' verifies an individual's identity based on physiological or behavioral attributes.

Question:
What is 'physiological traits'?

Answer:
'physiological traits' are physical attributes that are unique to the individual, and are reflected by 'what you are'.

Question:
What is a 'behavioral trait'?

Answer:
A 'behavioral trait' is a characteristic of an individual that is not guaranteed to be unique, such as signature, height or a walking gait, and is reflected by 'what you do'.

Question:
What is a 'type 1 biometric error'?

Answer:
A 'type 1 biometric error' is a biometric error that rejects an authorized individual.

Question:
What is a 'type 2 biometric error'?

Answer:
A 'type 2 biometric error' is a biometric error that accepts an unauthorized individual.

Question:
What is the 'False Rejection Rate, or FRR'?

Answer:
The 'False Rejection Rate, or FRR' increases when a type 1 error occurs.

Question:
What is the 'False Acceptance Rate, or FAR'?

Answer:
The 'False Acceptance Rate, or FAR' increases when a type 2 error occurs.

Identity and Access Management Domain

Question:
What is the 'Crossover Error Rate, or CER'?

Answer:
The 'Crossover Error Rate, or CER' is the point at which FRR = FAR.

Question:
What is 'fingerprints'?

Answer:
'fingerprints' is a complete record of ridges and valley on a finger.

Question:
What is a 'finger scan'?

Answer:
A 'finger scan' contains certain features of a fingerprint.

Question:
What is a 'palm scan'?

Answer:
A 'palm scan' includes fingerprint and the creases, ridges and grooves of the palm.

Question:
What is 'hand geometry'?

Answer:
'hand geometry' includes the shape, length and width of hand and fingers.

Question:
What is a 'retina scan'?

Answer:
A 'retina scan' records the blood-vessel patterns on the back of an eyeball, and is most invasive.

Question:
What is a 'iris scan'?

Answer:
A 'iris scan' records the colored portion surrounding the pupil, and is the most accurate.

Question:
What is 'signature dynamics'?

Answer:
'signature dynamics' are the speed and movements produced when signing a name.

Question:
What is 'keystroke dynamics'?

Answer:
'keystroke dynamics' are the speed and pauses between each keypress as a password is typed.

Identity and Access Management Domain

Question:
What is a 'voice print'?

Answer:
A 'voice print' is created by recording a number of words during enrollment.

Question:
What is a 'facial scan'?

Answer:
A 'facial scan' records the bone structure, nose ridge, eye widths, forehead size and chin shape.

Question:
What is 'hand topography'?

Answer:
'hand topography' is captured by a side camera looking at the contour of the palm and fingers.

Question:
What is 'electronic monitoring'?

Answer:
'electronic monitoring' occurs when an attacker sniffs network traffic or records keystrokes.

Question:
What is a 'password file'?

Answer:
A 'password file' is a file stored on the authentication server.

Question:
What is a 'brute-force attack'?

Answer:
A 'brute-force attack' is a password attack using an automated tool to try and login by cycling through many possible combinations of characters, numbers and symbols until a match is found.

Question:
What is a 'dictionary attack'?

Answer:
A 'dictionary attack' is a password attack in which words in the native language are used to guess the password.

Question:
What is a 'rainbow table'?

Answer:
A 'rainbow table' is used in an attack where all likely passwords exist in a table in a pre-hashed state.

Question:
What is 'social engineering'?

Answer:
'social engineering' is an attack where the attacker convinces the owner to reveal their password.

Identity and Access Management Domain

Question:
What is a 'clipping level'?

Answer:
A 'clipping level' is the number of failed authentication attempts before the system locks the account.

Question:
What is 'password aging'?

Answer:
'password aging' forces a user to change the password at recurring intervals.

Question:
What is a 'password checker'?

Answer:
A 'password checker' is a software tool that attempts to guess passwords.

Question:
What is a 'password cracker'?

Answer:
A 'password cracker' is the same as a password checker but is used by an attacker.

Question:
What is a 'shadow file'?

Answer:
A 'shadow file' is the location where Linux systems store passwords.

Question:
What is a 'cognitive password'?

Answer:
A 'cognitive password' is created when a user answers opinion-based questions during enrollment.

Question:
What is 'authentication by knowledge'?

Answer:
'authentication by knowledge' occurs when any password or phrase is used to authenticate.

Question:
What is 'CAPTCHA'?

Answer:
'CAPTCHA' is a technique in which a person is forced to enter information about a graphical image that is very difficult for computers to process.

Question:
What is a 'One-Time Password, or OTP'?

Answer:
A 'One-Time Password, or OTP' is a password that can be used once.

Identity and Access Management Domain

Question:
What is a 'synchronized device'?

Answer:
A 'synchronized device' is a device that will generate the same password simultaneously with the server.

Question:
What is a 'counter-synchronized, or event-based device'?

Answer:
A 'counter-synchronized, or event-based device' is a token device that requires the user to push a button, resulting in both server and device advancing to the next token.

Question:
What is a 'asynchronous token device'?

Answer:
A 'asynchronous token device' is a device which retrieves a nonce from the server, and when the user enters the same nonce, the device generates a shared key.

Question:
What is a 'soft token'?

Answer:
A 'soft token' is a software-only token generator, as opposed to a hardware device.

Question:
What is a 'passphrase'?

Answer:
A 'passphrase' is secret key made up of multiple words.

Question:
What is a 'memory card'?

Answer:
A 'memory card' is a card that stores data only.

Question:
What is a 'smart card'?

Answer:
A 'smart card' is a memory card with one or more chips.

Question:
What is a 'contact card'?

Answer:
A 'contact card' is a card which must be inserted into a reader and makes physical contact.

Question:
What is a 'contactless card'?

Answer:
A 'contactless card' is a card with an antenna around the perimeter and communicates via an electromagnetic field.

Identity and Access Management Domain

Question:
What is 'Radio Frequency Identification, or RFID'?

Answer:
'Radio Frequency Identification, or RFID' is a contactless card that is normally not encrypted due to power requirements.

Question:
What is a 'combi card'?

Answer:
A 'combi card' is a card with one chip supporting both connection methods.

Question:
What is a 'hybrid card'?

Answer:
A 'hybrid card' is a card with two chips, one for each connection method.

Question:
What is a 'side-channel attack'?

Answer:
A 'side-channel attack' is a non-invasive attack which leaves the environment alone and simply watches for behavioral differences.

Question:
What is 'differential power analysis'?

Answer:
'differential power analysis' is a side-channel attack in which the attacker monitors the power emissions during processing.

Question:
What is 'electromagnetic analysis'?

Answer:
'electromagnetic analysis' is a side-channel attack in which the attacker monitors the frequencies emitted.

Question:
What is 'timing analysis'?

Answer:
'timing analysis' is a side-channel attack in which the attacker monitors how long a process takes.

Question:
What is 'software attack'?

Answer:
'software attack' is a non-invasive attack that provides instructions to exploit a vulnerability.

Question:
What is a 'fault generation'?

Answer:
A 'fault generation' is an invasive card attack that changes the environment of the card, such as voltage, temperature or clock rate, and watches for differences.

Identity and Access Management Domain

Question:
What is 'microprobing'?

Answer:
'microprobing' is an invasive card attack that accesses the internal circuitry directly.

Question:
What is the 'ISO 14443-1'?

Answer:
The 'ISO 14443-1' is the ISO standard detailing card physical attributes.

Question:
What is the 'ISO 14443-2'?

Answer:
The 'ISO 14443-2' is the ISO standard detailing card initialization and anti-collision.

Question:
What is the 'ISO 14443-3'?

Answer:
The 'ISO 14443-3' is the ISO standard detailing card transmission protocols.

Question:
What is 'authorization'?

Answer:
'authorization' is the act of ensuring the subject is allowed to access an object.

Question:
What is 'access criteria'?

Answer:
'access criteria' are the rules used to determine if a subject has access to an object.

Question:
What is a 'role'?

Answer:
A 'role' represents access rights based on a subject's task.

Question:
What is a 'group'?

Answer:
A 'group' contains multiple roles.

Question:
What is 'physical location restriction'?

Answer:
'physical location restriction' is the act of restricting physical access to a device.

Identity and Access Management Domain

363

Question:
What is 'logical location restriction'?

Answer:
'logical location restriction' is the act of restricting access based on IP address.

Question:
What is 'time-of-day restriction'?

Answer:
'time-of-day restriction' is the act of restricting access so that an object is available only during business hours or week days.

Question:
What is 'temporal restriction'?

Answer:
'temporal restriction' is the act of restricting access based on the time of day.

Question:
What is 'transaction-type restriction'?

Answer:
'transaction-type restriction' is the act of restricting access depending on the activity the subject is engaged in.

Question:
What is 'Default to No Access'?

Answer:
'Default to No Access' is the approach that no features are allowed unless explicitly indicated.

Question:
What is 'need-to-know'?

Answer:
'need-to-know' is the approach that data is accessible only if the subject needs it.

Question:
What is 'least-privilege'?

Answer:
'least-privilege' is the approach that subjects should be given just enough access to get a job done, and no more.

Question:
What is 'authorization creep'?

Answer:
'authorization creep' is the tendency for an employee to gain more and more access over time as positions are changed.

Question:
What is 'Kerberos'?

Answer:
'Kerberos' is the most common SSO implementation.

Identity and Access Management Domain

Question:
What is the 'Authentication Service, or AS'?

Answer:
The 'Authentication Service, or AS' is a KDC component that authenticates a principal.

Question:
What is the 'Ticket Granting Service, or TGS'?

Answer:
The 'Ticket Granting Service, or TGS' is a KDC component that creates a ticket for a principal.

Question:
What is a 'Kerberos principal'?

Answer:
A 'Kerberos principal' is a user, application or network service.

Question:
What is a 'Kerberos ticket'?

Answer:
A 'Kerberos ticket' passes proof of identity from principal to principal.

Question:
What is a 'Kerberos authenticator'?

Answer:
A 'Kerberos authenticator' is a packet of data containing a principal's information.

Question:
What is a 'Kerberos realm'?

Answer:
A 'Kerberos realm' is a set of principals.

Question:
What is a 'security domain'?

Answer:
A 'security domain' is a logical groupings of resources that are managed by the same security policy.

Question:
What is a 'federated identity'?

Answer:
A 'federated identity' is a portable identity that can be used across organizational boundaries.

Question:
What is a 'portlet'?

Answer:
A 'portlet' is a browser-based plug-in.

Identity and Access Management Domain

Question:
What is 'eXtensible Markup Language, or XML'?

Answer:
'eXtensible Markup Language, or XML' is a text-based format used for data representation.

Question:
What is 'Hypertext Markup Language, or HTML'?

Answer:
'Hypertext Markup Language, or HTML' is used to create browser-based user interfaces.

Question:
What is 'Service Provisioning Markup Language, or SMPL'?

Answer:
'Service Provisioning Markup Language, or SMPL' is used for automated configuration of users and entitlements.

Question:
What is the 'Requesting Authority, or RA'?

Answer:
The 'Requesting Authority, or RA' is the software sending a change request to a PSP.

Question:
What is the 'Provisioning Service Provider, or PSP'?

Answer:
The 'Provisioning Service Provider, or PSP' is the software that will validate and distribute the change request to one or more PSTs.

Question:
What is the 'Provisioning Service Target, or PST'?

Answer:
The 'Provisioning Service Target, or PST' is the system acting on the change request.

Question:
What is 'Security Assertion Markup Language, or SAML'?

Answer:
'Security Assertion Markup Language, or SAML' is used for real-time authentication in a federation.

Question:
What is 'eXtensible Access Control Markup Language, or XACML'?

Answer:
'eXtensible Access Control Markup Language, or XACML' is a standardized way of communicating access rights and security policies.

Question:
What is 'web services'?

Answer:
'web services' are services that are accessible using HTTP across the web.

Identity and Access Management Domain

Question:
What is 'Representative State Transfer, or REST'?

Answer:
'Representative State Transfer, or REST' is a very simple web-based communication format that has low overhead but provides no security.

Question:
What is the 'Simple Object Access Protocol, or SOAP'?

Answer:
The 'Simple Object Access Protocol, or SOAP' is a very heavy web-based communication format that has considerable security built in.

Question:
What is a 'Service Oriented Approach, or SOA'?

Answer:
A 'Service Oriented Approach, or SOA' is a pattern for creating independent web-based services across business domains that can work together.

Question:
What is 'OpenID'?

Answer:
'OpenID' is a method for 2 sites to leverage the same set of credentials without having to trust each other.

Question:
What is an 'OpenID end user'?

Answer:
An 'OpenID end user' is a user wanting to access a resource party using an OpenID provider.

Question:
What is an 'OpenID resource party'?

Answer:
An 'OpenID resource party' is a site the end user wants to access, and is OpenID-enabled.

Question:
What is an 'OpenID provider'?

Answer:
An 'OpenID provider' is a third-party that stores end user's OpenID credentials.

Question:
What is 'OAuth'?

Answer:
'OAuth' is a standard that adds authorization capabilities to OpenID.

Identity and Access Management Domain

Question:
What is 'OAuth2'?

Answer:
'OAuth2' is an update to OAuth that implements both authentication and authorization, and is replacing OpenID.

Question:
What is 'Identity as a Service, or IaaS'?

Answer:
'Identity as a Service, or IaaS' is outsourced identity management that includes SSO, federated IdM and password-management services.

Question:
What is 'Access Control Models'?

Answer:
'Access Control Models' defines access rules and how they are applied to subjects and objects.

Question:
What is 'Discretionary Access Control, or DAC'?

Answer:
'Discretionary Access Control, or DAC' is a discretionary model that allows each user to dictate access to anything that user owns.

Question:
What is 'with DAC, the letter 'r''?

Answer:
'with DAC, the letter 'r'' represents 'read' in the Discretionary Access Control model.

Question:
What is 'with DAC, the letter 'w''?

Answer:
'with DAC, the letter 'w'' represents 'write' in the Discretionary Access Control model.

Question:
What is 'with DAC, the letter 'x''?

Answer:
'with DAC, the letter 'x'' represents 'execute' in the Discretionary Access Control model.

Question:
What is 'with DAC, the letter 'd''?

Answer:
'with DAC, the letter 'd'' represents 'delete' in the Discretionary Access Control model.

Question:
What is 'with DAC, the letter 'c''?

Answer:
'with DAC, the letter 'c'' represents 'change' in the Discretionary Access Control model.

Identity and Access Management Domain

Question:
What is 'Mandatory Access Control, or MAC'?

Answer:
'Mandatory Access Control, or MAC' is an access control model used primarily for high-security systems such as SE Linux and Trusted Solaris.

Question:
What is 'nondiscretionary'?

Answer:
'nondiscretionary' is an attribute dictating that the user cannot make decisions on access.

Question:
What is a 'security label, or sensitivity label'?

Answer:
A 'security label, or sensitivity label' is a label that is assigned to every subject and object to provide security.

Question:
What is a 'classification, or clearance level'?

Answer:
A 'classification, or clearance level' is assigned to each subject or object to provide security, but only one per.

Question:
What is a 'category'?

Answer:
A 'category' is assigned to each subject or object for security, and more than one is allowed.

Question:
What is a 'Multilevel Security System, or MLS'?

Answer:
A 'Multilevel Security System, or MLS' is a MAC system that allows a subject to access an object at a different classification.

Question:
What is 'domination'?

Answer:
'domination' occurs when an object's classification is at or below the subject's clearance, and can therefore be accessed.

Question:
What is a 'guard'?

Answer:
A 'guard' is a process that monitors the exchange of information and transfer of data between two systems.

Question:
What is 'Role-Based Access Control, or RBAC'?

Answer:
'Role-Based Access Control, or RBAC' is an access control model that provides roles.

Identity and Access Management Domain

Question:
What is a 'session'?

Answer:
A 'session' represents a user logging into an RBAC.

Question:
What is 'core RBAC'?

Answer:
'core RBAC' is an RBAC component that gathers all roles and permissions for a session.

Question:
What is 'hierarchical RBAC'?

Answer:
'hierarchical RBAC' is an RBAC component that allows the roles to be modeled on the actual organizational structure.

Question:
What is 'limited hierarchies'?

Answer:
'limited hierarchies' is a flavor of RBAC in which role inheritance is allowed only once; for example, Role 1 inherits from Role 2 but not from any other role.

Question:
What is 'general hierarchies'?

Answer:
'general hierarchies' is a flavor of RBAC in which role inheritance is allowed for multiple levels simultaneously; for example, Role 1 inherits from Role 2 AND from Role 3.

Question:
What is 'static separation of duty, or SSD'?

Answer:
'static separation of duty, or SSD' occurs in hierarchical RBAC when we constrain the combination of privileges; for example, a user cannot be a member of both 'dock worker' and 'manifest clerk'.

Question:
What is 'dynamic separation of duty, or DSD'?

Answer:
'dynamic separation of duty, or DSD' occurs in hierarchical RBAC when we constrain the combination of privileges that can be active within the same session; for example, a user can belong to both 'dock worker' and 'manifest clerk', but not at the same time.

Question:
What is 'non-RBAC'?

Answer:
'non-RBAC' is an RBAC management mode in which there are no roles; users are mapped directly to applications and no roles are used.

Identity and Access Management Domain

Question:
What is 'limited RBAC'?

Answer:
'limited RBAC' is an RBAC management mode in which roles are optional; users are mapped to multiple roles as well as being mapped to applications that do not have role-based support.

Question:
What is 'hybrid RBAC'?

Answer:
'hybrid RBAC' is an RBAC management mode in which we have pseudo roles; users are mapped to roles for multiple applications with only selected rights assigned.

Question:
What is 'full RBAC'?

Answer:
'full RBAC' is an RBAC management mode in which we have enterprise roles; users are mapped to enterprise roles.

Question:
What is 'privacy-aware RBAC'?

Answer:
'privacy-aware RBAC' is a special version of RBAC geared to PHI and PII.

Question:
What is 'Rule-Based Access Control, or RB-RBAC'?

Answer:
'Rule-Based Access Control, or RB-RBAC' is built on top of RBAC and extends its capabilities to include if...then rules.

Question:
What is a 'constrained user interface'?

Answer:
A 'constrained user interface' is a user interface that limits a user's ability to access data or functionality.

Question:
What is 'menus'?

Answer:
'menus' is a user interface constraint method that limits the options the user can chose from.

Question:
What is 'shells'?

Answer:
'shells' is a user interface constraint method that limits the commands available when a shell, or virtual environment, opens.

Question:
What is 'database views'?

Answer:
'database views' is a user interface constraint method that limits the data that can be viewed by creating a virtual view of the data.

Identity and Access Management Domain

Question:
What is 'physical constraints'?

Answer:
'physical constraints' is a user interface constraint method that limits the physical controls the user can access such as keys or touch-screen buttons.

Question:
What is an 'access control matrix'?

Answer:
An 'access control matrix' is a table of subjects and objects that dictates the level of access.

Question:
What is a 'capability table'?

Answer:
A 'capability table' specifies the rights a subject has to a specific object.

Question:
What is a 'capability'?

Answer:
A 'capability' is a term used to describe a token, ticket or key.

Question:
What is a 'capability component'?

Answer:
A 'capability component' is something that represents an object that a subject wishes to access.

Question:
What is an 'access control list, or ACL'?

Answer:
An 'access control list, or ACL' is a list of subjects who may access an object, and the permissions available for that subject.

Question:
What is a 'content-based access control'?

Answer:
A 'content-based access control' occurs when we control access based only on the content of an object.

Question:
What is a 'context-based access control'?

Answer:
A 'context-based access control' occurs when we add context decisions to content-based access control.

Question:
What is 'centralized access control administration'?

Answer:
'centralized access control administration' occurs when a single individual or department controls all access to resources.

Identity and Access Management Domain

Question:
What is 'Remote Authentication Dial-In User Service, or RADIUS'?

Answer:
'Remote Authentication Dial-In User Service, or RADIUS' is a network protocol that provides authentication and authorization services to remote clients.

Question:
What is 'Attribute Value Pairs, or AVPS'?

Answer:
'Attribute Value Pairs, or AVPS' is a flexible list of permissions implemented by access control systems.

Question:
What is 'Terminal Access Controller Access Control System, or TACACS'?

Answer:
'Terminal Access Controller Access Control System, or TACACS' is competitor to RADIUS.

Question:
What is 'eXtended TACACS, or XTACACS'?

Answer:
'eXtended TACACS, or XTACACS' is a successor to TACACS and separates authentication from authorization.

Question:
What is 'TACACS+'?

Answer:
'TACACS+' is a protocol that added many features to TACACS, including TCP, encryption, and allowed more AVPs.

Question:
What is 'Diameter'?

Answer:
'Diameter' is a protocol similar to TACACS+ but is peer-to-peer, and is the latest standard.

Question:
What is the 'Diameter base protocol'?

Answer:
The 'Diameter base protocol' is a Diameter protocol that covers just about everything but AAA.

Question:
What is 'Diameter extensions'?

Answer:
'Diameter extensions' is a Diameter protocol that allows other protocols to implement AAA.

Question:
What is a 'mobile IP'?

Answer:
A 'mobile IP' is a capability allowing a mobile device to move from network to network without changing its IP address.

Identity and Access Management Domain

Question:
What is a 'home IP address'?

Answer:
A 'home IP address' is a quasi-permanent IP that traffic can be sent to.

Question:
What is a 'care-of address'?

Answer:
A 'care-of address' is the current IP address of the mobile device.

Question:
What is 'decentralized access control administration'?

Answer:
'decentralized access control administration' occurs when we trust the data owners to take care of managing access to their own data.

Question:
What is 'administrative controls'?

Answer:
'administrative controls' are security controls that deal with personnel policies, employee training and periodic testing to make sure all controls are in-place and effective.

Question:
What is 'physical controls'?

Answer:
'physical controls' are security controls that deal with physically securing assets.

Question:
What is 'technical controls'?

Answer:
'technical controls' are security controls that always have a software component and are used to restrict access.

Question:
What is 'accountability'?

Answer:
'accountability' is the result of implementing audit tracking.

Question:
What is 'auditing'?

Answer:
'auditing' captures user actions, application events and system activities.

Question:
What is 'scrubbing'?

Answer:
'scrubbing' is the act of erasing log files entries after an attack.

Identity and Access Management Domain

Question:
What is 'simplex communication'?

Answer:
'simplex communication' is achieved by physically severing the "receive" pairs in an Ethernet cable.

Question:
What is 'cryptographic hash chaining'?

Answer:
'cryptographic hash chaining' allows us to detect the addition or removal of log entries by including the hash of the previous entry.

Question:
What is 'clipping'?

Answer:
'clipping' occurs when we apply the proper level of filtering such that only important details are logged.

Question:
What is an 'event-oriented log review'?

Answer:
An 'event-oriented log review' is a log review resulting from a disruption or security breach.

Question:
What is an 'audit trail log review'?

Answer:
An 'audit trail log review' is a periodic log review to detect unusual behaviors from users, applications or systems.

Question:
What is an 'real-time analysis log review'?

Answer:
An 'real-time analysis log review' is a log review in which an automated system correlates logs from various systems, such as SEM or SIEM.

Question:
What is an 'audit-reduction tool'?

Answer:
An 'audit-reduction tool' discards irrelevant data to make reviews easier.

Question:
What is 'Security Event Management, or SEM'?

Answer:
'Security Event Management, or SEM' automates the sifting and correlation of all logs.

Question:
What is 'Security Information and Event Management, or SIEM'?

Answer:
'Security Information and Event Management, or SIEM' is another name for SEM.

Identity and Access Management Domain

Question:
What is 'situational awareness'?

Answer:
'situational awareness' is the ability to make sense of the current state in spite of a large number of data points and complex relationships.

Question:
What is 'keystroke monitoring'?

Answer:
'keystroke monitoring' captures each keystroke and records the resulting characters in a file.

Question:
What is a 'dongle'?

Answer:
A 'dongle' is a device inserted between a wired keyboard connection and the computer.

Question:
What is a 'faraday cage'?

Answer:
A 'faraday cage' is a metal shield that prevents electronic signals from leaking out.

Question:
What is 'white noise'?

Answer:
'white noise' is the use of random electrical signals across the entire communication band to hide valid signals.

Question:
What is a 'control zone'?

Answer:
A 'control zone' is a room or building wrapped in a faraday cage.

Question:
What is 'TEMPEST'?

Answer:
'TEMPEST' is a standard that requires equipment to include a Faraday cage.

Question:
What is an 'Intrusion Detection System, or IDS'?

Answer:
An 'Intrusion Detection System, or IDS' is a system that detects intrusion attempts against network or network devices.

Question:
What is a 'sensor'?

Answer:
A 'sensor' within an IDS collects information and sends the resulting data to an analyzer.

Identity and Access Management Domain

Question:
What is an 'analyzer'?

Answer:
An 'analyzer' within an IDS looks for suspicious activity and send alerts to the administration interface.

Question:
What is an 'administration interface'?

Answer:
An 'administration interface' within an IDS processes alerts, which can result in an email, text message, phone call, a visual alert on a screen or sending a message to some other system.

Question:
What is 'promiscuous mode'?

Answer:
'promiscuous mode' is a NIC mode that captures all traffic whether it was intended for that device or not.

Question:
What is 'sniffing'?

Answer:
'sniffing' is the act of examining traffic as it passes by.

Question:
What is a 'protocol analyzer'?

Answer:
A 'protocol analyzer' understands and detects specific traffic protocols.

Question:
What is 'behavior blocking'?

Answer:
'behavior blocking' occurs when security vendors allow malicious software to execute on a host and then gather the changes that were made to the system.

Question:
What is 'ARP poisoning'?

Answer:
'ARP poisoning' is an attack in which a rogue client pretends to own an IP it does not.

Question:
What is a 'Loki attack'?

Answer:
A 'Loki attack' is an attack in which ICMP packets are used to hide data.

Question:
What is 'session hijacking'?

Answer:
'session hijacking' is an attack in which an attacker uses sequence numbers to jump in and take over a socket connection.

Identity and Access Management Domain

Question:
What is a 'Land attack'?

Answer:
A 'Land attack' is an attack in which the source and destination IP addresses are the same.

Question:
What is a 'Xmas attack'?

Answer:
A 'Xmas attack' is an attack in which all TCP header flags are set to '1'.

Question:
What is a 'Network-based IDS, or NIDS'?

Answer:
A 'Network-based IDS, or NIDS' is a device that watches network traffic.

Question:
What is a 'signature-based, or knowledge-based or pattern-matching'?

Answer:
A 'signature-based, or knowledge-based or pattern-matching' is a NIDS that compares traffic patterns in real-time to a list of patterns known to represent an attack.

Question:
What is an 'anomaly-based IDS or behavioral-based'?

Answer:
An 'anomaly-based IDS or behavioral-based' is a NIDS that detects new patterns relative to a known 'normal' baseline.

Question:
What is a 'protocol anomaly-based IDS'?

Answer:
A 'protocol anomaly-based IDS' is a NIDS that understands certain protocols, allowing it to add context to patterns.

Question:
What is a 'traffic anomaly-based IDS'?

Answer:
A 'traffic anomaly-based IDS' is a NIDS that watches for known patterns that are suspicious due to the time or frequency.

Question:
What is a 'rule-based IDS, or a heuristic-based IDS'?

Answer:
A 'rule-based IDS, or a heuristic-based IDS' is a NIDS that is considered to be an expert system.

Question:
What is 'rule-based facts'?

Answer:
'rule-based facts' describes any NIDS data that comes in from a sensor or system that is being monitored.

Identity and Access Management Domain

Question:
What is a 'rule-based knowledge base'?

Answer:
A 'rule-based knowledge base' is a collection of NIDS 'if...then' rules that analyze facts and takes action.

Question:
What is a 'rule-based inference engine'?

Answer:
A 'rule-based inference engine' uses 5th generation programming languages, such as artificial intelligence, and can infer relationships.

Question:
What is a 'Host-based IDS, or HIDS'?

Answer:
A 'Host-based IDS, or HIDS' is an IDS that watches everything on the local computer.

Question:
What is a 'HIDS state'?

Answer:
A 'HIDS state' is a snapshot of the contents of volatile and non-volatile memory within a host.

Question:
What is a 'stateful matching IDS'?

Answer:
A 'stateful matching IDS' is a host-based IDS which compares memory states to known attacks.

Question:
What is an 'Application-based IDS, or AIDS'?

Answer:
An 'Application-based IDS, or AIDS' is an IDS that watches certain software applications running on a host.

Question:
What is an 'Intrusion Prevention System, or IPS'?

Answer:
An 'Intrusion Prevention System, or IPS' is an AIDS that takes action according to some predefined rules.

Question:
What is 'enticement'?

Answer:
'enticement' is the act of redirecting an attacker's efforts that he or she has already determined to carry out.

Question:
What is 'entrapment'?

Answer:
'entrapment' is the act of convincing an attacker to take action by encouraging or tricking them.

Identity and Access Management Domain

Question:
What is a 'dictionary attack'?

Answer:
A 'dictionary attack' is an attack that iterates through all commonly used words or combinations of characters trying to guess a password.

Question:
What is a 'brute-force attack, or exhaustive attack'?

Answer:
A 'brute-force attack, or exhaustive attack' is an attack that iterates through every possible character in increasing lengths until a password match is found.

Question:
What is 'war-dialing'?

Answer:
'war-dialing' is an attack that automatically dials through a list of phone numbers until a modem answers.

Question:
What is a 'hybrid attack'?

Answer:
A 'hybrid attack' is an attack using a combination of dictionary and brute-force attacks.

Question:
What is a 'rainbow attack'?

Answer:
A 'rainbow attack' is an attack for which hashes for all relevant values are pre-computed into a 'rainbow table'.

Question:
What is 'spoofing at logon'?

Answer:
'spoofing at logon' is an attack in which a software program mimics an OS interface to collect credentials.

Identity and Access Management Domain

Quiz

Question:
What is the Key Distribution Center, or KDC, comprised of?

Answer:
'AS and TGS'.

Question:
What 4 steps are required to properly implement access control?

Answer:
'Identification, Authentication, Authorization, and Accountability'.

Question:
What are the 3 attributes of identity?

Answer:
'uniqueness, non-descriptive, issuance'.

Question:
What are the best practices for identities?

Answer:
'use unique names, have a standard naming scheme, do not describe position or task, and do not share across subjects'.

Question:
What are the 3 factors that can be used to authenticate a person?

Answer:
'something a person knows, has and is'.

Question:
What are the 2 types of biometric errors?

Answer:
'type 1 and type 2'.

Question:
How do you prevent a replay attack against voice print authentication?

Answer:
'By scrambling the recorded words that the user must repeat'.

Question:
Is hand topography unique enough to be used alone?

Answer:
'No, but it can often be used with hand geometry'.

Identity and Access Management Domain

Question:
What are the two types of cards?

Answer:
'memory and smart'.

Question:
What are the 2 types of card attacks?

Answer:
'non-invasive and invasive'.

Question:
What are the 3 behavior changes a side-channel attack looks for?

Answer:
'differential power analysis, electromagnetic analysis, timing'.

Question:
What are the 2 invasive card attacks?

Answer:
'fault generation, microprobing'.

Question:
What are the 3 primary components in Kerberos?

Answer:
'the KDC, principals and tickets'.

Question:
What attack is Kerberos vulnerable to and relies upon the OS to prevent?

Answer:
'Password guessing'.

Question:
What are 4 weaknesses of Kerberos?

Answer:
'is a single point of failure, can be a bottleneck, data not in tickets are not encrypted, and requires all clocks to be synchronized'.

Question:
What are the 4 attributes of a quality authentication mechanism?

Answer:
'transparent, scalable, reliable and secure'.

Question:
What are the 2 components to RBAC?

Answer:
'core RBAC and hierarchical RBAC'.

Identity and Access Management Domain

Question:
What are the 2 flavors of hierarchical RBAC?

Answer:
'limited hierarchies and general hierarchies'.

Question:
What are the 4 different ways in which RBAC can be managed?

Answer:
'non-RBAC, limited RBAC, hybrid RBAC and full RBAC'.

Question:
What are the 4 methods for constraining a user interface?

Answer:
'menus, shells, database views and physical constraints'.

Question:
What are the 3 types of log reviews?

Answer:
'event-oriented, audit trails and real-time analysis'.

Question:
What are the 3 types of IDSs?

Answer:
'network-based, host-based and application-based'.

Question:
What are the two filters can anomaly-based IDS can implement?

Answer:
'protocol filtering and traffic filtering'.

Question:
What are the 3 components of a rule-based NIDS?

Answer:
'facts, knowledge base and inference engine'.

Question:
Of enticement and entrapment, which is illegal?

Answer:
'entrapment'.

Security Assessment and Testing Domain

Definitions

Question:
What is an assessment of all security controls that protect a set of people, computers, processes and information?

Answer:
'security audit'

Question:
What provides outsourced services, such as insurance claim processing, data centers, ASPs, managed security providers and credit processing organizations?

Answer:
'Service Organization, or SO'

Question:
What is a standard that makes sure any SO claiming to protect a company's assets actually does so?

Answer:
'Statement on Auditing Standards No, 70, or SAS 70'

Question:
What is a framework consisting of SOC 1, SOC 2 and SOC 3?

Answer:
'Service Organization Controls, or SOC'

Question:
What is a SOC report that deals with financial controls?

Answer:
'SOC 1'

Question:
What is a detailed SOC report that deals with services such as security, privacy, confidentiality, integrity and availability?

Answer:
'SOC 2'

Question:
What is a SOC report that provides a pass/fail report about SOC 2?

Answer:
'SOC 3'

Question:
What identifies weaknesses that potentially could be exploited?

Answer:
'vulnerability testing'

Security Assessment and Testing Domain

Question:
What tests vulnerabilities to determine if they can be exploited?

Answer:
'penetration testing'

Question:
What occurs when the testing team has no prior knowledge of the environment?

Answer:
'black box test'

Question:
What occurs when the testing team has complete knowledge of and has complete access to the internal infrastructure?

Answer:
'white box test'

Question:
What is a hybrid of the black and white box approaches?

Answer:
'gray box test'

Question:
What is a type of vulnerability assessment that reviews employee tasks to identify weaknesses in policies and procedures?

Answer:
'personnel assessment'

Question:
What is a type of vulnerability assessment that tests facility and perimeter protection?

Answer:
'physical assessment'

Question:
What is a type of vulnerability assessment that employs an automated scanning tool to search for vulnerabilities?

Answer:
'system and networking assessment'

Question:
What examines the content resulting from a specific port scan and attempts to figure out what type or brand of service is running behind that port?

Answer:
'banner grabbing'

Question:
What uses banner grabbing to identify specific operating systems or applications?

Answer:
'fingerprinting'

Security Assessment and Testing Domain

Question:
What is a type of core vulnerability that can give the attacker a great deal of control?

Answer:
'kernel flaw'

Question:
What occurs when poorly implemented code allows an attacker to overwrite protected memory, resulting in launching an attacker's code?

Answer:
'buffer overflow'

Question:
What occurs when a file stub redirects to another location, allowing a back door path to access sensitive files?

Answer:
'symbolic link attack'

Question:
What occurs when operating systems consistently use the same numbers to represent open files, allowing an attacker to control input or output for these files?

Answer:
'file descriptor attack'

Question:
What occurs when a program's poor design can put it in a temporary vulnerable condition in which an attacker could force the program to execute an operation out of the intended order?

Answer:
'race condition attack'

Question:
What occurs when inadvertent system or user errors can result in file or directory permissions being lowered, allowing an attacker to access sensitive information?

Answer:
'file and directory permission vulnerability'

Question:
What is the process of simulating attacks on a network and its systems at the request of the senior management?

Answer:
'penetration testing'

Question:
What is a document carried by pen testing team members in case of being caught?

Answer:
'Get Out of Jail Free Card'

Security Assessment and Testing Domain

Question:
What is the pen testing step to footprint and gathering info about a target?

Answer:
'discovery step'

Question:
What is the pen testing step to scan ports and collect resource identification?

Answer:
'enumeration step'

Question:
What is the pen testing step to identify vulnerabilities?

Answer:
'vulnerability mapping step'

Question:
What is the pen testing step to gain unauthorized access by exploiting discovered vulnerabilities?

Answer:
'exploitation step'

Question:
What is the pen testing step to create and deliver documentation of test findings with suggested countermeasures?

Answer:
'report to management step'

Question:
What is the term for the type of box testing?

Answer:
'knowledge'

Question:
What is the level of box testing in which we know nothing about the environment or credentials?

Answer:
'zero knowledge'

Question:
What is the level of box testing in which we have partial knowledge of the environment or credentials?

Answer:
'partial knowledge'

Question:
What is the level of box testing in which we know everything about the environment and credentials?

Answer:
'full knowledge'

Security Assessment and Testing Domain

Question:
What occurs when testers only have public information available, but internal network staff are notified an attack is taking place?

Answer:
'blind assessment'

Question:
What occurs when testers only have public information available, and internal network staff are not notified?

Answer:
'double-blind assessment, or stealth assessment'

Question:
What occurs when both external and internal parties coordinate and test specific networks, systems or applications?

Answer:
'targeted assessment'

Question:
What produces decisions after a final testing report?

Answer:
'postmortem'

Question:
What is the examination of system log files to detect security events or verify effectiveness of security controls?

Answer:
'log review'

Question:
What is the service using UDP port 123 and allows servers to remain synchronized, which is important for logging?

Answer:
'Network Time Protocol, or NTP'

Question:
What is the most authoritative NTP level that includes atomic clocks, GPS, and radio clocks?

Answer:
'stratum 0'

Question:
What is the NTP level that includes highly accurate primary time sources with internal clocks directly connected to the stratum above?

Answer:
'stratum 1'

Question:
What is the NTP level that includes network servers such as NTP servers or domain controllers connected to the stratum above?

Answer:
'stratum 2'

Security Assessment and Testing Domain

Question:
What are the NTP levels that do not have a defined purpose?

Answer:
'stratum 3 and below'

Question:
What is a transaction initiated by a script to verify proper execution?

Answer:
'synthetic transaction'

Question:
What is an event that captures metrics such as delay, jitter and errors from a session conducted by a real person?

Answer:
'Real User Monitoring, or RUM'

Question:
What is a tool to graphically represent 'use cases'?

Answer:
'Unified Modeling Language, or UML'

Question:
What is a UML diagram showing an attacker executing malicious behavior?

Answer:
'misuse case'

Question:
What are the lines of software instructions that make up an application?

Answer:
'source code'

Question:
What is a systematic examination of application source code?

Answer:
'code review'

Question:
What is the habit of looking for opportunities for source code to go bad?

Answer:
'defensive coding'

Question:
What is a given set of exchange points between two systems?

Answer:
'interface'

Security Assessment and Testing Domain

Question:
What is the systematic evaluation of an interface to discover problems?

Answer:
'interface testing'

Question:
What are scenarios in-between known-good and known-bad use cases?

Answer:
'boundary conditions'

Question:
What is a written company policy informing users of precautions taken by the company?

Answer:
'Acceptable Use Policy, or AUP'

Question:
What occurs when a user account is assigned more rights than are necessary to complete his or her job?

Answer:
'privilege accumulation'

Question:
What are user-created and maintained files?

Answer:
'user data files'

Question:
What are large files in which server-based processes store data?

Answer:
'databases'

Question:
What is data contained on mail servers?

Answer:
'mailbox data'

Question:
What is the ability for an organization to continue operating following a serious incident?

Answer:
'Business Continuity, or BC'

Question:
What is a subset of BC and focuses on getting information systems back up after an incident?

Answer:
'Disaster Recovery, or DR'

Security Assessment and Testing Domain

390

Question:
What describes the steps to ensure DR?

Answer:
'Disaster Recovery Plan, or DRP'

Question:
What is the process of teaching security skills to security personnel?

Answer:
'security training'

Question:
What is the process of explaining security issues to all members of an organization?

Answer:
'security awareness training'

Question:
What is the process of manipulating a person such that they willingly violate security policies?

Answer:
'social engineering'

Question:
What is an attack in which the attacker provides a believable scenario in order to get a victim to give up information?

Answer:
'pretexting'

Question:
What are a high-level indicators of how well things are going from a security posture point of view?

Answer:
'Key Performance Indicators, or KPI'

Question:
What is the standard that outlines a process by which PKIs can be identified and 'calculated'?

Answer:
'ISO 27004'

Question:
What is an ISMS attribute that can change over time?

Answer:
'factor'

Question:
What is a factor's value at a specific point in time?

Answer:
'measurement'

Security Assessment and Testing Domain

Question:
What is a measurement that provides a point of reference going forward?

Answer:
'baseline'

Question:
What is a calculated value derived from either comparing a current measurement against a baseline, or comparing two or more current measurements to each other?

Answer:
'metric'

Question:
What is an interpretation of one or more metrics that communicate the effectiveness of the ISMS?

Answer:
'indicator, or PKI'

Question:
What is a threshold that should trigger something when exceeded?

Answer:
'Key Risk Indicator, or KRI'

Question:
What is created by applying a standard methodology to the specific context of a system being studied?

Answer:
'security assessment technical report'

Question:
What is the system being studied?

Answer:
'System Under Study, or SUS'

Question:
What is the method used to calculate the amount it would cost to acquire or replace a protected asset?

Answer:
'cost approach'

Question:
What is the method used to calculate the amount of revenue a protected asset is expected to contribute based on both the past and future business environment?

Answer:
'income approach'

Question:
What is the method used to calculate how much other organizations are paying for the same protected asset?

Answer:
'market approach'

Security Assessment and Testing Domain

Question:
What is a meeting for leadership to review the current management systems?

Answer:
'management review'

Question:
What is the standard that defines the plan-do-check-act?

Answer:
'ISO 9000'

Question:
What is the PDCA step that defines the objectives and processes to meet the objectives?

Answer:
'plan step'

Question:
What is the PDCA step that executes the plan?

Answer:
'do step'

Question:
What is the PDCA step that compares the expected results (PLAN) to the actual results (DO)?

Answer:
'check step'

Question:
What is the PDCA step that determines next actions based on CHECK; the next iteration of PLAN will take these into account?

Answer:
'act step'

Security Assessment and Testing Domain

Terms

Question:
What is a 'security audit'?

Answer:
A 'security audit' is an assessment of all security controls that protect a set of people, computers, processes and information.

Question:
What is a 'Service Organization, or SO'?

Answer:
A 'Service Organization, or SO' provides outsourced services, such as insurance claim processing, data centers, ASPs, managed security providers and credit processing organizations.

Question:
What is the 'Statement on Auditing Standards No, 70, or SAS 70'?

Answer:
The 'Statement on Auditing Standards No, 70, or SAS 70' is a standard that makes sure any SO claiming to protect a company's assets actually does so.

Question:
What is 'Service Organization Controls, or SOC'?

Answer:
'Service Organization Controls, or SOC' is a framework consisting of SOC 1, SOC 2 and SOC 3.

Question:
What is 'SOC 1'?

Answer:
'SOC 1' is a SOC report that deals with financial controls.

Question:
What is 'SOC 2'?

Answer:
'SOC 2' is a detailed SOC report that deals with services such as security, privacy, confidentiality, integrity and availability.

Question:
What is 'SOC 3'?

Answer:
'SOC 3' is a SOC report that provides a pass/fail report about SOC 2.

Question:
What is 'vulnerability testing'?

Answer:
'vulnerability testing' identifies weaknesses that potentially could be exploited.

Security Assessment and Testing Domain

Question:
What is 'penetration testing'?

Answer:
'penetration testing' tests vulnerabilities to determine if they can be exploited.

Question:
What is a 'black box test'?

Answer:
A 'black box test' occurs when the testing team has no prior knowledge of the environment.

Question:
What is a 'white box test'?

Answer:
A 'white box test' occurs when the testing team has complete knowledge of and has complete access to the internal infrastructure.

Question:
What is a 'gray box test'?

Answer:
A 'gray box test' is a hybrid of the black and white box approaches.

Question:
What is a 'personnel assessment'?

Answer:
A 'personnel assessment' is a type of vulnerability assessment that reviews employee tasks to identify weaknesses in policies and procedures.

Question:
What is a 'physical assessment'?

Answer:
A 'physical assessment' is a type of vulnerability assessment that tests facility and perimeter protection.

Question:
What is a 'system and networking assessment'?

Answer:
A 'system and networking assessment' is a type of vulnerability assessment that employs an automated scanning tool to search for vulnerabilities.

Question:
What is 'banner grabbing'?

Answer:
'banner grabbing' examines the content resulting from a specific port scan and attempts to figure out what type or brand of service is running behind that port.

Security Assessment and Testing Domain

Question:
What is 'fingerprinting'?

Answer:
'fingerprinting' uses banner grabbing to identify specific operating systems or applications.

Question:
What is a 'kernel flaw'?

Answer:
A 'kernel flaw' is a type of core vulnerability that can give the attacker a great deal of control.

Question:
What is a 'buffer overflow'?

Answer:
A 'buffer overflow' occurs when poorly implemented code allows an attacker to overwrite protected memory, resulting in launching an attacker's code.

Question:
What is a 'symbolic link attack'?

Answer:
A 'symbolic link attack' occurs when a file stub redirects to another location, allowing a back door path to access sensitive files.

Question:
What is a 'file descriptor attack'?

Answer:
A 'file descriptor attack' occurs when operating systems consistently use the same numbers to represent open files, allowing an attacker to control input or output for these files.

Question:
What is a 'race condition attack'?

Answer:
A 'race condition attack' occurs when a program's poor design can put it in a temporary vulnerable condition in which an attacker could force the program to execute an operation out of the intended order.

Question:
What is a 'file and directory permission vulnerability'?

Answer:
A 'file and directory permission vulnerability' occurs when inadvertent system or user errors can result in file or directory permissions being lowered, allowing an attacker to access sensitive information.

Question:
What is 'penetration testing'?

Answer:
'penetration testing' is the process of simulating attacks on a network and its systems at the request of the senior management.

Security Assessment and Testing Domain

Question:
What is a 'Get Out of Jail Free Card'?

Answer:
A 'Get Out of Jail Free Card' is a document carried by pen testing team members in case of being caught.

Question:
What is the 'discovery step'?

Answer:
The 'discovery step' is the pen testing step to footprint and gathering info about a target.

Question:
What is the 'enumeration step'?

Answer:
The 'enumeration step' is the pen testing step to scan ports and collect resource identification.

Question:
What is the 'vulnerability mapping step'?

Answer:
The 'vulnerability mapping step' is the pen testing step to identify vulnerabilities.

Question:
What is the 'exploitation step'?

Answer:
The 'exploitation step' is the pen testing step to gain unauthorized access by exploiting discovered vulnerabilities.

Question:
What is the 'report to management step'?

Answer:
The 'report to management step' is the pen testing step to create and deliver documentation of test findings with suggested countermeasures.

Question:
What is 'knowledge'?

Answer:
'knowledge' is the term for the type of box testing.

Question:
What is 'zero knowledge'?

Answer:
'zero knowledge' is the level of box testing in which we know nothing about the environment or credentials.

Question:
What is 'partial knowledge'?

Answer:
'partial knowledge' is the level of box testing in which we have partial knowledge of the environment or credentials.

Security Assessment and Testing Domain

Question:
What is 'full knowledge'?

Answer:
'full knowledge' is the level of box testing in which we know everything about the environment and credentials.

Question:
What is a 'blind assessment'?

Answer:
A 'blind assessment' occurs when testers only have public information available, but internal network staff are notified an attack is taking place.

Question:
What is a 'double-blind assessment, or stealth assessment'?

Answer:
A 'double-blind assessment, or stealth assessment' occurs when testers only have public information available, and internal network staff are not notified.

Question:
What is a 'targeted assessment'?

Answer:
A 'targeted assessment' occurs when both external and internal parties coordinate and test specific networks, systems or applications.

Question:
What is a 'postmortem'?

Answer:
A 'postmortem' produces decisions after a final testing report.

Question:
What is a 'log review'?

Answer:
A 'log review' is the examination of system log files to detect security events or verify effectiveness of security controls.

Question:
What is the 'Network Time Protocol, or NTP'?

Answer:
The 'Network Time Protocol, or NTP' is the service using UDP port 123 and allows servers to remain synchronized, which is important for logging.

Question:
What is 'stratum 0'?

Answer:
'stratum 0' is the most authoritative NTP level that includes atomic clocks, GPS, and radio clocks.

Security Assessment and Testing Domain

Question:
What is 'stratum 1'?

Answer:
'stratum 1' is the NTP level that includes highly accurate primary time sources with internal clocks directly connected to the stratum above.

Question:
What is 'stratum 2'?

Answer:
'stratum 2' is the NTP level that includes network servers such as NTP servers or domain controllers connected to the stratum above.

Question:
What is 'stratum 3 and below'?

Answer:
'stratum 3 and below' are the NTP levels that do not have a defined purpose.

Question:
What is a 'synthetic transaction'?

Answer:
A 'synthetic transaction' is a transaction initiated by a script to verify proper execution.

Question:
What is 'Real User Monitoring, or RUM'?

Answer:
'Real User Monitoring, or RUM' is an event that captures metrics such as delay, jitter and errors from a session conducted by a real person.

Question:
What is 'Unified Modeling Language, or UML'?

Answer:
'Unified Modeling Language, or UML' is a tool to graphically represent 'use cases'.

Question:
What is a 'misuse case'?

Answer:
A 'misuse case' is a UML diagram showing an attacker executing malicious behavior.

Question:
What is 'source code'?

Answer:
'source code' are the lines of software instructions that make up an application.

Question:
What is a 'code review'?

Answer:
A 'code review' is a systematic examination of application source code.

Security Assessment and Testing Domain

Question:
What is 'defensive coding'?

Answer:
'defensive coding' is the habit of looking for opportunities for source code to go bad.

Question:
What is an 'interface'?

Answer:
An 'interface' is a given set of exchange points between two systems.

Question:
What is 'interface testing'?

Answer:
'interface testing' is the systematic evaluation of an interface to discover problems.

Question:
What is 'boundary conditions'?

Answer:
'boundary conditions' are scenarios in-between known-good and known-bad use cases.

Question:
What is an 'Acceptable Use Policy, or AUP'?

Answer:
An 'Acceptable Use Policy, or AUP' is a written company policy informing users of precautions taken by the company.

Question:
What is 'privilege accumulation'?

Answer:
'privilege accumulation' occurs when a user account is assigned more rights than are necessary to complete his or her job.

Question:
What is 'user data files'?

Answer:
'user data files' are user-created and maintained files.

Question:
What is 'databases'?

Answer:
'databases' are large files in which server-based processes store data.

Question:
What is 'mailbox data'?

Answer:
'mailbox data' is data contained on mail servers.

Security Assessment and Testing Domain

400

Question:
What is 'Business Continuity, or BC'?

Answer:
'Business Continuity, or BC' is the ability for an organization to continue operating following a serious incident.

Question:
What is 'Disaster Recovery, or DR'?

Answer:
'Disaster Recovery, or DR' is a subset of BC and focuses on getting information systems back up after an incident.

Question:
What is 'Disaster Recovery Plan, or DRP'?

Answer:
'Disaster Recovery Plan, or DRP' describes the steps to ensure DR.

Question:
What is 'security training'?

Answer:
'security training' is the process of teaching security skills to security personnel.

Question:
What is 'security awareness training'?

Answer:
'security awareness training' is the process of explaining security issues to all members of an organization.

Question:
What is 'social engineering'?

Answer:
'social engineering' is the process of manipulating a person such that they willingly violate security policies.

Question:
What is 'pretexting'?

Answer:
'pretexting' is an attack in which the attacker provides a believable scenario in order to get a victim to give up information.

Question:
What is 'Key Performance Indicators, or KPI'?

Answer:
'Key Performance Indicators, or KPI' are a high-level indicators of how well things are going from a security posture point of view.

Question:
What is 'ISO 27004'?

Answer:
'ISO 27004' is the standard that outlines a process by which PKIs can be identified and 'calculated'.

Security Assessment and Testing Domain

401

Question:
What is a 'factor'?

Answer:
A 'factor' is an ISMS attribute that can change over time.

Question:
What is a 'measurement'?

Answer:
A 'measurement' is a factor's value at a specific point in time.

Question:
What is a 'baseline'?

Answer:
A 'baseline' is a measurement that provides a point of reference going forward.

Question:
What is a 'metric'?

Answer:
A 'metric' is a calculated value derived from either comparing a current measurement against a baseline, or comparing two or more current measurements to each other.

Question:
What is an 'indicator, or PKI'?

Answer:
An 'indicator, or PKI' is an interpretation of one or more metrics that communicate the effectiveness of the ISMS.

Question:
What is a 'Key Risk Indicator, or KRI'?

Answer:
A 'Key Risk Indicator, or KRI' is a threshold that should trigger something when exceeded.

Question:
What is a 'security assessment technical report'?

Answer:
A 'security assessment technical report' is created by applying a standard methodology to the specific context of a system being studied.

Question:
What is a 'System Under Study, or SUS'?

Answer:
A 'System Under Study, or SUS' is the system being studied.

Question:
What is the 'cost approach'?

Answer:
The 'cost approach' is the method used to calculate the amount it would cost to acquire or replace a protected asset.

Security Assessment and Testing Domain

Question:
What is the 'income approach'?

Answer:
The 'income approach' is the method used to calculate the amount of revenue a protected asset is expected to contribute based on both the past and future business environment.

Question:
What is the 'market approach'?

Answer:
The 'market approach' is the method used to calculate how much other organizations are paying for the same protected asset.

Question:
What is a 'management review'?

Answer:
A 'management review' is a meeting for leadership to review the current management systems.

Question:
What is 'ISO 9000'?

Answer:
'ISO 9000' is the standard that defines the plan-do-check-act.

Question:
What is the 'plan step'?

Answer:
The 'plan step' is the PDCA step that defines the objectives and processes to meet the objectives.

Question:
What is the 'do step'?

Answer:
The 'do step' is the PDCA step that executes the plan.

Question:
What is the 'check step'?

Answer:
The 'check step' is the PDCA step that compares the expected results (PLAN) to the actual results (DO).

Question:
What is the 'act step'?

Answer:
The 'act step' is the PDCA step that determines next actions based on CHECK; the next iteration of PLAN will take these into account.

Security Assessment and Testing Domain

Quiz

Question:
What are the 8 steps of the security audit process?

Answer:
'goals, people, scope, team, plan, conduct, document and report'.

Question:
What are the 3 types of vulnerability assessments?

Answer:
'personnel, physical and system and networking'.

Question:
What is the countermeasure to kernel flaws?

Answer:
'keeping OSs patched and up-to-date'.

Question:
What is the countermeasure to buffer overflows?

Answer:
'developer education, using strongly typed languages, and employing automated source code scanners'.

Question:
What is the countermeasure to symbolic link attacks?

Answer:
'ensure that programs and scripts are written to require the full path to the file'.

Question:
What is the countermeasure to file descriptor attacks?

Answer:
'developer education, performing application security testing, and using automated source code scanners'.

Question:
What is the countermeasure to race conditions attacks?

Answer:
'developer education, performing application security testing, and using automated source code scanners'.

Question:
What is the countermeasure to file and directory permissions attacks?

Answer:
'employ file integrity checkers that can alert on these changes before an attacker exploits them'.

Security Assessment and Testing Domain

Question:
What three items should the Get Out of Jail Free card contain?

Answer:
'The extent of testing authorized, contact information for key personnel, and a call tree in case something goes wrong'.

Question:
What are the 5 steps of penetration testing?

Answer:
'discovery, enumeration, vulnerability mapping, exploitation and report to management'.

Question:
What are the 3 levels of knowledge for box testing?

Answer:
'zero knowledge, partial knowledge and full knowledge'.

Question:
What are the 3 levels of coordination between the testing team and internal staff?

Answer:
'blind, double-blind and targeted'.

Question:
What are the 3 types of data involved in backups?

Answer:
'user data files, databases and mailbox data'.

Question:
What are the 7 backup testing steps?

Answer:
'Develop scenarios, develop a plan, use automation, minimize the impact, ensure coverage, document and fix'.

Question:
What are the 5 steps to test a DRP?

Answer:
'checklist, walk-through, simulation, parallel, full-interruption'.

Question:
What is the best process, consisting of 5 steps, for generating PKIs?

Answer:
'choose factors, measure, baseline, generate metrics and create indicators'.

Question:
What are the 3 approaches to deriving monetary value in an executive summary?

Answer:
'cost approach, income approach and market approach'.

Security Operations Domain

Definitions

Question:
What is a person who is responsible, careful, cautious and practical?

Answer:
'prudent man'

Question:
What results when we take reasonable precautions?

Answer:
'due care'

Question:
What results when we do everything within our power to prevent a bad thing from happening?

Answer:
'due diligence'

Question:
What is the act of managing personnel?

Answer:
'administrative management'

Question:
What is a role that works to achieve a highly available, performant infrastructure that meets user needs?

Answer:
'network administrator'

Question:
What is a role that works to ensure a highly-secure and controlled infrastructure?

Answer:
'security administrator'

Question:
What ensures that a given product is trustworthy?

Answer:
'assurance level'

Question:
What ensures that a product provides the necessary levels of protection based on its architecture, embedded features, and functionality?

Answer:
'operation assurance'

Security Operations Domain

Question:
What follows the development life-cycle of a product including specs, clipping levels, testing, configuration and distribution?

Answer:
'life-cycle assurance'

Question:
What is the ability to mitigate the damage resulting from unauthorized disclosure of information?

Answer:
'operational security'

Question:
What are systems that collect logs throughout the network and automatically correlates the information?

Answer:
'event management systems'

Question:
What happens when software starts up from an unexpected or expected shutdown?

Answer:
'Initial Program Load, or IPL'

Question:
What is a periodically measured value of a system that deviates significantly from the baseline measurements?

Answer:
'deviation from the standard'

Question:
What ensures that operations are carried out in the proper security context?

Answer:
'configuration management'

Question:
What is experienced when a system that unexpectedly shuts down comes back up in a secure state?

Answer:
'trusted recovery'

Question:
What occurs when the system shuts down in a controlled manner as a result of a kernel failure; examples might be insufficient memory or invalid data structures?

Answer:
'system reboot'

Question:
What occurs when the system shuts down in an uncontrolled manner?

Answer:
'emergency system restart'

Security Operations Domain

Question:
What occurs when the system shuts down and fails to execute a normal recovery procedure?

Answer:
'cold start'

Question:
What is a transaction that cannot be interrupted between input and output?

Answer:
'atomic transaction'

Question:
What is a system in which all features and services not required have been removed or disabled and remaining features have been configured to the most conservative setting that remains usable?

Answer:
'hardened system'

Question:
What is a standard hardened image that is cloned for new systems?

Answer:
'Gold Master, or GM'

Question:
What is the act of increasing the number of controls an attacker will have to compromise?

Answer:
'diversity of controls'

Question:
What are locks used in the primary personnel entrances and exits?

Answer:
'main locks'

Question:
What are locks used in areas such as side doors?

Answer:
'secondary locks'

Question:
What are locks used for doors such as delivery?

Answer:
'external locks'

Question:
What is a device that will only slow down a determined intruder?

Answer:
'delaying device'

Security Operations Domain

408

Question:
What is a basic padlock with a key?

Answer:
'warded lock'

Question:
What is a lock used on file cabinets, and uses wafers instead of pins; is fairly easy to beat?

Answer:
'basic wafer tumbler lock'

Question:
What is a common door lock, where the key raises individual pins, allowing the cylinder to rotate?

Answer:
'pin tumbler lock'

Question:
What is a lock used on safes, where moving levers are used to unlock the container?

Answer:
'lever tumbler lock'

Question:
What is a commercial and industrial lock grade?

Answer:
'grade 1 lock'

Question:
What is a heavy-duty residential and light-duty commercial lock grade?

Answer:
'grade 2 lock'

Question:
What is a residential and consumer lock grade?

Answer:
'grade 3 lock'

Question:
What is the security level for a cylinder lock with no resistance?

Answer:
'low security'

Question:
What is the security level for a cylinder lock with some resistance?

Answer:
'medium security'

Security Operations Domain

409

Question:
What is the security level for a cylinder lock with resistance provided through multiple mechanisms, but applies only to Grade 1 or Grade 2 locks?

Answer:
'high security'

Question:
What is a lock attack using an L-shaped tool that manipulates pins?

Answer:
'tension wrench attack'

Question:
What is a lock attack using a tool that applies pressure against pins while being quickly removed?

Answer:
'raking attack'

Question:
What is a lock attack using a tool that uses a bump key to force pins into the right position?

Answer:
'bumping attack'

Question:
What is a key that opens all locks?

Answer:
'master key'

Question:
What is a key that opens a specific range of doors?

Answer:
'submaster key'

Question:
What is a lock that has one or more internal spinning wheels that require an external spin control to be rotated both clockwise and counterclockwise by the operator?

Answer:
'combination lock'

Question:
What is a lock that has a keypad, and is really a small programmable computer?

Answer:
'cipher lock'

Question:
What is a cipher lock feature that triggers an alarm if the door is held open?

Answer:
'door delay'

Security Operations Domain

410

Question:
What is a cipher lock feature that allows a specific code to be used to override normal procedures?

Answer:
'key override'

Question:
What is a cipher lock feature that allows supervisors access to change codes and features?

Answer:
'master keying'

Question:
What is a cipher lock feature that accepts a special code to communicate duress?

Answer:
'hostage alarm'

Question:
What is a cipher lock capable of intelligently making access decisions based on external conditions, such as time of day or specific user codes?

Answer:
'smart lock'

Question:
What prevents hardware devices from being stolen or accessed?

Answer:
'device lock'

Question:
What covers on/off switches?

Answer:
'switch control'

Question:
What secures mobile systems to a stationary component using a steel cable?

Answer:
'slot lock'

Question:
What blocks access to disk drives or USB ports?

Answer:
'port control'

Question:
What inserts an on/off switch between a peripheral and the system?

Answer:
'peripheral switch control'

Security Operations Domain

Question:
What prevents removal of an I/O device by passing the device's cable through a lockable unit?

Answer:
'cable trap'

Question:
What are electronic devices that require authorization before allowing a person into a secured area?

Answer:
'personnel access controls'

Question:
What is a device that requires a user to initiate interaction?

Answer:
'user-activated reader'

Question:
What is a device that automatically senses an approaching person and reads the card wirelessly?

Answer:
'system sensing access control reader, or transponder'

Question:
What is a proximity detection device that identifies and authenticates a person?

Answer:
'Electronic Access Control token, or EAC token'

Question:
What occurs when an unauthorized person gains accessing by using another person's credentials with consent?

Answer:
'piggybacking'

Question:
What is similar to piggybacking, but occurs without the person's consent?

Answer:
'tailgating'

Question:
What controls pedestrian and vehicle flow, creates different security zones, provides delaying mechanisms and restricts control to entry points?

Answer:
'boundary protection mechanism'

Question:
What are represented by locks, card access systems and personnel awareness?

Answer:
'access control mechanisms'

Security Operations Domain

Question:
What is a type of boundary protection mechanism that includes fences, gates, walls and doors?

Answer:
'physical barrier mechanism'

Question:
What is a type of boundary protection mechanism that includes motion detectors?

Answer:
'intrusion detection mechanism'

Question:
What is a type of boundary protection mechanism that includes guards, CCTV, and anything else that requires a human?

Answer:
'assessment mechanism'

Question:
What is a type of boundary protection mechanism that includes guards and law enforcement?

Answer:
'response mechanism'

Question:
What is a type of boundary protection mechanism that includes signs, lighting and environmental design?

Answer:
'deterrent mechanism'

Question:
What is a measurement of a wire's thickness; the lower the gauge, the thicker the wire?

Answer:
'gauge'

Question:
What is a measurement of the spacing between wires; the smaller rating the more secure it will be?

Answer:
'mesh'

Question:
What is a fence that detects vibrations?

Answer:
'Perimeter Intrusion and Detection Assessment System, or PIDAS'

Question:
What is a class of gate strength designed for residential use?

Answer:
'Class I gate'

Security Operations Domain

Question:
What is a class of gate strength designed for commercial and general public access?

Answer:
'Class II gate'

Question:
What is a class of gate strength designed for industrial limited access?

Answer:
'Class III gate'

Question:
What is a class of gate strength designed for restricted access such as a prison gates?

Answer:
'Class IV gate'

Question:
What is a lighting best practice that states lighting should point toward the direction of potential attackers and away from security?

Answer:
'glare protection'

Question:
What is a lighting best practice that states an array of lighting provides the best, even amount of illumination?

Answer:
'continuous lighting'

Question:
What is a lighting best practice that states light should be prevented from bleeding over into unwanted areas?

Answer:
'controlled lighting'

Question:
What is a lighting best practice that encourages the use of systems to automatically turn lights on and off so that intruders think people are present?

Answer:
'standby lighting'

Question:
What is a lighting best practice that states backup lighting should be used in the event of power failure?

Answer:
'backup lighting'

Question:
What is a lighting best practice that states that lighting should be automatically turned on when an intruder is detected; this results in high false-positives so CCTV should also be used to allow remote verification if there is an actual problem?

Answer:
'responsive area illumination'

Security Operations Domain

414

Question:
What is a CCTV component that accepts multiple camera feeds and produces a single video feed to the monitor?

Answer:
'CCTV multiplexer'

Question:
What is a CCTV component that displays cameras feeds via the multiplexer?

Answer:
'CCTV monitor'

Question:
What is a CCTV component that compresses the video into a digital format for later review?

Answer:
'CCTV recording system'

Question:
What is a CCTV component that captures and sends video over a dedicated cable?

Answer:
'CCTV camera'

Question:
What is a device within a camera that converts light into an electrical signal?

Answer:
'Charge-Coupled Device, or CDD'

Question:
What is a camera attribute that determines how wide or narrow the captured image is?

Answer:
'focal length'

Question:
What allows images to be resized after an image has been captured, resulting in pixilation?

Answer:
'digital zoom'

Question:
What enlarges the field of view before an image is captured, resulting in greater detail?

Answer:
'optical zoom'

Question:
What controls whether objects that remain in focus are close or far away?

Answer:
'depth of focus'

Security Operations Domain

Question:
What is a camera mechanism that opens and closes around the lens to limit how much light is let in?

Answer:
'iris'

Question:
What is a type of iris that must be manually adjusted at the camera?

Answer:
'manual iris lens'

Question:
What is a type of iris that automatically adjusts based on the amount of light present?

Answer:
'auto iris lens'

Question:
What is a term used to indicate the minimum amount of light needed for a clear image in dark conditions?

Answer:
'lux'

Question:
What is the type of mount for a camera that must be manually adjusted to point in different directions?

Answer:
'fixed mount'

Question:
What is the type of mount for a camera that can be remotely moved around?

Answer:
'pan, tilt, zoom, or PTZ'

Question:
What is an intrusion detection system used for physical security?

Answer:
'perimeter scanning device'

Question:
What is a physical IDS that can detect changes in an environmental baseline, and is very sensitive?

Answer:
'volumetric IDS'

Question:
What is a physical IDS that can detect a change in some type of electrical or magnetic circuit, and is used to detect open doors and windows; a pressure pad is another example where weight sets off an alarm?

Answer:
'electromechanical IDS'

Security Operations Domain

Question:
What is a physical IDS that can detect a change in a light beam?

Answer:
'photoelectric IDS, or photometric system'

Question:
What is a physical IDS used to detect movement, that uses multiple beams of light, usually accomplished by mirrors bouncing the signal several times before reaching the detector?

Answer:
'cross-sectional photoelectric IDS'

Question:
What is a physical IDS used to detect people or active tools, by detecting changes in heat waves?

Answer:
'Passive Infrared IDS, or PIR IDS'

Question:
What is a physical IDS that uses microphones to detect changes in volume; these are very sensitive, and traffic and weather can set them off, so usually used for rooms far away from ambient noise?

Answer:
'acoustical detection IDS'

Question:
What is a physical IDS used for walls and vaults that can detect large vibrations such as drilling, cutting or a destructive force?

Answer:
'vibration sensor'

Question:
What is a physical IDS used for large rooms that can send out microwave, ultrasonic, or low frequency waves and expects it to return uninterrupted?

Answer:
'wave-pattern motion detector'

Question:
What is a physical IDS usually used for small areas such as cabinets or safes, that emits a magnetic field and alerts if interrupted; this is also an example of an Electrostatic IDS.?

Answer:
'proximity detector, or capacitance detector'

Question:
What is the standard that describes a secure supply chain?

Answer:
'ISO 28000'

Security Operations Domain

Question:
What is the component of a secure supply chain that states the manufacturer and supplier must be trusted to create a secure product?

Answer:
'trusted supplier'

Question:
What is the component of a secure supply chain that states the transportation mechanism between the supplier and the door must be secure?

Answer:
'trusted transportation network'

Question:
What is the component of a secure supply chain that states before hardware is allowed into inventory it must be inspected?

Answer:
'trusted inspection'

Question:
What is the process of establishing and maintaining a consistent baseline of all systems?

Answer:
'Configuration Management, or CM'

Question:
What is a measure of how long we expect a piece of equipment to continue operating in a usable manner without needing repair?

Answer:
'Mean Time Between Failure, or MTBF'

Question:
What is a measure of the lifetime of a product?

Answer:
'Mean Time To Failure, or MTTF'

Question:
What is a measure of the expected amount of time required to get a failed device back into a production state?

Answer:
'Mean Time To Repair, or MTTR'

Question:
What is a component that will cause a complete outage if it fails due to a lack of redundancy or backup measures?

Answer:
'single point of failure'

Question:
What is a configuration of multiple disks that mitigate data and up-time loss due to hardware failure?

Answer:
'Redundant Array of Independent Disks, or RAID'

Security Operations Domain

418

Question:
What is a RAID configuration that is striped over multiple drives for performance?

Answer:
'RAID 0'

Question:
What is a RAID configuration that is mirrored such that data is written to 2 drives simultaneously?

Answer:
'RAID 1'

Question:
What is a RAID configuration that has data striping at the bit level across all drives?

Answer:
'RAID 2'

Question:
What is a RAID configuration that has data striping with one parity drive at the byte level?

Answer:
'RAID 3'

Question:
What is a RAID configuration that has data striping with one parity drive at the block level?

Answer:
'RAID 4'

Question:
What is a RAID configuration that has data written in disk sector units to all drives along with parity?

Answer:
'RAID 5'

Question:
What is a RAID configuration that is the same as RAID 5 plus a second set of parity on all drives?

Answer:
'RAID 6'

Question:
What is a RAID configuration that is mirrored and striped across several drives?

Answer:
'RAID 10'

Question:
What is the most common type of magnetic hard drive, and any location on a DASD may be reached immediately?

Answer:
'Direct Access Storage Device, or DASD'

Security Operations Domain

Question:
What is a device such as a tape drive, where all locations in between the current and target location must be traversed before the data may be accessed?

Answer:
'Sequential Access Storage Device, or SASD'

Question:
What is a device that offers storage in the area of hundreds of terabytes and is write-optimized?

Answer:
'Massive Array of Inactive Disks, or MAID'

Question:
What is similar to RAID but uses tapes in a RAID 1 configuration instead of hard drives?

Answer:
'Redundant Array of Independent Tapes, or RAIT'

Question:
What is a very small, high-speed network between multiple storage devices?

Answer:
'Storage Area Network, or SAN'

Question:
What is a fault-tolerance technology similar to redundant servers, but where all servers take an active part?

Answer:
'clustering'

Question:
What results when geographically disparate systems focused on a single task dynamically join and leave a network?

Answer:
'grid computing'

Question:
What is a device that provides continuous online backups by combining hard disks with cheaper optical or tape jukeboxes?

Answer:
'Hierarchical Storage Management, or HSM'

Question:
What is data that is stored on slower media?

Answer:
'near-line'

Security Operations Domain

420

Question:
What is software that works by extracting a signature from files and comparing it to a known list of malware that is updated weekly?

Answer:
'antimalware, or antivirus'

Question:
What is the process for identifying, acquiring, installing and verifying patches for products and systems?

Answer:
'patch management'

Question:
What is a form of patch management implemented by allowing software to check for patches and updates and applying them unattended?

Answer:
'unmanaged patching'

Question:
What is a form of patch management where the application of patches is controlled from a central location?

Answer:
'centralized patch management'

Question:
What is a type of central patch management in which an agent runs on each device and contacts a central update server?

Answer:
'agent based central patching'

Question:
What is a type of central patch management in which one or more hosts connect to each device using network administrator credentials and install updates as-needed (Active Directory objects can be used for this as well)?

Answer:
'agentless central patching'

Question:
What is a type of central patch management in which a system monitors network traffic and infers the patch levels on networked devices; this is the least invasive but also the least effective?

Answer:
'passive central patching'

Question:
What is a client application that can be used to safely explore malicious web sites or links?

Answer:
'honeyclient'

Security Operations Domain

Question:
What is an application execution environment that abstracts the code away from the actual operating system?

Answer:
'sandbox, or emulation buffer'

Question:
What is any occurrence that can be observed, verified and documented?

Answer:
'event'

Question:
What is one or more related events that negatively affect a company and/or its security posture?

Answer:
'incident'

Question:
What is an organization which is a good resource for incident management processes?

Answer:
'Computer Emergency Response Team, or CERT'

Question:
What is an incident response team comprised of experts who have other responsibilities within the organization?

Answer:
'virtual response team'

Question:
What is an incident response team comprised of one or more people dedicated strictly to incident response?

Answer:
'permanent response team'

Question:
What is an incident response team comprised of one or more core permanent members with other experts on call as-needed?

Answer:
'hybrid response team'

Question:
What is the term for the steps of progression in almost all attacks?

Answer:
'kill chain'

Question:
What is the step in a kill chain in which deliberate information gathering occurs?

Answer:
'reconnaissance step'

Security Operations Domain

Question:
What is the step in a kill chain in which preparation and testing weapons based on reconnaissance occurs?

Answer:
'weaponization step'

Question:
What is the step in a kill chain in which the cyber weapon is delivered?

Answer:
'delivery step'

Question:
What is the step in a kill chain in which the malicious software executes on a CPU as a result of delivery?

Answer:
'exploitation step'

Question:
What is the step in a kill chain in which installation of the real payload occurs in a persisted manner by the malicious software?

Answer:
'installation step'

Question:
What is the step in a kill chain in which the payload phones home to check in and gather instructions?

Answer:
'Command and Control, or C&C step'

Question:
What is the step in a kill chain in which the payload carries out the instructions as directed?

Answer:
'actions on the objective step'

Question:
What is a step a response team takes to detect an attack, usually by using IDS alerts?

Answer:
'detection step'

Question:
What is a step a response team takes to gather data and find the root cause of the attack?

Answer:
'response step'

Question:
What is a step a response team takes to contain the damage done or about to be done to the most critical assets first?

Answer:
'mitigation step'

Security Operations Domain

423

Question:
What is the name of a strategy a response team can take to isolate the system(s), revise firewall rules and ACLs?

Answer:
'reactive response'

Question:
What is the name of a strategy a response team can take to activate a honeypot?

Answer:
'proactive response'

Question:
What is a step a response team takes to create the report that will be delivered after the event?

Answer:
'reporting step'

Question:
What is a step a response team takes to return all systems to a known-good state?

Answer:
'recovery step'

Question:
What is a step a response team takes to decide which measures executed during the Mitigation phase should become permanent.?

Answer:
'remediation step'

Question:
What is the standard covering the data that should be covered in a response team's report?

Answer:
'NIST SP 800-61'

Question:
What is a tool that response teams use to know if an attack is underway?

Answer:
'Indicators Of Attack, or IOA'

Question:
What is a tool that response teams use to know if a successful attack has already been completed?

Answer:
'Indicators Of Compromise, or IOC'

Question:
What is the overall time a company can survive without a given system running in an operational capacity?

Answer:
'Maximum Tolerable Downtime, or MTD'

Security Operations Domain

424

Question:
What is the longest time a business can survive without the affected process being restored to acceptable levels?

Answer:
'Recovery Time Objective, or RTO'

Question:
What is the time required to restore that data and complete all testing prior to going live?

Answer:
'Work Recovery Time, or WRT'

Question:
What is an event having a significant impact on a facility that remains operational in a reduced capacity?

Answer:
'non-disaster event'

Question:
What is an event that causes an entire facility to be unusable for one day or longer, and an alternate facility is required for the business to continue operating?

Answer:
'disaster event'

Question:
What is an event that results in a facility being a complete loss, and both short-term and long-term facilities are required?

Answer:
'catastrophe event'

Question:
What is a facility that the company owns and maintains, and is sometimes called a mirrored site?

Answer:
'redundant site'

Question:
What is a mobile data center contained in a large truck or trailer with self-contained communications capability?

Answer:
'rolling hot site'

Question:
What is a scenario in which two or more centers in different regions are used continuously?

Answer:
'multiple processing centers'

Question:
What is a facility that is maintained by a third-party, but it is dedicated to the company?

Answer:
'rented offsite installation'

Security Operations Domain

425

Question:
What is a company-owned site that is always ready to go at a moment's notice, complete with hardware?

Answer:
'hot site'

Question:
What is a company-owned site that is always ready to go at a moment's notice, but has no hardware?

Answer:
'warm site'

Question:
What is a company-owned site that is essentially an empty data center?

Answer:
'cold site'

Question:
What is a company that provides a rented offsite installation?

Answer:
'service bureau'

Question:
What is a company that provides raw materials such as generator fuel or backup communication services?

Answer:
'contingency company'

Question:
What is a 'backup for the backup', or a Plan B when Plan A fails?

Answer:
'tertiary site'

Question:
What is a disaster plan in which the company enters into an agreement with another company to share their facilities if needed?

Answer:
'reciprocal agreement'

Question:
What is a disaster plan in which 3 or more companies agree to aid each other in times of crisis?

Answer:
'mutual aid agreement'

Question:
What is a file-level flag that indicates if the file has been changed?

Answer:
'archive bit'

Security Operations Domain

426

Question:
What is a data backup strategy in which all files are backed up regardless of the archive bit?

Answer:
'full backup'

Question:
What is a data backup strategy in which all files are backed up that have changed since the last full backup but does not clear the archive bit?

Answer:
'differential backup'

Question:
What is a data backup strategy in which all files are backed up that have changed since the last full back up or differential backup, and also clears the archive bit?

Answer:
'incremental backup'

Question:
What is a system configuration having multiple disk controllers for fail-over?

Answer:
'disk duplexing'

Question:
What is a system configuration in which all data is simultaneously written to two disks?

Answer:
'disk shadowing'

Question:
What is a type of disk shadowing in which two disks have the exact same data and configuration, but appear as one disk?

Answer:
'disk mirroring'

Question:
What makes copies of files in real-time as they are modified and periodically writes them in a bulk fashion to an offsite backup facility?

Answer:
'electronic vaulting'

Question:
What moves the journal or transaction logs (files that contain the delta only) to an offsite facility in real-time, as opposed to operating in batches like electronic vaulting?

Answer:
'remote journaling'

Security Operations Domain

Question:
What backs up data to a tape, where it is then manually transferred to an offsite facility for storage?

Answer:
'tape vaulting'

Question:
What allows data to be transferred to a remote offsite tape backup facility over a connection, but personnel in the remote facility are responsible for swapping tapes when necessary?

Answer:
'electronic tape vaulting, or automatic tape vaulting'

Question:
What is a capability built into most modern DBs that allow them to automatically replicate their data to a remote instance of the database?

Answer:
'database replication'

Question:
What is a type of database replication in which the two copies may be out of sync for a period of time (seconds to days)?

Answer:
'asynchronous database replication '

Question:
What is a type of database replication in which the two repositories are never out of sync?

Answer:
'synchronous database replication '

Question:
What is a combination of technologies that ensures a system or process is always running?

Answer:
'High Availability, or HA'

Question:
What provides alternative options in real-time?

Answer:
'redundancy'

Question:
What is a capability of a technology to switch 'over' to a working system in case the primary system fails?

Answer:
'failover'

Security Operations Domain

Question:
What is a type of failover in which multiple identical systems are linked in real-time such that if one fails, the other systems take over?

Answer:
'clustering'

Question:
What is a type of failover in which multiple identical systems all share in servicing the same types of requests as instructed by some type of centralized connection point?

Answer:
'load balancing'

Question:
What is the probability that a system will perform its function for a specific time under specific conditions?

Answer:
'reliability'

Question:
What insures losses caused by DoS, malware, hackers, electronic theft and privacy-related lawsuits?

Answer:
'cyber insurance'

Question:
What is a type of insurance that will pay for specified expenses and income loss if a company is out of business past a specific length of time?

Answer:
'business interruption insurance'

Question:
What is a type of insurance that covers part or all of the losses if a company cannot collect on its accounts?

Answer:
'accounts receivables insurance'

Question:
What is a step in the BCP recovery process that assesses the original site and determine next steps?

Answer:
'BCP damage assessment phase'

Question:
What is a step in the BCP recovery process that brings an alternate site online?

Answer:
'BCP restoration phase'

Security Operations Domain

Question:
What is a step in the BCP recovery process that brings the original site back into a production level?

Answer:
'BCP salvage phase'

Question:
What is a step in the BCP recovery process that brings the company as a whole back to full capacity as soon as possible?

Answer:
'BCP recovery phase '

Question:
What is a step in the BCP recovery process that takes the company back into the original site?

Answer:
'BCP reconstitution phase'

Question:
What is the recovery, authentication and analysis of electronic data with the express purpose of carrying out a digital criminal investigation?

Answer:
'computer forensics'

Question:
What is a superset of computer forensics and includes network forensics, electronic data discovery, cyber-forensics and forensic computing?

Answer:
'digital forensics'

Question:
What is any result of computer forensic, network or code analysis?

Answer:
'digital evidence'

Question:
What is an organization that ensures all other organizations have a consistent approach to forensics?

Answer:
'Scientific Working Group on Digital Evidence, or SWGDE'

Question:
What is an acronym for motive, opportunity and means?

Answer:
'MOM'

Question:
What is the typical pattern a criminal follows in all of his or her crimes?

Answer:
'Modus Operandi, or MO'

Security Operations Domain

430

Question:
What is a saying that every criminal always takes something from a crime scene, and leaves something behind?

Answer:
'Locard's exchange principal'

Question:
What is an image of original media stored in a library?

Answer:
'primary image'

Question:
What is a secondary image of original media to be used during the investigation?

Answer:
'working image'

Question:
What is a list of all actions showing a complete history of how evidence was collected, analyzed, transported and preserved?

Answer:
'chain of custody'

Question:
What is the term for analysis taking place on-site?

Answer:
'live forensics'

Question:
What is the term for analysis taking place in a lab?

Answer:
'dead forensics'

Question:
What is a term for secondhand evidence?

Answer:
'hearsay evidence'

Question:
What is a digital evidence criterion stating the evidence must have a reasonable relationship to the findings?

Answer:
'relevant evidence'

Question:
What is a digital evidence criterion stating the evidence must communicate the whole truth?

Answer:
'complete evidence'

Security Operations Domain

Question:
What is a digital evidence criterion stating the evidence validity must be convincing to a reasonable person?

Answer:
'sufficient evidence'

Question:
What is a digital evidence criterion stating the evidence must be consistent with the facts, and be factual itself?

Answer:
'reliable evidence'

Question:
What is a type of computer surveillance that uses network sniffers, keyboard monitors, wiretaps and line monitoring?

Answer:
'passive monitoring'

Question:
What is a type of computer surveillance that is invasive and gathers evidence directly?

Answer:
'active monitoring'

Question:
What is a law that allows law enforcement to immediately seize potential evidence if it is about to be destroyed?

Answer:
'exigent circumstances'

Question:
What is liability that a company offering services may encounter if it does not exercise due care and due diligence to make sure its customers cannot sue it down the road?

Answer:
'downstream liability'

Question:
What is the obvious cause of a claim?

Answer:
'proximate cause'

Question:
What is the first step in getting a vendor to provide a solution?

Answer:
'Request for Proposal, or RFP'

Question:
What is the process of monitoring and developing a relationship with a vendor?

Answer:
'vendor management'

Security Operations Domain

432

Question:
What is a program that aligns governance, risk and compliance to see how well the three are integrated?

Answer:
'Governance, Risk and Compliance, or GRC'

Security Operations Domain

Terms

Question:
What is a 'prudent man'?

Answer:
A 'prudent man' is a person who is responsible, careful, cautious and practical.

Question:
What is 'due care'?

Answer:
'due care' results when we take reasonable precautions.

Question:
What is 'due diligence'?

Answer:
'due diligence' results when we do everything within our power to prevent a bad thing from happening.

Question:
What is 'administrative management'?

Answer:
'administrative management' is the act of managing personnel.

Question:
What is a 'network administrator'?

Answer:
A 'network administrator' is a role that works to achieve a highly available, performant infrastructure that meets user needs.

Question:
What is a 'security administrator'?

Answer:
A 'security administrator' is a role that works to ensure a highly-secure and controlled infrastructure.

Question:
What is the 'assurance level'?

Answer:
The 'assurance level' ensures that a given product is trustworthy.

Question:
What is 'operation assurance'?

Answer:
'operation assurance' ensures that a product provides the necessary levels of protection based on its architecture, embedded features, and functionality.

Security Operations Domain

Question:
What is 'life-cycle assurance'?

Answer:
'life-cycle assurance' follows the development life-cycle of a product including specs, clipping levels, testing, configuration and distribution.

Question:
What is 'operational security'?

Answer:
'operational security' is the ability to mitigate the damage resulting from unauthorized disclosure of information.

Question:
What is 'event management systems'?

Answer:
'event management systems' are systems that collect logs throughout the network and automatically correlates the information.

Question:
What is the 'Initial Program Load, or IPL'?

Answer:
The 'Initial Program Load, or IPL' happens when software starts up from an unexpected or expected shutdown.

Question:
What is 'deviation from the standard'?

Answer:
'deviation from the standard' is a periodically measured value of a system that deviates significantly from the baseline measurements.

Question:
What is 'configuration management'?

Answer:
'configuration management' ensures that operations are carried out in the proper security context.

Question:
What is a 'trusted recovery'?

Answer:
A 'trusted recovery' is experienced when a system that unexpectedly shuts down comes back up in a secure state.

Question:
What is a 'system reboot'?

Answer:
A 'system reboot' occurs when the system shuts down in a controlled manner as a result of a kernel failure; examples might be insufficient memory or invalid data structures.

Security Operations Domain

Question:
What is an 'emergency system restart'?

Answer:
An 'emergency system restart' occurs when the system shuts down in an uncontrolled manner.

Question:
What is a 'cold start'?

Answer:
A 'cold start' occurs when the system shuts down and fails to execute a normal recovery procedure.

Question:
What is an 'atomic transaction'?

Answer:
An 'atomic transaction' is a transaction that cannot be interrupted between input and output.

Question:
What is a 'hardened system'?

Answer:
A 'hardened system' is a system in which all features and services not required have been removed or disabled and remaining features have been configured to the most conservative setting that remains usable.

Question:
What is a 'Gold Master, or GM'?

Answer:
A 'Gold Master, or GM' is a standard hardened image that is cloned for new systems.

Question:
What is 'diversity of controls'?

Answer:
'diversity of controls' is the act of increasing the number of controls an attacker will have to compromise.

Question:
What is 'main locks'?

Answer:
'main locks' are locks used in the primary personnel entrances and exits.

Question:
What is 'secondary locks'?

Answer:
'secondary locks' are locks used in areas such as side doors.

Question:
What is 'external locks'?

Answer:
'external locks' are locks used for doors such as delivery.

Security Operations Domain

Question:
What is a 'delaying device'?

Answer:
A 'delaying device' is a device that will only slow down a determined intruder.

Question:
What is a 'warded lock'?

Answer:
A 'warded lock' is a basic padlock with a key.

Question:
What is a 'basic wafer tumbler lock'?

Answer:
A 'basic wafer tumbler lock' is a lock used on file cabinets, and uses wafers instead of pins; is fairly easy to beat.

Question:
What is a 'pin tumbler lock'?

Answer:
A 'pin tumbler lock' is a common door lock, where the key raises individual pins, allowing the cylinder to rotate.

Question:
What is a 'lever tumbler lock'?

Answer:
A 'lever tumbler lock' is a lock used on safes, where moving levers are used to unlock the container.

Question:
What is a 'grade 1 lock'?

Answer:
A 'grade 1 lock' is a commercial and industrial lock grade.

Question:
What is a 'grade 2 lock'?

Answer:
A 'grade 2 lock' is a heavy-duty residential and light-duty commercial lock grade.

Question:
What is a 'grade 3 lock'?

Answer:
A 'grade 3 lock' is a residential and consumer lock grade.

Question:
What is 'low security'?

Answer:
'low security' is the security level for a cylinder lock with no resistance.

Security Operations Domain

437

Question:
What is 'medium security'?

Answer:
'medium security' is the security level for a cylinder lock with some resistance.

Question:
What is 'high security'?

Answer:
'high security' is the security level for a cylinder lock with resistance provided through multiple mechanisms, but applies only to Grade 1 or Grade 2 locks.

Question:
What is a 'tension wrench attack'?

Answer:
A 'tension wrench attack' is a lock attack using an L-shaped tool that manipulates pins.

Question:
What is a 'raking attack'?

Answer:
A 'raking attack' is a lock attack using a tool that applies pressure against pins while being quickly removed.

Question:
What is a 'bumping attack'?

Answer:
A 'bumping attack' is a lock attack using a tool that uses a bump key to force pins into the right position.

Question:
What is a 'master key'?

Answer:
A 'master key' is a key that opens all locks.

Question:
What is a 'submaster key'?

Answer:
A 'submaster key' is a key that opens a specific range of doors.

Question:
What is a 'combination lock'?

Answer:
A 'combination lock' is a lock that has one or more internal spinning wheels that require an external spin control to be rotated both clockwise and counterclockwise by the operator.

Question:
What is a 'cipher lock'?

Answer:
A 'cipher lock' is a lock that has a keypad, and is really a small programmable computer.

Security Operations Domain

Question:
What is 'door delay'?

Answer:
'door delay' is a cipher lock feature that triggers an alarm if the door is held open.

Question:
What is 'key override'?

Answer:
'key override' is a cipher lock feature that allows a specific code to be used to override normal procedures.

Question:
What is 'master keying'?

Answer:
'master keying' is a cipher lock feature that allows supervisors access to change codes and features.

Question:
What is 'hostage alarm'?

Answer:
'hostage alarm' is a cipher lock feature that accepts a special code to communicate duress.

Question:
What is a 'smart lock'?

Answer:
A 'smart lock' is a cipher lock capable of intelligently making access decisions based on external conditions, such as time of day or specific user codes.

Question:
What is a 'device lock'?

Answer:
A 'device lock' prevents hardware devices from being stolen or accessed.

Question:
What is a 'switch control'?

Answer:
A 'switch control' covers on/off switches.

Question:
What is a 'slot lock'?

Answer:
A 'slot lock' secures mobile systems to a stationary component using a steel cable.

Question:
What is a 'port control'?

Answer:
A 'port control' blocks access to disk drives or USB ports.

Security Operations Domain

Question:
What is a 'peripheral switch control'?

Answer:
A 'peripheral switch control' inserts an on/off switch between a peripheral and the system.

Question:
What is a 'cable trap'?

Answer:
A 'cable trap' prevents removal of an I/O device by passing the device's cable through a lockable unit.

Question:
What is 'personnel access controls'?

Answer:
'personnel access controls' are electronic devices that require authorization before allowing a person into a secured area.

Question:
What is a 'user-activated reader'?

Answer:
A 'user-activated reader' is a device that requires a user to initiate interaction.

Question:
What is a 'system sensing access control reader, or transponder'?

Answer:
A 'system sensing access control reader, or transponder' is a device that automatically senses an approaching person and reads the card wirelessly.

Question:
What is an 'Electronic Access Control token, or EAC token'?

Answer:
An 'Electronic Access Control token, or EAC token' is a proximity detection device that identifies and authenticates a person.

Question:
What is 'piggybacking'?

Answer:
'piggybacking' occurs when an unauthorized person gains accessing by using another person's credentials with consent.

Question:
What is 'tailgating'?

Answer:
'tailgating' is similar to piggybacking, but occurs without the person's consent.

Question:
What is a 'boundary protection mechanism'?

Answer:
A 'boundary protection mechanism' controls pedestrian and vehicle flow, creates different security zones, provides delaying mechanisms and restricts control to entry points.

Security Operations Domain

440

Question:
What is 'access control mechanisms'?

Answer:
'access control mechanisms' are represented by locks, card access systems and personnel awareness.

Question:
What is a 'physical barrier mechanism'?

Answer:
A 'physical barrier mechanism' is a type of boundary protection mechanism that includes fences, gates, walls and doors.

Question:
What is an 'intrusion detection mechanism'?

Answer:
An 'intrusion detection mechanism' is a type of boundary protection mechanism that includes motion detectors.

Question:
What is an 'assessment mechanism'?

Answer:
An 'assessment mechanism' is a type of boundary protection mechanism that includes guards, CCTV, and anything else that requires a human.

Question:
What is a 'response mechanism'?

Answer:
A 'response mechanism' is a type of boundary protection mechanism that includes guards and law enforcement.

Question:
What is a 'deterrent mechanism'?

Answer:
A 'deterrent mechanism' is a type of boundary protection mechanism that includes signs, lighting and environmental design.

Question:
What is 'gauge'?

Answer:
'gauge' is a measurement of a wire's thickness; the lower the gauge, the thicker the wire.

Question:
What is 'mesh'?

Answer:
'mesh' is a measurement of the spacing between wires; the smaller rating the more secure it will be.

Question:
What is 'Perimeter Intrusion and Detection Assessment System, or PIDAS'?

Answer:
'Perimeter Intrusion and Detection Assessment System, or PIDAS' is a fence that detects vibrations.

Security Operations Domain

Question:
What is a 'Class I gate'?

Answer:
A 'Class I gate' is a class of gate strength designed for residential use.

Question:
What is a 'Class II gate'?

Answer:
A 'Class II gate' is a class of gate strength designed for commercial and general public access.

Question:
What is a 'Class III gate'?

Answer:
A 'Class III gate' is a class of gate strength designed for industrial limited access.

Question:
What is a 'Class IV gate'?

Answer:
A 'Class IV gate' is a class of gate strength designed for restricted access such as a prison gates.

Question:
What is 'glare protection'?

Answer:
'glare protection' is a lighting best practice that states lighting should point toward the direction of potential attackers and away from security.

Question:
What is 'continuous lighting'?

Answer:
'continuous lighting' is a lighting best practice that states an array of lighting provides the best, even amount of illumination.

Question:
What is 'controlled lighting'?

Answer:
'controlled lighting' is a lighting best practice that states light should be prevented from bleeding over into unwanted areas.

Question:
What is 'standby lighting'?

Answer:
'standby lighting' is a lighting best practice that encourages the use of systems to automatically turn lights on and off so that intruders think people are present.

Question:
What is 'backup lighting'?

Answer:
'backup lighting' is a lighting best practice that states backup lighting should be used in the event of power failure.

Security Operations Domain

442

Question:
What is 'responsive area illumination'?

Answer:
'responsive area illumination' is a lighting best practice that states that lighting should be automatically turned on when an intruder is detected; this results in high false-positives so CCTV should also be used to allow remote verification if there is an actual problem.

Question:
What is a 'CCTV multiplexer'?

Answer:
A 'CCTV multiplexer' is a CCTV component that accepts multiple camera feeds and produces a single video feed to the monitor.

Question:
What is a 'CCTV monitor'?

Answer:
A 'CCTV monitor' is a CCTV component that displays cameras feeds via the multiplexer.

Question:
What is a 'CCTV recording system'?

Answer:
A 'CCTV recording system' is a CCTV component that compresses the video into a digital format for later review.

Question:
What is a 'CCTV camera'?

Answer:
A 'CCTV camera' is a CCTV component that captures and sends video over a dedicated cable.

Question:
What is a 'Charge-Coupled Device, or CDD'?

Answer:
A 'Charge-Coupled Device, or CDD' is a device within a camera that converts light into an electrical signal.

Question:
What is 'focal length'?

Answer:
'focal length' is a camera attribute that determines how wide or narrow the captured image is.

Question:
What is 'digital zoom'?

Answer:
'digital zoom' allows images to be resized after an image has been captured, resulting in pixilation.

Question:
What is 'optical zoom'?

Answer:
'optical zoom' enlarges the field of view before an image is captured, resulting in greater detail.

Security Operations Domain

443

Question:
What is the 'depth of focus'?

Answer:
The 'depth of focus' controls whether objects that remain in focus are close or far away.

Question:
What is an 'iris'?

Answer:
An 'iris' is a camera mechanism that opens and closes around the lens to limit how much light is let in.

Question:
What is a 'manual iris lens'?

Answer:
A 'manual iris lens' is a type of iris that must be manually adjusted at the camera.

Question:
What is an 'auto iris lens'?

Answer:
An 'auto iris lens' is a type of iris that automatically adjusts based on the amount of light present.

Question:
What is 'lux'?

Answer:
'lux' is a term used to indicate the minimum amount of light needed for a clear image in dark conditions.

Question:
What is 'fixed mount'?

Answer:
'fixed mount' is the type of mount for a camera that must be manually adjusted to point in different directions.

Question:
What is 'pan, tilt, zoom, or PTZ'?

Answer:
'pan, tilt, zoom, or PTZ' is the type of mount for a camera that can be remotely moved around.

Question:
What is a 'perimeter scanning device'?

Answer:
A 'perimeter scanning device' is an intrusion detection system used for physical security.

Question:
What is a 'volumetric IDS'?

Answer:
A 'volumetric IDS' is a physical IDS that can detect changes in an environmental baseline, and is very sensitive.

Security Operations Domain

Question:
What is an 'electromechanical IDS'?

Answer:
An 'electromechanical IDS' is a physical IDS that can detect a change in some type of electrical or magnetic circuit, and is used to detect open doors and windows; a pressure pad is another example where weight sets off an alarm.

Question:
What is a 'photoelectric IDS, or photometric system'?

Answer:
A 'photoelectric IDS, or photometric system' is a physical IDS that can detect a change in a light beam.

Question:
What is a 'cross-sectional photoelectric IDS'?

Answer:
A 'cross-sectional photoelectric IDS' is a physical IDS used to detect movement, that uses multiple beams of light, usually accomplished by mirrors bouncing the signal several times before reaching the detector.

Question:
What is a 'Passive Infrared IDS, or PIR IDS'?

Answer:
A 'Passive Infrared IDS, or PIR IDS' is a physical IDS used to detect people or active tools, by detecting changes in heat waves.

Question:
What is an 'acoustical detection IDS'?

Answer:
An 'acoustical detection IDS' is a physical IDS that uses microphones to detect changes in volume; these are very sensitive, and traffic and weather can set them off, so usually used for rooms far away from ambient noise.

Question:
What is a 'vibration sensor'?

Answer:
A 'vibration sensor' is a physical IDS used for walls and vaults that can detect large vibrations such as drilling, cutting or a destructive force.

Question:
What is a 'wave-pattern motion detector'?

Answer:
A 'wave-pattern motion detector' is a physical IDS used for large rooms that can send out microwave, ultrasonic, or low frequency waves and expects it to return uninterrupted.

Question:
What is a 'proximity detector, or capacitance detector'?

Answer:
A 'proximity detector, or capacitance detector' is a physical IDS usually used for small areas such as cabinets or safes, that emits a magnetic field and alerts if interrupted; this is also an example of an Electrostatic IDS..

Security Operations Domain

Question:
What is 'ISO 28000'?

Answer:
'ISO 28000' is the standard that describes a secure supply chain.

Question:
What is a 'trusted supplier'?

Answer:
A 'trusted supplier' is the component of a secure supply chain that states the manufacturer and supplier must be trusted to create a secure product.

Question:
What is a 'trusted transportation network'?

Answer:
A 'trusted transportation network' is the component of a secure supply chain that states the transportation mechanism between the supplier and the door must be secure.

Question:
What is a 'trusted inspection'?

Answer:
A 'trusted inspection' is the component of a secure supply chain that states before hardware is allowed into inventory it must be inspected.

Question:
What is 'Configuration Management, or CM'?

Answer:
'Configuration Management, or CM' is the process of establishing and maintaining a consistent baseline of all systems.

Question:
What is the 'Mean Time Between Failure, or MTBF'?

Answer:
The 'Mean Time Between Failure, or MTBF' is a measure of how long we expect a piece of equipment to continue operating in a usable manner without needing repair.

Question:
What is the 'Mean Time To Failure, or MTTF'?

Answer:
The 'Mean Time To Failure, or MTTF' is a measure of the lifetime of a product.

Question:
What is the 'Mean Time To Repair, or MTTR'?

Answer:
The 'Mean Time To Repair, or MTTR' is a measure of the expected amount of time required to get a failed device back into a production state.

Security Operations Domain

446

Question:
What is a 'single point of failure'?

Answer:
A 'single point of failure' is a component that will cause a complete outage if it fails due to a lack of redundancy or backup measures.

Question:
What is a 'Redundant Array of Independent Disks, or RAID'?

Answer:
A 'Redundant Array of Independent Disks, or RAID' is a configuration of multiple disks that mitigate data and up-time loss due to hardware failure.

Question:
What is 'RAID 0'?

Answer:
'RAID 0' is a RAID configuration that is striped over multiple drives for performance.

Question:
What is 'RAID 1'?

Answer:
'RAID 1' is a RAID configuration that is mirrored such that data is written to 2 drives simultaneously.

Question:
What is 'RAID 2'?

Answer:
'RAID 2' is a RAID configuration that has data striping at the bit level across all drives.

Question:
What is 'RAID 3'?

Answer:
'RAID 3' is a RAID configuration that has data striping with one parity drive at the byte level.

Question:
What is 'RAID 4'?

Answer:
'RAID 4' is a RAID configuration that has data striping with one parity drive at the block level.

Question:
What is 'RAID 5'?

Answer:
'RAID 5' is a RAID configuration that has data written in disk sector units to all drives along with parity.

Question:
What is 'RAID 6'?

Answer:
'RAID 6' is a RAID configuration that is the same as RAID 5 plus a second set of parity on all drives.

Security Operations Domain

447

Question:
What is 'RAID 10'?

Answer:
'RAID 10' is a RAID configuration that is mirrored and striped across several drives.

Question:
What is a 'Direct Access Storage Device, or DASD'?

Answer:
A 'Direct Access Storage Device, or DASD' is the most common type of magnetic hard drive, and any location on a DASD may be reached immediately.

Question:
What is a 'Sequential Access Storage Device, or SASD'?

Answer:
A 'Sequential Access Storage Device, or SASD' is a device such as a tape drive, where all locations in between the current and target location must be traversed before the data may be accessed.

Question:
What is a 'Massive Array of Inactive Disks, or MAID'?

Answer:
A 'Massive Array of Inactive Disks, or MAID' is a device that offers storage in the area of hundreds of terabytes and is write-optimized.

Question:
What is a 'Redundant Array of Independent Tapes, or RAIT'?

Answer:
A 'Redundant Array of Independent Tapes, or RAIT' is similar to RAID but uses tapes in a RAID 1 configuration instead of hard drives.

Question:
What is a 'Storage Area Network, or SAN'?

Answer:
A 'Storage Area Network, or SAN' is a very small, high-speed network between multiple storage devices.

Question:
What is 'clustering'?

Answer:
'clustering' is a fault-tolerance technology similar to redundant servers, but where all servers take an active part.

Question:
What is 'grid computing'?

Answer:
'grid computing' results when geographically disparate systems focused on a single task dynamically join and leave a network.

Security Operations Domain

448

Question:
What is 'Hierarchical Storage Management, or HSM'?

Answer:
'Hierarchical Storage Management, or HSM' is a device that provides continuous online backups by combining hard disks with cheaper optical or tape jukeboxes.

Question:
What is 'near-line'?

Answer:
'near-line' is data that is stored on slower media.

Question:
What is 'antimalware, or antivirus'?

Answer:
'antimalware, or antivirus' is software that works by extracting a signature from files and comparing it to a known list of malware that is updated weekly.

Question:
What is 'patch management'?

Answer:
'patch management' is the process for identifying, acquiring, installing and verifying patches for products and systems.

Question:
What is 'unmanaged patching'?

Answer:
'unmanaged patching' is a form of patch management implemented by allowing software to check for patches and updates and applying them unattended.

Question:
What is 'centralized patch management'?

Answer:
'centralized patch management' is a form of patch management where the application of patches is controlled from a central location.

Question:
What is 'agent based central patching'?

Answer:
'agent based central patching' is a type of central patch management in which an agent runs on each device and contacts a central update server.

Question:
What is 'agentless central patching'?

Answer:
'agentless central patching' is a type of central patch management in which one or more hosts connect to each device using network administrator credentials and install updates as-needed (Active Directory objects can be used for this as well).

Security Operations Domain

Question:
What is 'passive central patching'?

Answer:
'passive central patching' is a type of central patch management in which a system monitors network traffic and infers the patch levels on networked devices; this is the least invasive but also the least effective.

Question:
What is a 'honeyclient'?

Answer:
A 'honeyclient' is a client application that can be used to safely explore malicious web sites or links.

Question:
What is a 'sandbox, or emulation buffer'?

Answer:
A 'sandbox, or emulation buffer' is an application execution environment that abstracts the code away from the actual operating system.

Question:
What is an 'event'?

Answer:
An 'event' is any occurrence that can be observed, verified and documented.

Question:
What is an 'incident'?

Answer:
An 'incident' is one or more related events that negatively affect a company and/or its security posture.

Question:
What is the 'Computer Emergency Response Team, or CERT'?

Answer:
The 'Computer Emergency Response Team, or CERT' is an organization which is a good resource for incident management processes.

Question:
What is a 'virtual response team'?

Answer:
A 'virtual response team' is an incident response team comprised of experts who have other responsibilities within the organization.

Question:
What is a 'permanent response team'?

Answer:
A 'permanent response team' is an incident response team comprised of one or more people dedicated strictly to incident response.

Security Operations Domain

450

Question:
What is a 'hybrid response team'?

Answer:
A 'hybrid response team' is an incident response team comprised of one or more core permanent members with other experts on call as-needed.

Question:
What is a 'kill chain'?

Answer:
A 'kill chain' is the term for the steps of progression in almost all attacks.

Question:
What is the 'reconnaissance step'?

Answer:
The 'reconnaissance step' is the step in a kill chain in which deliberate information gathering occurs.

Question:
What is the 'weaponization step'?

Answer:
The 'weaponization step' is the step in a kill chain in which preparation and testing weapons based on reconnaissance occurs.

Question:
What is the 'delivery step'?

Answer:
The 'delivery step' is the step in a kill chain in which the cyber weapon is delivered.

Question:
What is the 'exploitation step'?

Answer:
The 'exploitation step' is the step in a kill chain in which the malicious software executes on a CPU as a result of delivery.

Question:
What is the 'installation step'?

Answer:
The 'installation step' is the step in a kill chain in which installation of the real payload occurs in a persisted manner by the malicious software.

Question:
What is the 'Command and Control, or C&C step'?

Answer:
The 'Command and Control, or C&C step' is the step in a kill chain in which the payload phones home to check in and gather instructions.

Security Operations Domain

451

Question:
What is the 'actions on the objective step'?

Answer:
The 'actions on the objective step' is the step in a kill chain in which the payload carries out the instructions as directed.

Question:
What is the 'detection step'?

Answer:
The 'detection step' is a step a response team takes to detect an attack, usually by using IDS alerts.

Question:
What is the 'response step'?

Answer:
The 'response step' is a step a response team takes to gather data and find the root cause of the attack.

Question:
What is the 'mitigation step'?

Answer:
The 'mitigation step' is a step a response team takes to contain the damage done or about to be done to the most critical assets first.

Question:
What is a 'reactive response'?

Answer:
A 'reactive response' is the name of a strategy a response team can take to isolate the system(s), revise firewall rules and ACLs.

Question:
What is a 'proactive response'?

Answer:
A 'proactive response' is the name of a strategy a response team can take to activate a honeypot.

Question:
What is the 'reporting step'?

Answer:
The 'reporting step' is a step a response team takes to create the report that will be delivered after the event.

Question:
What is the 'recovery step'?

Answer:
The 'recovery step' is a step a response team takes to return all systems to a known-good state.

Question:
What is the 'remediation step'?

Answer:
The 'remediation step' is a step a response team takes to decide which measures executed during the Mitigation phase should become permanent.

Security Operations Domain

Question:
What is 'NIST SP 800-61'?

Answer:
'NIST SP 800-61' is the standard covering the data that should be covered in a response team's report.

Question:
What is 'Indicators Of Attack, or IOA'?

Answer:
'Indicators Of Attack, or IOA' is a tool that response teams use to know if an attack is underway.

Question:
What is 'Indicators Of Compromise, or IOC'?

Answer:
'Indicators Of Compromise, or IOC' is a tool that response teams use to know if a successful attack has already been completed.

Question:
What is the 'Maximum Tolerable Downtime, or MTD'?

Answer:
The 'Maximum Tolerable Downtime, or MTD' is the overall time a company can survive without a given system running in an operational capacity.

Question:
What is the 'Recovery Time Objective, or RTO'?

Answer:
The 'Recovery Time Objective, or RTO' is the longest time a business can survive without the affected process being restored to acceptable levels.

Question:
What is the 'Work Recovery Time, or WRT'?

Answer:
The 'Work Recovery Time, or WRT' is the time required to restore that data and complete all testing prior to going live.

Question:
What is a 'non-disaster event'?

Answer:
A 'non-disaster event' is an event having a significant impact on a facility that remains operational in a reduced capacity.

Question:
What is a 'disaster event'?

Answer:
A 'disaster event' is an event that causes an entire facility to be unusable for one day or longer, and an alternate facility is required for the business to continue operating.

Security Operations Domain

Question:
What is a 'catastrophe event'?

Answer:
A 'catastrophe event' is an event that results in a facility being a complete loss, and both short-term and long-term facilities are required.

Question:
What is a 'redundant site'?

Answer:
A 'redundant site' is a facility that the company owns and maintains, and is sometimes called a mirrored site.

Question:
What is a 'rolling hot site'?

Answer:
A 'rolling hot site' is a mobile data center contained in a large truck or trailer with self-contained communications capability.

Question:
What is 'multiple processing centers'?

Answer:
'multiple processing centers' is a scenario in which two or more centers in different regions are used continuously.

Question:
What is a 'rented offsite installation'?

Answer:
A 'rented offsite installation' is a facility that is maintained by a third-party, but it is dedicated to the company.

Question:
What is a 'hot site'?

Answer:
A 'hot site' is a company-owned site that is always ready to go at a moment's notice, complete with hardware.

Question:
What is a 'warm site'?

Answer:
A 'warm site' is a company-owned site that is always ready to go at a moment's notice, but has no hardware.

Question:
What is a 'cold site'?

Answer:
A 'cold site' is a company-owned site that is essentially an empty data center.

Question:
What is a 'service bureau'?

Answer:
A 'service bureau' is a company that provides a rented offsite installation.

Security Operations Domain

Question:
What is a 'contingency company'?

Answer:
A 'contingency company' is a company that provides raw materials such as generator fuel or backup communication services.

Question:
What is a 'tertiary site'?

Answer:
A 'tertiary site' is a 'backup for the backup', or a Plan B when Plan A fails.

Question:
What is a 'reciprocal agreement'?

Answer:
A 'reciprocal agreement' is a disaster plan in which the company enters into an agreement with another company to share their facilities if needed.

Question:
What is a 'mutual aid agreement'?

Answer:
A 'mutual aid agreement' is a disaster plan in which 3 or more companies agree to aid each other in times of crisis.

Question:
What is an 'archive bit'?

Answer:
An 'archive bit' is a file-level flag that indicates if the file has been changed.

Question:
What is a 'full backup'?

Answer:
A 'full backup' is a data backup strategy in which all files are backed up regardless of the archive bit.

Question:
What is a 'differential backup'?

Answer:
A 'differential backup' is a data backup strategy in which all files are backed up that have changed since the last full backup but does not clear the archive bit.

Question:
What is an 'incremental backup'?

Answer:
An 'incremental backup' is a data backup strategy in which all files are backed up that have changed since the last full back up or differential backup, and also clears the archive bit.

Security Operations Domain

Question:
What is 'disk duplexing'?

Answer:
'disk duplexing' is a system configuration having multiple disk controllers for fail-over.

Question:
What is 'disk shadowing'?

Answer:
'disk shadowing' is a system configuration in which all data is simultaneously written to two disks.

Question:
What is 'disk mirroring'?

Answer:
'disk mirroring' is a type of disk shadowing in which two disks have the exact same data and configuration, but appear as one disk.

Question:
What is 'electronic vaulting'?

Answer:
'electronic vaulting' makes copies of files in real-time as they are modified and periodically writes them in a bulk fashion to an offsite backup facility.

Question:
What is 'remote journaling'?

Answer:
'remote journaling' moves the journal or transaction logs (files that contain the delta only) to an offsite facility in real-time, as opposed to operating in batches like electronic vaulting.

Question:
What is 'tape vaulting'?

Answer:
'tape vaulting' backs up data to a tape, where it is then manually transferred to an offsite facility for storage.

Question:
What is 'electronic tape vaulting, or automatic tape vaulting'?

Answer:
'electronic tape vaulting, or automatic tape vaulting' allows data to be transferred to a remote offsite tape backup facility over a connection, but personnel in the remote facility are responsible for swapping tapes when necessary.

Question:
What is 'database replication'?

Answer:
'database replication' is a capability built into most modern DBs that allow them to automatically replicate their data to a remote instance of the database.

Security Operations Domain

Question:
What is 'asynchronous database replication '?

Answer:
'asynchronous database replication ' is a type of database replication in which the two copies may be out of sync for a period of time (seconds to days).

Question:
What is 'synchronous database replication '?

Answer:
'synchronous database replication ' is a type of database replication in which the two repositories are never out of sync.

Question:
What is 'High Availability, or HA'?

Answer:
'High Availability, or HA' is a combination of technologies that ensures a system or process is always running.

Question:
What is 'redundancy'?

Answer:
'redundancy' provides alternative options in real-time.

Question:
What is 'failover'?

Answer:
'failover' is a capability of a technology to switch 'over' to a working system in case the primary system fails.

Question:
What is 'clustering'?

Answer:
'clustering' is a type of failover in which multiple identical systems are linked in real-time such that if one fails, the other systems take over.

Question:
What is 'load balancing'?

Answer:
'load balancing' is a type of failover in which multiple identical systems all share in servicing the same types of requests as instructed by some type of centralized connection point.

Question:
What is 'reliability'?

Answer:
'reliability' is the probability that a system will perform its function for a specific time under specific conditions.

Security Operations Domain

457

Question:
What is 'cyber insurance'?

Answer:
'cyber insurance' insures losses caused by DoS, malware, hackers, electronic theft and privacy-related lawsuits.

Question:
What is 'business interruption insurance'?

Answer:
'business interruption insurance' is a type of insurance that will pay for specified expenses and income loss if a company is out of business past a specific length of time.

Question:
What is 'accounts receivables insurance'?

Answer:
'accounts receivables insurance' is a type of insurance that covers part or all of the losses if a company cannot collect on its accounts.

Question:
What is the 'BCP damage assessment phase'?

Answer:
The 'BCP damage assessment phase' is a step in the BCP recovery process that assesses the original site and determine next steps.

Question:
What is the 'BCP restoration phase'?

Answer:
The 'BCP restoration phase' is a step in the BCP recovery process that brings an alternate site online.

Question:
What is the 'BCP salvage phase'?

Answer:
The 'BCP salvage phase' is a step in the BCP recovery process that brings the original site back into a production level.

Question:
What is the 'BCP recovery phase '?

Answer:
The 'BCP recovery phase ' is a step in the BCP recovery process that brings the company as a whole back to full capacity as soon as possible.

Question:
What is the 'BCP reconstitution phase'?

Answer:
The 'BCP reconstitution phase' is a step in the BCP recovery process that takes the company back into the original site.

Security Operations Domain

Question:
What is 'computer forensics'?

Answer:
'computer forensics' is the recovery, authentication and analysis of electronic data with the express purpose of carrying out a digital criminal investigation.

Question:
What is 'digital forensics'?

Answer:
'digital forensics' is a superset of computer forensics and includes network forensics, electronic data discovery, cyber-forensics and forensic computing.

Question:
What is 'digital evidence'?

Answer:
'digital evidence' is any result of computer forensic, network or code analysis.

Question:
What is the 'Scientific Working Group on Digital Evidence, or SWGDE'?

Answer:
The 'Scientific Working Group on Digital Evidence, or SWGDE' is an organization that ensures all other organizations have a consistent approach to forensics.

Question:
What is 'MOM'?

Answer:
'MOM' is an acronym for motive, opportunity and means.

Question:
What is 'Modus Operandi, or MO'?

Answer:
'Modus Operandi, or MO' is the typical pattern a criminal follows in all of his or her crimes.

Question:
What is 'Locard's exchange principal'?

Answer:
'Locard's exchange principal' is a saying that every criminal always takes something from a crime scene, and leaves something behind.

Question:
What is the 'primary image'?

Answer:
The 'primary image' is an image of original media stored in a library.

Security Operations Domain

Question:
What is the 'working image'?

Answer:
The 'working image' is a secondary image of original media to be used during the investigation.

Question:
What is the 'chain of custody'?

Answer:
The 'chain of custody' is a list of all actions showing a complete history of how evidence was collected, analyzed, transported and preserved.

Question:
What is 'live forensics'?

Answer:
'live forensics' is the term for analysis taking place on-site.

Question:
What is 'dead forensics'?

Answer:
'dead forensics' is the term for analysis taking place in a lab.

Question:
What is 'hearsay evidence'?

Answer:
'hearsay evidence' is a term for secondhand evidence.

Question:
What is 'relevant evidence'?

Answer:
'relevant evidence' is a digital evidence criterion stating the evidence must have a reasonable relationship to the findings.

Question:
What is 'complete evidence'?

Answer:
'complete evidence' is a digital evidence criterion stating the evidence must communicate the whole truth.

Question:
What is 'sufficient evidence'?

Answer:
'sufficient evidence' is a digital evidence criterion stating the evidence validity must be convincing to a reasonable person.

Question:
What is 'reliable evidence'?

Answer:
'reliable evidence' is a digital evidence criterion stating the evidence must be consistent with the facts, and be factual itself.

Security Operations Domain

Question:
What is 'passive monitoring'?

Answer:
'passive monitoring' is a type of computer surveillance that uses network sniffers, keyboard monitors, wiretaps and line monitoring.

Question:
What is 'active monitoring'?

Answer:
'active monitoring' is a type of computer surveillance that is invasive and gathers evidence directly.

Question:
What is 'exigent circumstances'?

Answer:
'exigent circumstances' is a law that allows law enforcement to immediately seize potential evidence if it is about to be destroyed.

Question:
What is 'downstream liability'?

Answer:
'downstream liability' is liability that a company offering services may encounter if it does not exercise due care and due diligence to make sure its customers cannot sue it down the road.

Question:
What is the 'proximate cause'?

Answer:
The 'proximate cause' is the obvious cause of a claim.

Question:
What is a 'Request for Proposal, or RFP'?

Answer:
A 'Request for Proposal, or RFP' is the first step in getting a vendor to provide a solution.

Question:
What is 'vendor management'?

Answer:
'vendor management' is the process of monitoring and developing a relationship with a vendor.

Question:
What is 'Governance, Risk and Compliance, or GRC'?

Answer:
'Governance, Risk and Compliance, or GRC' is a program that aligns governance, risk and compliance to see how well the three are integrated.

… Security Operations Domain

Quiz

Question:
What Does disk shadowing or disk mirroring provide better performance?

Answer:
'disk mirroring'.

Question:
What Of disk shadowing and mirroring, which one is cheaper but provides less fault tolerance?

Answer:
'disk shadowing'.

Question:
What Which type of database replication can negatively impact performance?

Answer:
'synchronous database replication '.

Question:
What are the 3 reasons for IPL?

Answer:
'intentional, unintentional and malicious'.

Question:
What are the 3 responses an OS might when it intentionally halts operation?

Answer:
'system reboot, emergency system restart and cold start'.

Question:
What are the 3 categories of locks?

Answer:
'main, secondary and external'.

Question:
What are the 3 types of wafer tumbler locks?

Answer:
'wafer tumbler, pin tumbler and lever tumbler'.

Question:
What are the three construction grades of locks?

Answer:
'grades 1 through 3'.

Security Operations Domain

462

Question:
What are the 3 security levels for cylinder locks?

Answer:
'low, medium and high'.

Question:
What are the 3 attack methods for locks?

Answer:
'tension wrench, raking and bumping'.

Question:
What are the 4 features that cipher locks provide?

Answer:
'door delay, key override, master keying and hostage alarm'.

Question:
What are the 6 types of boundary protection mechanisms?

Answer:
'access control mechanisms, physical barriers, intrusion detection, assessment, response and deterrents'.

Question:
What are the 4 classes of gate strengths?

Answer:
'class I, class II, class III and class IV'.

Question:
What are the 5 factors to consider when choosing CCTV systems?

Answer:
'purpose, environment, field of view, amount of lighting and integration'.

Question:
What are the 4 components of a CCTV system?

Answer:
'multiplexer, monitor, recording System and camera'.

Question:
What is the best security mechanism?

Answer:
'security guards'.

Question:
What data should be noted when reviewing logs?

Answer:
'Date/time, entry point, user ID and if the access was unsuccessful'.

Security Operations Domain

Question:
What are the 3 aspects of a secure supply chain?

Answer:
'Trusted supplier, trusted transportation network and trusted inspection'.

Question:
What are the 2 problems created by pirated or unlicensed software?

Answer:
'The company is liable for unpaid copies, and may contain backdoors or trojan horses'.

Question:
What are the 4 solutions to unlicensed or pirated software?

Answer:
'Application whitelisting, use gold masters, enforce least privilege and automated scanning'.

Question:
What are the top 6 best practices for configuration management?

Answer:
'Request a change to take place, Approve, Document, Implement, Test and Report to management'.

Question:
What are the 4 primary components to network and resource availability?

Answer:
'Redundant hardware, Fault-tolerance, Service level agreements, or SLAs and Solid operational procedures'.

Question:
What is the most common type of RAID?

Answer:
'RAID 5'.

Question:
What are the 5 steps to select the appropriate preventative measures?

Answer:
'Understand the risk, use the right controls, use the controls correctly, manage your configuration and assess your operation'.

Question:
What are the 4 risks of unmanaged patching?

Answer:
'Credentials, configuration management, bandwidth utilization and service availability'.

Question:
What are the 3 approaches to centralized patch management?

Answer:
'Agent based, Agentless and Passive'.

Security Operations Domain

Question:
What are the 3 types of Incident response teams?

Answer:
'Virtual team, permanent team and hybrid team'.

Question:
What 7 items should the incident response team be equipped with?

Answer:
'outside agencies to contact, an outline of roles, a call tree, a list experts to contact, steps to preserve evidence, items to include in a report and the systems mentioned in the policy'.

Question:
What are the 7 steps in a kill chain?

Answer:
'Reconnaissance, Weaponization, Delivery, Exploitation, Installation, Command and Control, or C&C and Actions on the Objective'.

Question:
What are the 6 steps a response teams should follow when responding to an attack?

Answer:
'Detection, Response, Mitigation, Reporting, Recovery and Remediation'.

Question:
What are the 2 strategies the response team's mitigation step can take?

Answer:
'reactive or proactive'.

Question:
What is the formula for calculating Work Recovery Time?

Answer:
'WRT = MTD - RTO'.

Question:
What are the 3 main types of disruption that the Business Continuity team must address?

Answer:
'Non-disaster, Disaster and Catastrophe'.

Question:
What are the 3 types of rented sites?

Answer:
'hot site, warm site and cold site'.

Question:
What are the 3 types of backup strategies?

Answer:
'full backup, differential backup and incremental backup'.

Security Operations Domain

Question:
What backup strategy takes the longest time create and but is the simplest to restore?

Answer:
'full backup'.

Question:
What backup strategy is the quickest to create but is the most complex to restore?

Answer:
'incremental backup'.

Question:
What 2 backup strategies cannot be mixed due to the archive bit?

Answer:
'differential and incremental'.

Question:
What are the 8 BCP teams?

Answer:
'Damage assessment, Legal, Media relations, Restoration, Relocation, Recovery, Salvage and Security'.

Question:
What are the 5 steps in BCP recovery process?

Answer:
'Damage assessment, Restoration, Salvage, Recovery and Reconstitution'.

Question:
What 4 things should each goal in a BCP address?

Answer:
'Responsibility, Authority, Priorities and Implementation and testing'.

Question:
What 5 sections should a good BCP have?

Answer:
'Initiation phase, Activation phase, Recovery phase, Reconstruction phase and Appendixes'.

Question:
What 5 types of memory are considered to be volatile data?

Answer:
'Registers and cache, Process tables and ARP cache, System memory (RAM), Temporary file systems, Special disk sectors'.

Question:
What are the four types of assessments an investigator can perform?

Answer:
'Network analysis, Media analysis, Software analysis, Hardware device analysis'.

Security Operations Domain

Question:
What are the 7 steps of the Forensic Investigation Process?

Answer:
'Identification, Preservation, Collection, Examination, Analysis, Presentation, Decision'.

Question:
What 4 criteria must digital evidence meet before being allowed as admissible evidence in court?

Answer:
'Relevant, Complete, Sufficient, Reliable'.

Question:
What are the 4 steps of evidence lifecycle?

Answer:
'Collection, Storage, Presentation, Return'.

Question:
What are the 2 types of surveillance associated with computer crimes?

Answer:
'Physical surveillance and computer surveillance'.

Software Development Security Domain

Definitions

Question:
What is a term describing how fit for a purpose something is?

Answer:
'quality'

Question:
What creates a repeatable and predictable process that development teams will follow?

Answer:
'software development life cycle'

Question:
What is the SLDC step in which we figure out what the product will do when completed?

Answer:
'requirements gathering step'

Question:
What is the SLDC step in which we plan how the product will be put together?

Answer:
'design step'

Question:
What is the SLDC step in which we put the product together?

Answer:
'development step'

Question:
What is the SLDC step in which we make sure the product does what the requirements said it should do?

Answer:
'testing and validation step'

Question:
What is the SLDC step in which we ship the product and update as-needed?

Answer:
'release and maintenance step'

Question:
What ties together all of the pieces required to deliver a product?

Answer:
'project management'

Software Development Security Domain

Question:
What is one part of project management, in which a security plan is created from the beginning?

Answer:
'security management'

Question:
What is a contract for a specific customer that clarifies requirements?

Answer:
'Statement of Work, or SOW'

Question:
What is the addition of new requirements that seem to creep out of the woodwork but were not originally envisioned?

Answer:
'scope creep'

Question:
What is the collection of tasks and subtasks that are required to meet the stated requirements?

Answer:
'Work Breakdown Structure, or WBS'

Question:
What is the term for figuring out what the finished product should be capable of, what it should look like and how it should behave?

Answer:
'requirements gathering'

Question:
What is the process of examining the data the product will be handling in terms of privacy?

Answer:
'privacy risk assessment'

Question:
What is the rating that a privacy risk assessment assigns to each element?

Answer:
'privacy impact rating'

Question:
What is the categorization assigned to PII that is routinely handled and stored?

Answer:
'p1, or High Privacy Risk'

Question:
What is the categorization assigned to PII that is handled in a one-time, user-initiated data transfer?

Answer:
'p2, or Moderate Privacy Risk'

Software Development Security Domain

Question:
What is the categorization assigned when no PII is handled or stored?

Answer:
'p3, or Low Privacy Risk'

Question:
What is a requirements model that lists the type of information to be processed and how they are processed?

Answer:
'informational model'

Question:
What is a requirements model that lists the tasks and functions an application needs to provide?

Answer:
'functional model'

Question:
What is a requirements model that lists the states the application will be in during and after specific transactions take place?

Answer:
'behavioral model'

Question:
What is the portion of the application visible to an attacker?

Answer:
'attack surface'

Question:
What is an automated scan of an application resulting in a report?

Answer:
'attack surface analysis'

Question:
What occurs when we imagine various malicious scenarios and design the software to counteract the threats?

Answer:
'threat modeling'

Question:
What is a tool to visualize and document various attack vectors into the software?

Answer:
'threat tree'

Question:
What occurs after the design is broken down into scheduled deliverables, and developers get down to work?

Answer:
'development step'

Software Development Security Domain

Question:
What is a tool can often be used to auto-generate code, create automated tests and handle debugging activities?

Answer:
'Computer-Aided Software Engineering, or CASE'

Question:
What is the act of exploiting a process or configuration setting to gain access to resources that normally are off limits to the process or user?

Answer:
'privilege escalation'

Question:
What is the process of examining the source code for defects or security policy violations?

Answer:
'static analysis'

Question:
What is an approach in which the unit test is written first, followed by the source code that will pass the test?

Answer:
'Test-Driven Development, or TDD'

Question:
What occurs when testing individual components?

Answer:
'unit testing'

Question:
What occurs when testing multiple components working together?

Answer:
'integration testing'

Question:
What occurs when testing to ensure the application meets the customer's requirements?

Answer:
'acceptance testing'

Question:
What occurs after a change by rerunning all previously passing tests to ensure the application is still on solid footing?

Answer:
'regression testing'

Question:
What is a technique in which a large amount of randomly malformed and unexpected inputs is provided to an application?

Answer:
'fuzzing'

Software Development Security Domain

471

Question:
What occurs when we evaluate an application in real-time as it is running?

Answer:
'dynamic analysis'

Question:
What is the act of ensuring that the product meets the requirements as written?

Answer:
'verification'

Question:
What is the act of ensuring that the product meets the original goal as it was envisioned?

Answer:
'validation'

Question:
What is an issue that does not yet have a resolution?

Answer:
'zero-day vulnerability'

Question:
What is a software update that is released after a product has been released into production?

Answer:
'patch'

Question:
What is a software development model that is used when a development team follows no formal SDLC model?

Answer:
'build and fix model'

Question:
What is a software development model that uses a linear-sequential life-cycle approach?

Answer:
'waterfall model'

Question:
What is a software development model that is similar to Waterfall but allows testing to start earlier and continue throughout the entire SDLC?

Answer:
'V-shaped, or V-model'

Question:
What is a software development model that creates a simple model of a complex idea?

Answer:
'prototype model'

Software Development Security Domain

Question:
What is a software development model that creates a 'throwaway' product with just enough functionality to decide whether it is worth pursuing?

Answer:
'rapid prototype'

Question:
What is a software development model that creates a product that is incrementally improved upon until it reaches full maturity and can be placed into production?

Answer:
'evolutionary prototype model'

Question:
What is a software development model that is the same as the evolutionary model but can be placed into production immediately and is enhanced on-the-fly?

Answer:
'operational prototype model'

Question:
What is a software development model that is useful when unknown requirements prevent commitment to a given path?

Answer:
'incremental model'

Question:
What is a software development model that is used for complex projects in which requirements change often?

Answer:
'spiral model'

Question:
What is a software development model that has the intent to use the product to elicit requirements?

Answer:
'Rapid Application Development, or RAD'

Question:
What is a software development model that emphasizes incremental product deliveries built on continuous-feedback from the customer?

Answer:
'agile'

Question:
What is a simple description of a single feature written by an end-user?

Answer:
'user story'

Software Development Security Domain

Question:
What is the most widely recognized Agile model?

Answer:
'scrum'

Question:
What is a Scrum pre-defined interval (usually 2 weeks) during which the customer is not allowed to make changes?

Answer:
'sprint'

Question:
What is a Scrum prioritized list of user stories?

Answer:
'backlog'

Question:
What is a software development model using pair programming, in which developers work in pairs, with one developer telling the other what to type?

Answer:
'eXtreme Programming, or XP'

Question:
What is a software development model that stresses a visual tracking of development tasks, resulting in a just-in-time delivery of features?

Answer:
'Kanban'

Question:
What is a software development model that is used when the goals of a project are not well-known, but final specifications that the product must meet are known?

Answer:
'exploratory model'

Question:
What is a software development model that is used when non-developers are able to dedicate their full time to the project and sit with the development team as work progresses?

Answer:
'Joint Application Development, or JAD'

Question:
What is a software development model that assumes that existing prototypes have already been created and are progressively enhanced?

Answer:
'reuse model'

Software Development Security Domain

Question:
What is a software development model that is used when preventing errors and mistakes is the highest priority?

Answer:
'cleanroom model'

Question:
What is a team made up of the development team plus representatives from each stakeholder?

Answer:
'Integrated Product Team, or IPT'

Question:
What is used as a set of guidelines on establishing a mature software development process?

Answer:
'Capability Maturity Model Integration, or CMMI'

Question:
What is a CMMI maturity level in which the process is unpredictable, poorly controlled and reactive?

Answer:
'CMMI level 1 - Initial'

Question:
What is a CMMI maturity level in which the process within a project is repeatable?

Answer:
'CMMI level 2 - Repeatable'

Question:
What is a CMMI maturity level in which the process within an organization is repeatable?

Answer:
'CMMI level 3 - Defined'

Question:
What is a CMMI maturity level in which the process is quantitatively measured and controlled?

Answer:
'CMMI level 4 - Managed'

Question:
What is a CMMI maturity level in which the organization has a focus on continually improving the process?

Answer:
'CMMI level 5 - Optimizing'

Question:
What is the process of controlling any changes that take place during a product's lifetime and documenting the activities that result?

Answer:
'change control'

Software Development Security Domain

Question:
What is a tool providing traceability for a project by tracking change requests as they are entered, approved and delivered to the customer?

Answer:
'Software Configuration Management, or SCM'

Question:
What is a process that keeps track of each change made to a file?

Answer:
'versioning'

Question:
What allows more than one developer to work on the same project simultaneously, but with different files?

Answer:
'synchronization'

Question:
What is a tool to protect a company in the event that a partner company goes out of business or violates a contract?

Answer:
'software escrow'

Question:
What is something that humans can understand but is easily translated into binary so computers can understand it?

Answer:
'programming language'

Question:
What is the language generation that is the binary language computers speak?

Answer:
'1st Generation, or Machine language'

Question:
What is the language generation that is one step above machine language?

Answer:
'2nd Generation, or Assembly language'

Question:
What is the language generation that introduced languages capable of running on multiple processors, and added if...then statements?

Answer:
'3rd Generation, or High-level languages'

Question:
What is the language generation that introduced garbage collectors and SQL?

Answer:
'4th Generation, or Very high-level languages'

Software Development Security Domain

Question:
What is the language generation that defines problems to be solved?

Answer:
'5th Generation, or Natural language'

Question:
What is software that converts assembly language into machine language?

Answer:
'assembler'

Question:
What is software that converts a high-level language into a machine-level format that is targeted for specific hardware?

Answer:
'compiler'

Question:
What is an intermediate format that is converted at run-time into a machine-level format?

Answer:
'interpreted language'

Question:
What is a process carries out memory allocation and deallocation automatically?

Answer:
'garbage-collector'

Question:
What is the term for Java intermediate code?

Answer:
'bytecode'

Question:
What is a type of programming that is focused on objects instead procedural code?

Answer:
'object-oriented concepts'

Question:
What is a type of writing code that executes in a linear fashion, with one entry and one exit point?

Answer:
'procedural'

Question:
What is the act of hiding complexity behind an interface?

Answer:
'encapsulation'

Software Development Security Domain

Question:
What is how outside code communicates and provides input to an object?

Answer:
'message'

Question:
What is internal code that is executed in response to a message?

Answer:
'method'

Question:
What is a term describing the results of a message being processed through a method?

Answer:
'behavior'

Question:
What is a collection of methods that define some behavior?

Answer:
'class'

Question:
What is a single run-time creation of a class in-memory?

Answer:
'instance'

Question:
What is a pattern in which methods from a parent class are inherited by a child class?

Answer:
'inheritance'

Question:
What is a pattern in which an object not having a method to handle a given message will forward, or delegate, that message to another object?

Answer:
'delegation'

Question:
What is a characteristic of an object that allows it to respond with different behaviors to the same message?

Answer:
'polymorphism'

Question:
What is a measure of the strength of the relationship between methods of the same class?

Answer:
'cohesion'

Software Development Security Domain

Question:
What is the level of required interaction between objects?

Answer:
'coupling'

Question:
What views the data independently from code?

Answer:
'data modeling'

Question:
What looks at the logical relationships between data and how it is presented to code?

Answer:
'data structure'

Question:
What hides complex details from being seen, leaving only the bare minimum necessary for interaction?

Answer:
'abstraction'

Question:
What provides a reusable component by abstracting complexity?

Answer:
'Application Programming Interface, or API'

Question:
What is a remote solution that has at least two components separated by a network?

Answer:
'distributed computing'

Question:
What describes the architecture when only two components are used?

Answer:
'client/server'

Question:
What is used when a client invokes a service on a remote computer?

Answer:
'Remote Procedure Call, or RPC'

Question:
What was the first attempt to provide a standard method for distributing computer communication?

Answer:
'Distributed Computing Environment, or DCE'

Software Development Security Domain

479

Question:
What is a string of characters that is unique to a system?

Answer:
'Universal Unique Identifier, or UID'

Question:
What is an open-standard that defines the distributed communication API and protocols?

Answer:
'Common Object Request Broker Architecture, or CORBA'

Question:
What is the organization that created CORBA?

Answer:
'Object Management Group, or OMG'

Question:
What are processes responsible for knowing where CORBA objects live?

Answer:
'Object Request Brokers, or ORBs'

Question:
What is a standard that allows inter-process communication, or IPC on a single Windows computer?

Answer:
'Component Object Model, or COM'

Question:
What is a standard that extends COM so that it can work over a Windows network?

Answer:
'Distributed Component Object Model, or DCOM'

Question:
What is a standard based on COM, and allows objects such as images, spreadsheets and Word documents to be shared on a Windows computer?

Answer:
'Object Linking and Embedding, or OLE'

Question:
What occurs when one Windows program calls another in real-time?

Answer:
'linked'

Question:
What is the term that describes a foreign object that is fully contained inside of a native application?

Answer:
'embedded'

Software Development Security Domain

480

Question:
What is technology created by Oracle to extend the Java language across the network on multiple platforms?

Answer:
'Java Platform, Enterprise Edition'

Question:
What is a pattern used to create reusable services, usually web services?

Answer:
'Service-Oriented Architecture, or SOA'

Question:
What is a protocol based on HTTP using WSDL, and provides heavy security?

Answer:
'Simple Object Access Protocol, or SOAP'

Question:
What is an XML document that describes a SOAP service?

Answer:
'Web Services Description Language, or WSDL'

Question:
What is a protocol based on HTTP that is very lightweight with no security?

Answer:
'Representational State Transfer, or REST'

Question:
What is any type of code that can be transmitted through a network?

Answer:
'mobile code'

Question:
What is Java bytecode that is downloaded across the network?

Answer:
'applet'

Question:
What is a compiled Windows COM object that is downloaded in a native format specific to the machine?

Answer:
'ActiveX'

Question:
What is a process that allows applications to execute within a browser?

Answer:
'component container'

Software Development Security Domain

481

Question:
What is an attack carried out by inserting the '/' characters into a URL, causing the web server to access inappropriate directories?

Answer:
'directory traversal attack, or dot-dot-slash attack'

Question:
What is an attack in which URL characters are encoded as Unicode instead of ASCII text?

Answer:
'Unicode encoding'

Question:
What is an attack in which URL characters are encoded as URL characters instead of ASCII text?

Answer:
'URL encoding'

Question:
What occurs when an attacker puts SQL commands into a text field and submits a form?

Answer:
'SQL injection'

Question:
What occurs when an attacker gets their own script to execute inside of a user's browser?

Answer:
'script injection, or Cross-site scripting, or XSS'

Question:
What occurs when an attacker convinces the web server to emit HTML that downloads a rogue script from another site?

Answer:
'non-persistent XSS vulnerability, or reflected vulnerability'

Question:
What occurs when an attacker convinces a server to store their malicious data in a database field?

Answer:
'persistent XSS vulnerability'

Question:
What occurs when an attacker dynamically generates content within the browser using the DOM?

Answer:
'document object model XSS attack'

Question:
What occurs when client code ensures that all required fields are provided and checks for invalid values?

Answer:
'client-side validation'

Software Development Security Domain

Question:
What occurs when the server examines and validates values that are assumed to be beyond the ability of a user to change?

Answer:
'parameter validation'

Question:
What occurs when a server generates a unique session ID the first time a browser connects, and requires the browser to always send back the session ID for any subsequent request?

Answer:
'session management'

Question:
What occurs when an attacker sniffs a current session ID and uses it in their own packets?

Answer:
'session hijacking'

Question:
What is a collection of persisted data which users can view and modify as-needed?

Answer:
'database'

Question:
What is software that exposes the database, enforces access control, provides data integrity and redundancy, and provides procedures for data manipulation?

Answer:
'database management system, or DMS'

Question:
What is a database model that combines records and fields in a tree structure without using indexes (LDAP)?

Answer:
'hierarchical data model'

Question:
What is a database model that uses attributes, called columns, and tuples, called rows, to store data in 2-dimensional tables?

Answer:
'relational database model, or RDBM'

Question:
What is the intersection of a column and a row?

Answer:
'cell'

Question:
What is a field that provides a unique value to every record in the table?

Answer:
'primary key'

Software Development Security Domain

Question:
What is used to speed up database searches?

Answer:
'index'

Question:
What is a database model built on the hierarchical data model and is useful for many parent/many child relationships?

Answer:
'network database model'

Question:
What is a database model designed to handle multiple data types as objects, with each object having properties and methods?

Answer:
'Object-Oriented Database, or OOD'

Question:
What is an RDBM that is fronted with a business logic layer?

Answer:
'Object-Relational Database, or ORD'

Question:
What is a database programming interface that uses a database-specific driver to translate a common language (SQL) to the database language?

Answer:
'Open Database Connectivity, or ODBC'

Question:
What is a database programming interface that is Microsoft's replacement for ODBC that can access any data source?

Answer:
'Object Linking and Embedding Database, or OLE DB'

Question:
What is a database programming interface that is the official API for OLE DB?

Answer:
'ActiveX Data Objects, or ADO'

Question:
What is a database programming interface that implements ODBC for Java apps?

Answer:
'Java Database Connectivity, or JDBC'

Question:
What is a database language that defines the structure and schema in a database?

Answer:
'Data Definition Language, or DDL'

Software Development Security Domain

Question:
What represents table details such as properties and data types?

Answer:
'schema'

Question:
What represents everything outside of tables, such as table size, index size, views, and table relationships?

Answer:
'structure'

Question:
What is a database language that provides access to data?

Answer:
'Data Manipulation Language, or DML'

Question:
What is a database language that defines the internal organization of the database?

Answer:
'Data Control Language, or DCL'

Question:
What is a database language that allows users to make requests - SQL is based on this?

Answer:
'ad hoc Query Language, or QL'

Question:
What is a database tool that produces printouts of data in a user-defined format?

Answer:
'report generator'

Question:
What is a centralized collection of information about all users, user roles, tables, indexes and privileges, and is used to provide access controls?

Answer:
'data dictionary'

Question:
What is a unique value across all records in a table, used for indexing?

Answer:
'primary key'

Question:
What is a relationship where Table A has a column that matches a primary key in Table B?

Answer:
'foreign key'

Software Development Security Domain

485

Question:
What occurs when multiple users try to modify the same data at the same time?

Answer:
'concurrency'

Question:
What is a database method for blocking access to data so that only one user can modify the value?

Answer:
'lock'

Question:
What ensures the database's structure remains secure by enforcing data types, logical values, uniqueness constraints and operations?

Answer:
'semantic integrity'

Question:
What ensures that all foreign keys within a database reference a valid primary key?

Answer:
'referential integrity'

Question:
What ensures that all primary keys have a unique value within the table?

Answer:
'entity integrity'

Question:
What is a sequence of operations performed as a single unit of work?

Answer:
'transaction'

Question:
What occurs when we cancel the current transaction and revert the database to the state it was before the transaction started?

Answer:
'rollback'

Question:
What occurs when we complete a transaction and execute all changes just made within the transaction?

Answer:
'commit'

Question:
What is a process for transactions in a distributed environment, in which all databases make a 'pre-commit', and once all databases have reported back successfully, they all perform a 'commit'?

Answer:
'two-phase commit'

Software Development Security Domain

Question:
What occurs when requests for database changes are put into a queue and executed all at once?

Answer:
'batch processing'

Question:
What provides fault tolerance and better performance with clustered databases?

Answer:
'Online Transaction Processing, or OLTP'

Question:
What is a series of attributes that OLTP must implement?

Answer:
'ACID'

Question:
What is an attribute in ACID that states all changes take effect or none do?

Answer:
'atomicity attribute'

Question:
What is an attribute in ACID that states all data remains consistent in all databases?

Answer:
'consistency attribute'

Question:
What is an attribute in ACID that states transactions execute in isolation until completed?

Answer:
'isolation attribute'

Question:
What is an attribute in ACID that states once the transaction is committed it cannot be rolled back?

Answer:
'durability attribute'

Question:
What is a periodic save of a database that can be restored in case of severe interruption; this can be triggered based on elapsed time or for every number of completed transactions?

Answer:
'savepoint'

Question:
What is a savepoint triggered when the database fills up a specific amount of memory?

Answer:
'checkpoint'

Question:

Software Development Security Domain

What is a virtual table comprised of one or more underlying tables that restrict or aggregate data according to access control policy?

Answer:
'database view'

Question:
What occurs when interactively creating two instances of the same object with different attributes?

Answer:
'polyinstantiation'

Question:
What is a process that combines data from two or more databases into a single large database for follow-up analysis?

Answer:
'data warehousing'

Question:
What shows trends and relationships in warehoused data not evident in the raw sources?

Answer:
'metadata'

Question:
What is the process of creating metadata?

Answer:
'data mining'

Question:
What defines 3 approaches to data mining?

Answer:
'Knowledge Discovery in Database, or KDD'

Question:
What is a KDD pattern identification approach that groups data according to similarities?

Answer:
'classification'

Question:
What is a KDD pattern identification approach that identifies relationships and calculates probabilities?

Answer:
'probalistic'

Question:
What is a KDD pattern identification approach that identifies relationships and uses rule discovery?

Answer:
'statistical'

Software Development Security Domain

Question:
What are very large data sets that are unsuitable for traditional analysis techniques?

Answer:
'big data'

Question:
What occurs when data types are not standardized?

Answer:
'heterogeneity'

Question:
What occurs when there are many different relationships between data?

Answer:
'complexity'

Question:
What is present when some sources are verbose while others are sparse?

Answer:
'variability'

Question:
What is present when the reliability of the source is not known?

Answer:
'lack of reliability'

Question:
What is a small application that infects software and can replicate itself?

Answer:
'virus'

Question:
What is the term used to describe the ability of a virus to install itself?

Answer:
'insertion ability'

Question:
What is the term used to describe the ability of a virus to avoid detection?

Answer:
'avoidance ability'

Question:
What is the term used to describe the ability of a virus to remove itself after the payload has been delivered?

Answer:
'eradication ability'

Software Development Security Domain

Question:
What is the term used to describe the ability of a virus to make copies of itself and spread?

Answer:
'replication ability'

Question:
What is the term used to describe the ability of a virus to use an event to execute the payload?

Answer:
'trigger ability'

Question:
What is the term used to describe the ability of a virus to carry out its function?

Answer:
'payload ability'

Question:
What is written in a macro language such as Visual Basic or VBScript?

Answer:
'macro virus'

Question:
What infects the boot sector of a computer?

Answer:
'boot sector virus'

Question:
What intercepts requests for a file and presents a forged version of itself to antimalware products?

Answer:
'tunneling virus'

Question:
What is a tunneling virus that can hide the size of its file and move around to avoid detection?

Answer:
'stealth virus'

Question:
What can alter its appearance in an effort to outwit virus scanners?

Answer:
'polymorphic virus'

Question:
What has several components that are distributed in multiple locations on each system?

Answer:
'multipart virus'

Software Development Security Domain

490

Question:
What is an email that gets spread quickly around the Internet?

Answer:
'meme virus'

Question:
What is a virus sent in script as an interpreted language?

Answer:
'script virus'

Question:
What is a self-contained program and can reproduce without requiring a host application?

Answer:
'worm'

Question:
What is a bundle of tools an attacker uploads to an infected system for later use?

Answer:
'rootkit'

Question:
What replaces valid files with malicious alternatives?

Answer:
'trojan program'

Question:
What removes traces of the attacker's movements from the system log files?

Answer:
'log scrubber'

Question:
What is malware that exists to simply gather information about a victim?

Answer:
'spyware'

Question:
What is malware that automatically generates advertisements?

Answer:
'adware'

Question:
What is malware that is installed through infected email, drive-by-downloads, Trojan horses or shared media?

Answer:
'bot'

Software Development Security Domain

491

Question:
What is a network of bots?

Answer:
'botnet'

Question:
What is the owner of a botnet?

Answer:
'bot herder'

Question:
What are the servers that send instructions to a botnet?

Answer:
'Command-and-Control, or C&C'

Question:
What is an evasion technique used to continually be on the move by updating DNS entries?

Answer:
'fast flux'

Question:
What is a program that is set to go off and execute its payload whenever a specific trigger is activated?

Answer:
'logic bomb'

Question:
What is a program that is disguised as another program?

Answer:
'Trojan Horse'

Question:
What is a program that allows an intruder to access and use a system remotely?

Answer:
'Remote Access Trojan, or RAT'

Question:
What is the receipt of unsolicited junk email?

Answer:
'spam'

Question:
What is used to apply statistical modeling to the words in an email message to detect spam?

Answer:
'bayesian filtering'

Software Development Security Domain

492

Question:
What scans incoming SMTP, HTTP and FTP traffic for malware?

Answer:
'virus wall'

Software Development Security Domain

Terms

Question:
What is 'quality'?

Answer:
'quality' is a term describing how fit for a purpose something is.

Question:
What is the 'software development life cycle'?

Answer:
The 'software development life cycle' creates a repeatable and predictable process that development teams will follow.

Question:
What is the 'requirements gathering step'?

Answer:
The 'requirements gathering step' is the SLDC step in which we figure out what the product will do when completed.

Question:
What is the 'design step'?

Answer:
The 'design step' is the SLDC step in which we plan how the product will be put together.

Question:
What is the 'development step'?

Answer:
The 'development step' is the SLDC step in which we put the product together.

Question:
What is the 'testing and validation step'?

Answer:
The 'testing and validation step' is the SLDC step in which we make sure the product does what the requirements said it should do.

Question:
What is the 'release and maintenance step'?

Answer:
The 'release and maintenance step' is the SLDC step in which we ship the product and update as-needed.

Question:
What is 'project management'?

Answer:
'project management' ties together all of the pieces required to deliver a product.

Software Development Security Domain

494

Question:
What is 'security management'?

Answer:
'security management' is one part of project management, in which a security plan is created from the beginning.

Question:
What is the 'Statement of Work, or SOW'?

Answer:
The 'Statement of Work, or SOW' is a contract for a specific customer that clarifies requirements.

Question:
What is 'scope creep'?

Answer:
'scope creep' is the addition of new requirements that seem to creep out of the woodwork but were not originally envisioned.

Question:
What is the 'Work Breakdown Structure, or WBS'?

Answer:
The 'Work Breakdown Structure, or WBS' is the collection of tasks and subtasks that are required to meet the stated requirements.

Question:
What is 'requirements gathering'?

Answer:
'requirements gathering' is the term for figuring out what the finished product should be capable of, what it should look like and how it should behave.

Question:
What is a 'privacy risk assessment'?

Answer:
A 'privacy risk assessment' is the process of examining the data the product will be handling in terms of privacy.

Question:
What is a 'privacy impact rating'?

Answer:
A 'privacy impact rating' is the rating that a privacy risk assessment assigns to each element.

Question:
What is 'p1, or High Privacy Risk'?

Answer:
'p1, or High Privacy Risk' is the categorization assigned to PII that is routinely handled and stored.

Question:
What is 'p2, or Moderate Privacy Risk'?

Answer:
'p2, or Moderate Privacy Risk' is the categorization assigned to PII that is handled in a one-time, user-initiated data transfer.

Software Development Security Domain

Question:
What is 'p3, or Low Privacy Risk'?

Answer:
'p3, or Low Privacy Risk' is the categorization assigned when no PII is handled or stored.

Question:
What is an 'informational model'?

Answer:
An 'informational model' is a requirements model that lists the type of information to be processed and how they are processed.

Question:
What is a 'functional model'?

Answer:
A 'functional model' is a requirements model that lists the tasks and functions an application needs to provide.

Question:
What is a 'behavioral model'?

Answer:
A 'behavioral model' is a requirements model that lists the states the application will be in during and after specific transactions take place.

Question:
What is the 'attack surface'?

Answer:
The 'attack surface' is the portion of the application visible to an attacker.

Question:
What is an 'attack surface analysis'?

Answer:
An 'attack surface analysis' is an automated scan of an application resulting in a report.

Question:
What is 'threat modeling'?

Answer:
'threat modeling' occurs when we imagine various malicious scenarios and design the software to counteract the threats.

Question:
What is a 'threat tree'?

Answer:
A 'threat tree' is a tool to visualize and document various attack vectors into the software.

Question:
What is the 'development step'?

Answer:
The 'development step' occurs after the design is broken down into scheduled deliverables, and developers get down to work.

Software Development Security Domain

Question:
What is 'Computer-Aided Software Engineering, or CASE'?

Answer:
'Computer-Aided Software Engineering, or CASE' is a tool can often be used to auto-generate code, create automated tests and handle debugging activities.

Question:
What is 'privilege escalation'?

Answer:
'privilege escalation' is the act of exploiting a process or configuration setting to gain access to resources that normally are off limits to the process or user.

Question:
What is 'static analysis'?

Answer:
'static analysis' is the process of examining the source code for defects or security policy violations.

Question:
What is 'Test-Driven Development, or TDD'?

Answer:
'Test-Driven Development, or TDD' is an approach in which the unit test is written first, followed by the source code that will pass the test.

Question:
What is 'unit testing'?

Answer:
'unit testing' occurs when testing individual components.

Question:
What is 'integration testing'?

Answer:
'integration testing' occurs when testing multiple components working together.

Question:
What is 'acceptance testing'?

Answer:
'acceptance testing' occurs when testing to ensure the application meets the customer's requirements.

Question:
What is 'regression testing'?

Answer:
'regression testing' occurs after a change by rerunning all previously passing tests to ensure the application is still on solid footing.

Software Development Security Domain

497

Question:
What is 'fuzzing'?

Answer:
'fuzzing' is a technique in which a large amount of randomly malformed and unexpected inputs is provided to an application.

Question:
What is 'dynamic analysis'?

Answer:
'dynamic analysis' occurs when we evaluate an application in real-time as it is running.

Question:
What is 'verification'?

Answer:
'verification' is the act of ensuring that the product meets the requirements as written.

Question:
What is 'validation'?

Answer:
'validation' is the act of ensuring that the product meets the original goal as it was envisioned.

Question:
What is a 'zero-day vulnerability'?

Answer:
A 'zero-day vulnerability' is an issue that does not yet have a resolution.

Question:
What is a 'patch'?

Answer:
A 'patch' is a software update that is released after a product has been released into production.

Question:
What is the 'build and fix model'?

Answer:
The 'build and fix model' is a software development model that is used when a development team follows no formal SDLC model.

Question:
What is the 'waterfall model'?

Answer:
The 'waterfall model' is a software development model that uses a linear-sequential life-cycle approach.

Question:
What is the 'V-shaped, or V-model'?

Answer:
The 'V-shaped, or V-model' is a software development model that is similar to Waterfall but allows testing to start earlier and continue throughout the entire SDLC.

Software Development Security Domain

Question:
What is the 'prototype model'?

Answer:
The 'prototype model' is a software development model that creates a simple model of a complex idea.

Question:
What is the 'rapid prototype'?

Answer:
The 'rapid prototype' is a software development model that creates a 'throwaway' product with just enough functionality to decide whether it is worth pursuing.

Question:
What is the 'evolutionary prototype model'?

Answer:
The 'evolutionary prototype model' is a software development model that creates a product that is incrementally improved upon until it reaches full maturity and can be placed into production.

Question:
What is the 'operational prototype model'?

Answer:
The 'operational prototype model' is a software development model that is the same as the evolutionary model but can be placed into production immediately and is enhanced on-the-fly.

Question:
What is the 'incremental model'?

Answer:
The 'incremental model' is a software development model that is useful when unknown requirements prevent commitment to a given path.

Question:
What is the 'spiral model'?

Answer:
The 'spiral model' is a software development model that is used for complex projects in which requirements change often.

Question:
What is 'Rapid Application Development, or RAD'?

Answer:
'Rapid Application Development, or RAD' is a software development model that has the intent to use the product to elicit requirements.

Question:
What is 'agile'?

Answer:
'agile' is a software development model that emphasizes incremental product deliveries built on continuous-feedback from the customer.

Software Development Security Domain

Question:
What is a 'user story'?

Answer:
A 'user story' is a simple description of a single feature written by an end-user.

Question:
What is 'scrum'?

Answer:
'scrum' is the most widely recognized Agile model.

Question:
What is a 'sprint'?

Answer:
A 'sprint' is a Scrum pre-defined interval (usually 2 weeks) during which the customer is not allowed to make changes.

Question:
What is a 'backlog'?

Answer:
A 'backlog' is a Scrum prioritized list of user stories.

Question:
What is 'eXtreme Programming, or XP'?

Answer:
'eXtreme Programming, or XP' is a software development model using pair programming, in which developers work in pairs, with one developer telling the other what to type.

Question:
What is 'Kanban'?

Answer:
'Kanban' is a software development model that stresses a visual tracking of development tasks, resulting in a just-in-time delivery of features.

Question:
What is the 'exploratory model'?

Answer:
The 'exploratory model' is a software development model that is used when the goals of a project are not well-known, but final specifications that the product must meet are known.

Question:
What is 'Joint Application Development, or JAD'?

Answer:
'Joint Application Development, or JAD' is a software development model that is used when non-developers are able to dedicate their full time to the project and sit with the development team as work progresses.

Software Development Security Domain

500

Question:
What is the 'reuse model'?

Answer:
The 'reuse model' is a software development model that assumes that existing prototypes have already been created and are progressively enhanced.

Question:
What is the 'cleanroom model'?

Answer:
The 'cleanroom model' is a software development model that is used when preventing errors and mistakes is the highest priority.

Question:
What is an 'Integrated Product Team, or IPT'?

Answer:
An 'Integrated Product Team, or IPT' is a team made up of the development team plus representatives from each stakeholder.

Question:
What is the 'Capability Maturity Model Integration, or CMMI'?

Answer:
The 'Capability Maturity Model Integration, or CMMI' is used as a set of guidelines on establishing a mature software development process.

Question:
What is 'CMMI level 1 - Initial'?

Answer:
'CMMI level 1 - Initial' is a CMMI maturity level in which the process is unpredictable, poorly controlled and reactive.

Question:
What is 'CMMI level 2 - Repeatable'?

Answer:
'CMMI level 2 - Repeatable' is a CMMI maturity level in which the process within a project is repeatable.

Question:
What is 'CMMI level 3 - Defined'?

Answer:
'CMMI level 3 - Defined' is a CMMI maturity level in which the process within an organization is repeatable.

Question:
What is 'CMMI level 4 - Managed'?

Answer:
'CMMI level 4 - Managed' is a CMMI maturity level in which the process is quantitatively measured and controlled.

Question:
What is 'CMMI level 5 - Optimizing'?

Answer:
'CMMI level 5 - Optimizing' is a CMMI maturity level in which the organization has a focus on continually improving the process.

Software Development Security Domain

501

Question:
What is 'change control'?

Answer:
'change control' is the process of controlling any changes that take place during a product's lifetime and documenting the activities that result.

Question:
What is 'Software Configuration Management, or SCM'?

Answer:
'Software Configuration Management, or SCM' is a tool providing traceability for a project by tracking change requests as they are entered, approved and delivered to the customer.

Question:
What is 'versioning'?

Answer:
'versioning' is a process that keeps track of each change made to a file.

Question:
What is 'synchronization'?

Answer:
'synchronization' allows more than one developer to work on the same project simultaneously, but with different files.

Question:
What is 'software escrow'?

Answer:
'software escrow' is a tool to protect a company in the event that a partner company goes out of business or violates a contract.

Question:
What is a 'programming language'?

Answer:
A 'programming language' is something that humans can understand but is easily translated into binary so computers can understand it.

Question:
What is '1st Generation, or Machine language'?

Answer:
'1st Generation, or Machine language' is the language generation that is the binary language computers speak.

Question:
What is '2nd Generation, or Assembly language'?

Answer:
'2nd Generation, or Assembly language' is the language generation that is one step above machine language.

Software Development Security Domain

Question:
What is '3rd Generation, or High-level languages'?

Answer:
'3rd Generation, or High-level languages' is the language generation that introduced languages capable of running on multiple processors, and added if...then statements.

Question:
What is '4th Generation, or Very high-level languages'?

Answer:
'4th Generation, or Very high-level languages' is the language generation that introduced garbage collectors and SQL.

Question:
What is '5th Generation, or Natural language'?

Answer:
'5th Generation, or Natural language' is the language generation that defines problems to be solved.

Question:
What is an 'assembler'?

Answer:
An 'assembler' is software that converts assembly language into machine language.

Question:
What is a 'compiler'?

Answer:
A 'compiler' is software that converts a high-level language into a machine-level format that is targeted for specific hardware.

Question:
What is 'interpreted language'?

Answer:
'interpreted language' is an intermediate format that is converted at run-time into a machine-level format.

Question:
What is a 'garbage-collector'?

Answer:
A 'garbage-collector' is a process carries out memory allocation and deallocation automatically.

Question:
What is 'bytecode'?

Answer:
'bytecode' is the term for Java intermediate code.

Question:
What is 'object-oriented concepts'?

Answer:
'object-oriented concepts' is a type of programming that is focused on objects instead procedural code.

Software Development Security Domain

Question:
What is 'procedural'?

Answer:
'procedural' is a type of writing code that executes in a linear fashion, with one entry and one exit point.

Question:
What is 'encapsulation'?

Answer:
'encapsulation' is the act of hiding complexity behind an interface.

Question:
What is a 'message'?

Answer:
A 'message' is how outside code communicates and provides input to an object.

Question:
What is a 'method'?

Answer:
A 'method' is internal code that is executed in response to a message.

Question:
What is 'behavior'?

Answer:
'behavior' is a term describing the results of a message being processed through a method.

Question:
What is a 'class'?

Answer:
A 'class' is a collection of methods that define some behavior.

Question:
What is an 'instance'?

Answer:
An 'instance' is a single run-time creation of a class in-memory.

Question:
What is 'inheritance'?

Answer:
'inheritance' is a pattern in which methods from a parent class are inherited by a child class.

Question:
What is 'delegation'?

Answer:
'delegation' is a pattern in which an object not having a method to handle a given message will forward, or delegate, that message to another object.

Software Development Security Domain

504

Question:
What is 'polymorphism'?

Answer:
'polymorphism' is a characteristic of an object that allows it to respond with different behaviors to the same message.

Question:
What is 'cohesion'?

Answer:
'cohesion' is a measure of the strength of the relationship between methods of the same class.

Question:
What is 'coupling'?

Answer:
'coupling' is the level of required interaction between objects.

Question:
What is 'data modeling'?

Answer:
'data modeling' views the data independently from code.

Question:
What is a 'data structure'?

Answer:
A 'data structure' looks at the logical relationships between data and how it is presented to code.

Question:
What is 'abstraction'?

Answer:
'abstraction' hides complex details from being seen, leaving only the bare minimum necessary for interaction.

Question:
What is an 'Application Programming Interface, or API'?

Answer:
An 'Application Programming Interface, or API' provides a reusable component by abstracting complexity.

Question:
What is 'distributed computing'?

Answer:
'distributed computing' is a remote solution that has at least two components separated by a network.

Question:
What is 'client/server'?

Answer:
'client/server' describes the architecture when only two components are used.

Software Development Security Domain

Question:
What is a 'Remote Procedure Call, or RPC'?

Answer:
A 'Remote Procedure Call, or RPC' is used when a client invokes a service on a remote computer.

Question:
What is a 'Distributed Computing Environment, or DCE'?

Answer:
A 'Distributed Computing Environment, or DCE' was the first attempt to provide a standard method for distributing computer communication.

Question:
What is a 'Universal Unique Identifier, or UID'?

Answer:
A 'Universal Unique Identifier, or UID' is a string of characters that is unique to a system.

Question:
What is the 'Common Object Request Broker Architecture, or CORBA'?

Answer:
The 'Common Object Request Broker Architecture, or CORBA' is an open-standard that defines the distributed communication API and protocols.

Question:
What is the 'Object Management Group, or OMG'?

Answer:
The 'Object Management Group, or OMG' is the organization that created CORBA.

Question:
What is 'Object Request Brokers, or ORBs'?

Answer:
'Object Request Brokers, or ORBs' are processes responsible for knowing where CORBA objects live.

Question:
What is the 'Component Object Model, or COM'?

Answer:
The 'Component Object Model, or COM' is a standard that allows inter-process communication, or IPC on a single Windows computer.

Question:
What is the 'Distributed Component Object Model, or DCOM'?

Answer:
The 'Distributed Component Object Model, or DCOM' is a standard that extends COM so that it can work over a Windows network.

Software Development Security Domain

506

Question:
What is 'Object Linking and Embedding, or OLE'?

Answer:
'Object Linking and Embedding, or OLE' is a standard based on COM, and allows objects such as images, spreadsheets and Word documents to be shared on a Windows computer.

Question:
What is 'linked'?

Answer:
'linked' occurs when one Windows program calls another in real-time.

Question:
What is 'embedded'?

Answer:
'embedded' is the term that describes a foreign object that is fully contained inside of a native application.

Question:
What is 'Java Platform, Enterprise Edition'?

Answer:
'Java Platform, Enterprise Edition' is technology created by Oracle to extend the Java language across the network on multiple platforms.

Question:
What is 'Service-Oriented Architecture, or SOA'?

Answer:
'Service-Oriented Architecture, or SOA' is a pattern used to create reusable services, usually web services.

Question:
What is 'Simple Object Access Protocol, or SOAP'?

Answer:
'Simple Object Access Protocol, or SOAP' is a protocol based on HTTP using WSDL, and provides heavy security.

Question:
What is 'Web Services Description Language, or WSDL'?

Answer:
'Web Services Description Language, or WSDL' is an XML document that describes a SOAP service.

Question:
What is 'Representational State Transfer, or REST'?

Answer:
'Representational State Transfer, or REST' is a protocol based on HTTP that is very lightweight with no security.

Question:
What is 'mobile code'?

Answer:
'mobile code' is any type of code that can be transmitted through a network.

Software Development Security Domain

507

Question:
What is an 'applet'?

Answer:
An 'applet' is Java bytecode that is downloaded across the network.

Question:
What is 'ActiveX'?

Answer:
'ActiveX' is a compiled Windows COM object that is downloaded in a native format specific to the machine.

Question:
What is a 'component container'?

Answer:
A 'component container' is a process that allows applications to execute within a browser.

Question:
What is a 'directory traversal attack, or dot-dot-slash attack'?

Answer:
A 'directory traversal attack, or dot-dot-slash attack' is an attack carried out by inserting the '/' characters into a URL, causing the web server to access inappropriate directories.

Question:
What is 'Unicode encoding'?

Answer:
'Unicode encoding' is an attack in which URL characters are encoded as Unicode instead of ASCII text.

Question:
What is 'URL encoding'?

Answer:
'URL encoding' is an attack in which URL characters are encoded as URL characters instead of ASCII text.

Question:
What is 'SQL injection'?

Answer:
'SQL injection' occurs when an attacker puts SQL commands into a text field and submits a form.

Question:
What is 'script injection, or Cross-site scripting, or XSS'?

Answer:
'script injection, or Cross-site scripting, or XSS' occurs when an attacker gets their own script to execute inside of a user's browser.

Question:
What is a 'non-persistent XSS vulnerability, or reflected vulnerability'?

Answer:
A 'non-persistent XSS vulnerability, or reflected vulnerability' occurs when an attacker convinces the web server to emit HTML that downloads a rogue script from another site.

Software Development Security Domain

Question:
What is a 'persistent XSS vulnerability'?

Answer:
A 'persistent XSS vulnerability' occurs when an attacker convinces a server to store their malicious data in a database field.

Question:
What is a 'document object model XSS attack'?

Answer:
A 'document object model XSS attack' occurs when an attacker dynamically generates content within the browser using the DOM.

Question:
What is 'client-side validation'?

Answer:
'client-side validation' occurs when client code ensures that all required fields are provided and checks for invalid values.

Question:
What is 'parameter validation'?

Answer:
'parameter validation' occurs when the server examines and validates values that are assumed to be beyond the ability of a user to change.

Question:
What is 'session management'?

Answer:
'session management' occurs when a server generates a unique session ID the first time a browser connects, and requires the browser to always send back the session ID for any subsequent request.

Question:
What is 'session hijacking'?

Answer:
'session hijacking' occurs when an attacker sniffs a current session ID and uses it in their own packets.

Question:
What is a 'database'?

Answer:
A 'database' is a collection of persisted data which users can view and modify as-needed.

Question:
What is a 'database management system, or DMS'?

Answer:
A 'database management system, or DMS' is software that exposes the database, enforces access control, provides data integrity and redundancy, and provides procedures for data manipulation.

Software Development Security Domain

Question:
What is a 'hierarchical data model'?

Answer:
A 'hierarchical data model' is a database model that combines records and fields in a tree structure without using indexes (LDAP).

Question:
What is a 'relational database model, or RDBM'?

Answer:
A 'relational database model, or RDBM' is a database model that uses attributes, called columns, and tuples, called rows, to store data in 2-dimensional tables.

Question:
What is a 'cell'?

Answer:
A 'cell' is the intersection of a column and a row.

Question:
What is a 'primary key'?

Answer:
A 'primary key' is a field that provides a unique value to every record in the table.

Question:
What is an 'index'?

Answer:
An 'index' is used to speed up database searches.

Question:
What is a 'network database model'?

Answer:
A 'network database model' is a database model built on the hierarchical data model and is useful for many parent/many child relationships.

Question:
What is an 'Object-Oriented Database, or OOD'?

Answer:
An 'Object-Oriented Database, or OOD' is a database model designed to handle multiple data types as objects, with each object having properties and methods.

Question:
What is an 'Object-Relational Database, or ORD'?

Answer:
An 'Object-Relational Database, or ORD' is an RDBM that is fronted with a business logic layer.

Software Development Security Domain

Question:
What is 'Open Database Connectivity, or ODBC'?

Answer:
'Open Database Connectivity, or ODBC' is a database programming interface that uses a database-specific driver to translate a common language (SQL) to the database language.

Question:
What is an 'Object Linking and Embedding Database, or OLE DB'?

Answer:
An 'Object Linking and Embedding Database, or OLE DB' is a database programming interface that is Microsoft's replacement for ODBC that can access any data source.

Question:
What is 'ActiveX Data Objects, or ADO'?

Answer:
'ActiveX Data Objects, or ADO' is a database programming interface that is the official API for OLE DB.

Question:
What is 'Java Database Connectivity, or JDBC'?

Answer:
'Java Database Connectivity, or JDBC' is a database programming interface that implements ODBC for Java apps.

Question:
What is 'Data Definition Language, or DDL'?

Answer:
'Data Definition Language, or DDL' is a database language that defines the structure and schema in a database.

Question:
What is a 'schema'?

Answer:
A 'schema' represents table details such as properties and data types.

Question:
What is a 'structure'?

Answer:
A 'structure' represents everything outside of tables, such as table size, index size, views, and table relationships.

Question:
What is 'Data Manipulation Language, or DML'?

Answer:
'Data Manipulation Language, or DML' is a database language that provides access to data.

Question:
What is 'Data Control Language, or DCL'?

Answer:
'Data Control Language, or DCL' is a database language that defines the internal organization of the database.

Software Development Security Domain

511

Question:
What is 'ad hoc Query Language, or QL'?

Answer:
'ad hoc Query Language, or QL' is a database language that allows users to make requests - SQL is based on this.

Question:
What is a 'report generator'?

Answer:
A 'report generator' is a database tool that produces printouts of data in a user-defined format.

Question:
What is a 'data dictionary'?

Answer:
A 'data dictionary' is a centralized collection of information about all users, user roles, tables, indexes and privileges, and is used to provide access controls.

Question:
What is a 'primary key'?

Answer:
A 'primary key' is a unique value across all records in a table, used for indexing.

Question:
What is a 'foreign key'?

Answer:
A 'foreign key' is a relationship where Table A has a column that matches a primary key in Table B.

Question:
What is 'concurrency'?

Answer:
'concurrency' occurs when multiple users try to modify the same data at the same time.

Question:
What is a 'lock'?

Answer:
A 'lock' is a database method for blocking access to data so that only one user can modify the value.

Question:
What is 'semantic integrity'?

Answer:
'semantic integrity' ensures the database's structure remains secure by enforcing data types, logical values, uniqueness constraints and operations.

Question:
What is 'referential integrity'?

Answer:
'referential integrity' ensures that all foreign keys within a database reference a valid primary key.

Software Development Security Domain

Question:
What is 'entity integrity'?

Answer:
'entity integrity' ensures that all primary keys have a unique value within the table.

Question:
What is a 'transaction'?

Answer:
A 'transaction' is a sequence of operations performed as a single unit of work.

Question:
What is a 'rollback'?

Answer:
A 'rollback' occurs when we cancel the current transaction and revert the database to the state it was before the transaction started.

Question:
What is a 'commit'?

Answer:
A 'commit' occurs when we complete a transaction and execute all changes just made within the transaction.

Question:
What is a 'two-phase commit'?

Answer:
A 'two-phase commit' is a process for transactions in a distributed environment, in which all databases make a 'pre-commit', and once all databases have reported back successfully, they all perform a 'commit'.

Question:
What is 'batch processing'?

Answer:
'batch processing' occurs when requests for database changes are put into a queue and executed all at once.

Question:
What is 'Online Transaction Processing, or OLTP'?

Answer:
'Online Transaction Processing, or OLTP' provides fault tolerance and better performance with clustered databases.

Question:
What is 'ACID'?

Answer:
'ACID' is a series of attributes that OLTP must implement.

Question:
What is the 'atomicity attribute'?

Answer:
The 'atomicity attribute' is an attribute in ACID that states all changes take effect or none do.

Software Development Security Domain

Question:
What is the 'consistency attribute'?

Answer:
The 'consistency attribute' is an attribute in ACID that states all data remains consistent in all databases.

Question:
What is the 'isolation attribute'?

Answer:
The 'isolation attribute' is an attribute in ACID that states transactions execute in isolation until completed.

Question:
What is the 'durability attribute'?

Answer:
The 'durability attribute' is an attribute in ACID that states once the transaction is committed it cannot be rolled back.

Question:
What is a 'savepoint'?

Answer:
A 'savepoint' is a periodic save of a database that can be restored in case of severe interruption; this can be triggered based on elapsed time or for every number of completed transactions.

Question:
What is a 'checkpoint'?

Answer:
A 'checkpoint' is a savepoint triggered when the database fills up a specific amount of memory.

Question:
What is a 'database view'?

Answer:
A 'database view' is a virtual table comprised of one or more underlying tables that restrict or aggregate data according to access control policy.

Question:
What is 'polyinstantiation'?

Answer:
'polyinstantiation' occurs when interactively creating two instances of the same object with different attributes.

Question:
What is 'data warehousing'?

Answer:
'data warehousing' is a process that combines data from two or more databases into a single large database for follow-up analysis.

Question:
What is 'metadata'?

Answer:
'metadata' shows trends and relationships in warehoused data not evident in the raw sources.

Software Development Security Domain

Question:
What is 'data mining'?

Answer:
'data mining' is the process of creating metadata.

Question:
What is 'Knowledge Discovery in Database, or KDD'?

Answer:
'Knowledge Discovery in Database, or KDD' defines 3 approaches to data mining.

Question:
What is 'classification'?

Answer:
'classification' is a KDD pattern identification approach that groups data according to similarities.

Question:
What is 'probalistic'?

Answer:
'probalistic' is a KDD pattern identification approach that identifies relationships and calculates probabilities.

Question:
What is 'statistical'?

Answer:
'statistical' is a KDD pattern identification approach that identifies relationships and uses rule discovery.

Question:
What is 'big data'?

Answer:
'big data' are very large data sets that are unsuitable for traditional analysis techniques.

Question:
What is 'heterogeneity'?

Answer:
'heterogeneity' occurs when data types are not standardized.

Question:
What is 'complexity'?

Answer:
'complexity' occurs when there are many different relationships between data.

Question:
What is 'variability'?

Answer:
'variability' is present when some sources are verbose while others are sparse.

Software Development Security Domain

515

Question:
What is 'lack of reliability'?

Answer:
'lack of reliability' is present when the reliability of the source is not known.

Question:
What is a 'virus'?

Answer:
A 'virus' is a small application that infects software and can replicate itself.

Question:
What is the 'insertion ability'?

Answer:
The 'insertion ability' is the term used to describe the ability of a virus to install itself.

Question:
What is the 'avoidance ability'?

Answer:
The 'avoidance ability' is the term used to describe the ability of a virus to avoid detection.

Question:
What is the 'eradication ability'?

Answer:
The 'eradication ability' is the term used to describe the ability of a virus to remove itself after the payload has been delivered.

Question:
What is the 'replication ability'?

Answer:
The 'replication ability' is the term used to describe the ability of a virus to make copies of itself and spread.

Question:
What is the 'trigger ability'?

Answer:
The 'trigger ability' is the term used to describe the ability of a virus to use an event to execute the payload.

Question:
What is the 'payload ability'?

Answer:
The 'payload ability' is the term used to describe the ability of a virus to carry out its function.

Question:
What is a 'macro virus'?

Answer:
A 'macro virus' is written in a macro language such as Visual Basic or VBScript.

Software Development Security Domain

Question:
What is a 'boot sector virus'?

Answer:
A 'boot sector virus' infects the boot sector of a computer.

Question:
What is a 'tunneling virus'?

Answer:
A 'tunneling virus' intercepts requests for a file and presents a forged version of itself to antimalware products.

Question:
What is a 'stealth virus'?

Answer:
A 'stealth virus' is a tunneling virus that can hide the size of its file and move around to avoid detection.

Question:
What is a 'polymorphic virus'?

Answer:
A 'polymorphic virus' can alter its appearance in an effort to outwit virus scanners.

Question:
What is a 'multipart virus'?

Answer:
A 'multipart virus' has several components that are distributed in multiple locations on each system.

Question:
What is a 'meme virus'?

Answer:
A 'meme virus' is an email that gets spread quickly around the Internet.

Question:
What is a 'script virus'?

Answer:
A 'script virus' is a virus sent in script as an interpreted language.

Question:
What is a 'worm'?

Answer:
A 'worm' is a self-contained program and can reproduce without requiring a host application.

Question:
What is a 'rootkit'?

Answer:
A 'rootkit' is a bundle of tools an attacker uploads to an infected system for later use.

Software Development Security Domain

517

Question:
What is a 'trojan program'?

Answer:
A 'trojan program' replaces valid files with malicious alternatives.

Question:
What is a 'log scrubber'?

Answer:
A 'log scrubber' removes traces of the attacker's movements from the system log files.

Question:
What is 'spyware'?

Answer:
'spyware' is malware that exists to simply gather information about a victim.

Question:
What is 'adware'?

Answer:
'adware' is malware that automatically generates advertisements.

Question:
What is a 'bot'?

Answer:
A 'bot' is malware that is installed through infected email, drive-by-downloads, Trojan horses or shared media.

Question:
What is a 'botnet'?

Answer:
A 'botnet' is a network of bots.

Question:
What is a 'bot herder'?

Answer:
A 'bot herder' is the owner of a botnet.

Question:
What is 'Command-and-Control, or C&C'?

Answer:
'Command-and-Control, or C&C' are the servers that send instructions to a botnet.

Question:
What is 'fast flux'?

Answer:
'fast flux' is an evasion technique used to continually be on the move by updating DNS entries.

Software Development Security Domain

518

Question:
What is a 'logic bomb'?

Answer:
A 'logic bomb' is a program that is set to go off and execute its payload whenever a specific trigger is activated.

Question:
What is a 'Trojan Horse'?

Answer:
A 'Trojan Horse' is a program that is disguised as another program.

Question:
What is a 'Remote Access Trojan, or RAT'?

Answer:
A 'Remote Access Trojan, or RAT' is a program that allows an intruder to access and use a system remotely.

Question:
What is 'spam'?

Answer:
'spam' is the receipt of unsolicited junk email.

Question:
What is 'bayesian filtering'?

Answer:
'bayesian filtering' is used to apply statistical modeling to the words in an email message to detect spam.

Question:
What is a 'virus wall'?

Answer:
A 'virus wall' scans incoming SMTP, HTTP and FTP traffic for malware.

Software Development Security Domain

Quiz

Question:
If a class limits the scope of what it accomplishes, does it have a high or low cohesion?

Answer:
'high cohesion'.

Question:
Which type of cohesion is better for software design?

Answer:
'high cohesion'.

What If a class is less dependent on another class, does it have low or high coupling?

Answer:
'low coupling '.

Question:
Which type of coupling is better software design?

Answer:
'low coupling '.

Question:
What are the 5 steps in the software development lifecycle?

Answer:
'Requirements gathering, Design, Development, Testing/validation, Release/maintenance'.

Question:
What are the 4 tasks that should be completed by the time that the requirements phase has ended?

Answer:
'Security requirements, Security risk assessment, Privacy risk assessment, Risk-level acceptance'.

Question:
What are the 3 models used when documenting requirements?

Answer:
'informational, functional, and behavioral'.

Question:
What are the 3 outputs from the design phase?

Answer:
'Data design, Architectural design, Procedural design'.

Question:
What are the 4 elements of an application that should be made as small as possible to reduce the attack surface?

Answer:
'The amount of code running, Entry points, Privilege levels, Unnecessary services'.

Software Development Security Domain

Question:
What are the 4 types of software testing?

Answer:
'unit, integration, acceptance, regression'.

Question:
What are the 5 CMMI levels?

Answer:
'level 1 - Initial, level 2 - Repeatable, level 3 - Defined, level 4 - Managed, level 5 - Optimizing'.

Question:
What are the 4 components in ACID?

Answer:
'Atomicity, Consistency, Isolation, Durability'.

Question:
What is used to stop inference attacks?

Answer:
'polyinstantiation'.

Question:
What are the 3 approached that KDD defines to identify patterns?

Answer:
'classification, probalistic, statistical'.

Question:
What are the 5 attributes of big data?

Answer:
'heterogeneity, complexity, variability, lack of reliability, volume'.

Question:
What are the 6 primary components of a virus?

Answer:
'insertion, avoidance, eradication, replication, trigger, payload'.

What's Next?

One of the issues with testing yourself from a list of questions, is that eventually you learn subconsciously to key in on subtle clues that have nothing to do with actually learning the material. For example, one question may reference an acronym that helps you answer the next question – while you may provide the right answer to the second question, you may not have actually learned the material.

I was tempted to include a second section that completely randomized the questions to help you overcome this challenge, but the sheer size of the book would become unmanageable. However, in September 2017 an Audible version of this book will be coming out that WILL include a second randomized list of questions. If you think it would help, I encourage you to look for this audio book and use it to negate this possible block to properly learning the material. Bonus, you get to hear my awesome Texan accent!

Good luck on your exam!
- Phil Martin

Made in the USA
San Bernardino, CA
15 June 2019